Grace Under Pressure

Grace Under Pressure

The Emergence of Women in Sport

Adrianne Blue

Sidgwick & Jackson
London

For my mother and father,
RUBY and HENNY

First published in Great Britain in 1987 by
Sidgwick & Jackson Limited

Copyright © 1987 Adrianne Blue

ISBN 0-283-99306-5 (hardcover)
ISBN 0-283-99583-1 (softcover)

Design by Lynda Smith

Phototypeset by Falcon Graphic Art Ltd
Wallington, Surrey
Printed in Great Britain by
St Edmundsbury Press, Bury St Edmunds, Suffolk
for Sidgwick & Jackson Limited
1 Tavistock Chambers, Bloomsbury Way
London WC1A 2SG

Contents

Acknowledgements

The expertise of others, generously donated, has helped incalculably.

I would like first to thank the many sports champions for their time and their candour during interviews over the years. Their patient coaches, advisors and families have been interviewed too.

The too classicists Professor Mary R. Lefkowitz of Wellesley College and Dr Judith Swaddling of the British Museum provided reliable ancient history in a field that is strewn with wishful thinking. The two athletics correspondents Cliff Temple of *The Sunday Times* and Pat Butcher of *The Times* provided perspective on more recent history, as did Paul Colston of *Soviet Weekly*. Anne McArthur shared her knowledge and love of tennis; Hazel Wearmouth hers of gymnastics.

I would like to acknowledge the invaluable help of Madeleine Harmsworth and Jane Kirwan who commented on the manuscript as I was writing it, and that of Carey Smith, Libby Joy and Anne Cohen of Sidgwick & Jackson. I am grateful, too, to Alison Turnbull, Caradoc King, Celia Brackenridge, Margaret Talbot, Dr Anita White, Phillip Boys, Frances Borzello, Harriett Gilbert, Peter Ball, Caroline Silver and Heather Dallas. Finally, my thanks to the British Library, the Fawcett Library, and the public libraries of London, New York and West Palm Beach, and to the Women's Sports Foundation.

List of Illustrations

Sculpture of girl athlete (*Ancient Art & Architecture Collection*)
Atalanta and Peleus (*Ancient Art & Architecture Collection*)
Roman Mosaic (*Paul Watkins*)
Nadia Comaneci (*The Photo Source*)
Mary Queen of Scots (*The Mansell Collection*)
Sophie Armant Blanchard (*Mary Evans Picture Library*)
Victorian cyclist (*The Mansell Collection*)
Gertrude Ederle (*Mary Evans Picture Library*)
Princess Elizabeth (*Popperfoto*)
Virginia Holgate Leng (*Colorsport*)
The Young Rower (*Rochdale Art Gallery*)

Lottie Dod and Ernest Renshaw (*Wimbledon Lawn Tennis Museum*)
Chris Evert (*Colorific!*)
Suzanne Lenglen (*The Photo Source*)
Althea Gibson (*BBC Hulton Picture Library*)
Steffi Graf (*All Sport*)
Martina Navratilova (*The Photo Source*)
Ingrid Kristiansen (*Sporting Pictures (UK) Ltd*)
Mary Decker Slaney and Zola Budd (*Colorsport*)
Fanny Blankers-Koen (*All Sport*)
Joan Benoit (*Sporting Pictures (UK) Ltd*)
Bev Francis (*All Sport*)
Judy Oakes (*All Sport*)
Fatima Whitbread (*Sporting Pictures (UK) Ltd*)
Tamara Press (*The Photo Source*)
Karen Briggs (*Chris Smith*)

Key Dates

1500 BC	In Crete female bulljumpers defy death.
1000 BC	Atalanta outwrestles Peleus.
1000 BC	Women run at the all-female Herean Games in Greece.
440 BC	Kallipateira sneaks into the Olympics; the men institute the first Olympic sex test aimed at keeping women out.
396 BC	The Spartan princess Kyniska becomes the first female Olympic champion when her horses win the chariot race.
1200 AD	Gleemaidens tour Europe performing gymnastic feats on and off stage.
1424	Madame Margot outplays the men of Paris at *jeu de paume*, a version of tennis.
1591	Queen Elizabeth shoots deer with a crossbow.
1600	Sporting women at Elizabeth's court are observed to have easier labour than more sedentary types.
1714	Queen Anne, an excellent horsewoman, invents official racing for money.
1792	Mary Wollstonecraft argues in *A Vindication of Women* that women who are allowed to exercise will look better; unfortunately she mentions they will think more independently too.
1805	Sophie Armant Blanchard soloes in a gas-powered balloon.
1849	Bloomers are invented by busy New York feminists.
1885	Sharp-shooter Annie Oakley joins Buffalo Bill's Wild West Show.
1888	Lottie Dod defeats the Wimbledon champion Ernest Renshaw.
1890s	Bicycling is the rage.
1900	Tennis player Charlotte Cooper is the first female Olympic champion of the new Games.

1919	Suzanne Lenglen makes her début at Wimbledon, leaving her corset in Nice.
1926	Gertrude Ederle swims the English Channel.
1932	Amelia Earhart flies solo across the Atlantic.
1932	Texan Babe 'Don't-call-me-Mildred' Didriksen dominates the Los Angeles Olympics.
1948	Fanny Blankers-Koen is the top star of the London Olympics.
1956	Althea Gibson breaks the colour bar in tennis.
1966	Sex tests for women introduced in international sport.
1972	Title IX of the US Higher Education Act guarantees equal facilities for girls' sports.
1972	Billie Jean King earns $100,000 – a lot 'for a woman'.
1972	Gymnast Olga Korbut cries on television, launching an acceptably girlish sport in the West.
1973	Billie Jean King wins the tennis Battle of the Sexes.
1973	Maria Pepe, aged twelve, goes to court to stay on the Little League baseball team; generations of American girls win.
1975	Female tennis players win pay parity at US Open.
1978	Theresa Bennett loses in a court case to keep her place on the under-12 Mushkam United football team; generations of British girls lose too.
1977-1978	Naomi James sails around the world alone.
1984	Joan Benoit wins first women's Olympic marathon.
1987	First women's weight-lifting World Championships.
1988	Women's 5,000 metres introduced at the Olympics.
1992	Women's judo becomes a fully fledged Olympic sport.

The State of Play: A Summary

As a sports writer I have spent most of my time in the land of macho, chiefly as the motor-cycle racing correspondent of the *Sunday Times*. I did not want to be boxed into the women's pages, into women's subjects, into women's issues – which is ironic because the most important sport story of our era has been the emergence of women in sport.

Most of the media have missed it; all of them have under-reported it. I too might have missed it, but the sports editor of the *Sunday Times*, John Lovesey, urged me to write articles about the emerging champions. When he sent me to Oregon, in 1980, to interview the American star runner Mary Decker (now Decker Slaney), few people in Britain had ever heard of her – including me.

Women are everywhere in sport now – at sea, on the mountains, in the air; in the triathlon, and in the body-building arena. They are weight-lifters, discus throwers, shot putters, rodeo-riders, footballers, cricketers, basketball players, wrestlers, judoka, and tennis players, riders, runners, swimmers, golfers, gymnasts. Indeed the only places from which women are missing in fair numbers are the sports pages and the television screen.

* BBC television's sports round-up of the year in 1985 lasted 90 minutes – 3 minutes 45 seconds were devoted to women.
* BBC television's 1986 programme ran over by 20 minutes to about 110 minutes – fewer than 10 minutes were devoted to women, even though the public had voted the javelin thrower Fatima Whitbread runner-up BBC Sports Personality of the Year.
* *Sportsweek*, the new magazine that faltered, stuck to the old ways when it came to women – an article on the heptathlete Judy Simpson was all about how she knits sweaters for the male runners between her events; a profile of Liz Hobbs, twice world

high-speed water-skiing champion, *focussed* on her sideline as a fashion model.

* A *Times* athletics correspondent mentioned to me he had done a long feature article on Mary Decker Slaney, the runner, in 1985. The *Times* secretary, looking it up, said she was certain there wasn't one – but she had noticed an article he had done about Decker Slaney's husband.

* *USA Today*, the American newspaper, did a front-page feature on a female triathlon champion. Her husband, too, figured large.

I could go on and on. Far more interesting, though, is an account of what the sportswomen themselves are and are not doing. This book is an informal social history of the emergence of women in sport and an analysis of the state of play.

Sport was created for men. Its story is usually told as the triumphs of men, with a nod, and occasionally even a bow to the ladies. Most of the books by those of us who love sport ignore the anabolic steroids, the outright cheating, the role of sport as a pawn in world politics. They stick to chronicling the stereotype: sportsmen who are dedicated, defiant, assertive, and utterly fearless. He-men.

This book is about women who are dedicated, defiant, assertive and fearless. They are not He-men. They are a new and privileged breed of woman.

Some of them use steroids; some of them cheat; and in this decade some have even become the centre of political hurricanes. These sportstars are, without even wanting to be, increasingly role models for women today. Their stories, even in the sports you never hear much about, are often astounding.

In the midst of the gruelling 3,107-mile 1986 bicycle Race Across America, the defending champion, a 32-year-old nurse, paused to save a life. Sue Notorangelo's long, nearly sleepless ride had started in Huntington Beach, California. In Arkansas, well past midnight, the ABC–TV cameraman fell off the cameratruck, striking his head and losing consciousness. Sue Notorangelo, who had been riding twenty-one hours a day for a week, jumped off her bike. 'I'm usually conscious of my bike at all times, but I just threw it off the road,' she said. 'I cleared his airway of blood with a finger, then held his tongue back so he could breathe.' The cameraman was rushed to hospital with a fractured skull. She got back on her bike and rode on to Atlantic City, finishing the race in second place.

Like the men, female sports superstars are paid ridiculous amounts. In the 1990s, they will be earning three, maybe four, times as much as they do today. No matter how grudging the TV and newspaper sports writers continue to be in giving sportswomen their fair share of coverage, in the 1990s the female champions will be getting much more media time too.

I have focussed upon the sports that interest me particularly and on the ones that I believe are central to the story. Much has had to be left out. This is a disclaimer in many books. I now understand why.

It was tennis, a sport first played in corsets and crinolines by well-bred ladies, which fomented the revolution – high competitive pressure, high visibility, exquisite skill, gargantuan money – in top-level women's sport. The women of tennis have attained commercial power. Earnest, bespectacled, energetic, able Billie Jean King smashed a lot of the prejudices which for generations kept women on the sidelines of sport. As the *New York Times* sports writer Dave Anderson put it, 'She has been a woman of history, not merely tennis history.' And half a century before King, another tennis player served the first ball in the modern revolution in women's sport. That was Suzanne Lenglen, a French woman with a penchant for fur coats and glitz.

Olympic athletes have recently graduated from 'shamateurism' to pro standing. These champions, particularly the runners, have attained glory, and are following tennis into the modern era of Big Sport. Olympic sport is big business now – it always secretly has been; but it is still the arena of the East–West sporting war.

The history of women in sport is a history of ambivalence. Queens have been horsewomen, hunters, golfers; ordinary women have more often stuck to their embroidery in dim light. As women began to play sport, they instinctively developed apologetic tactics to counter the prejudices they faced.

Like male champions, women have achieved excellence at great personal sacrifice. They have endured pain, exhaustion, defeat. They have altered their bodies with chemicals. They have, for sport, submitted to the surgeon's knife. In the 'amateur' sports, they have endured the indignity and participated in the lie of under-the-table money. The women who have become champions are no better than they should be; no better than the men. They have followed the male competitive model; they have won at all costs.

They are in a sense, however, *more heroic than the men*. A male sportstar has only to show courage at his sport, to show grace under pressure. The women have shown grace under the pressure of sport and grace under the pressure of prejudice. They have won through. Theirs is a story of excellence and of excess; an occasion for celebration and for some regret. It is an enlightening as well as a thrilling story.

1

Golden Racket

La Prototype

When she runs for the ball, you can glimpse bare thigh above Suzanne Lenglen's knee-length stockings. When she stretches for a difficult shot, the accordion pleats of her loose dress cling tellingly to her body. They may be less shocked on the Riviera, her home ground, but here at her first Wimbledon, in 1919, men are blushing and women mumble 'indecent'. Her dress stops short at mid-calf. Her arms are 'disgracefully' bare – from the upper arm down. One woman and her husband stalk out when Lenglen, jumping to reach a high ball, kicks her foot into the air like a *Folies Bergère* chorus girl. Under her skirt, there is just one little lace-hemmed slip. Instead of a corset and petticoats, La Grande Suzanne has opted for mobility.

Several more dismayed Britons attending this first post-war Wimbledon final stiffen their lips when, during the break between sets, the dark-haired foreigner takes out her make-up and begins to retouch her face. There is annoyance too when she swallows a sip of brandy. But Suzanne Lenglen is getting away with it. She is about to become the first superstar of women's sport. The Lenglen Legend is being born. It is not an easy birth.

The match lasts two hours. Standing squarely at the back of the court, the defending champion, Dorothea Lambert Chambers, sends her merciless dipped forehand cross-court again and again. Since well before the Great War, the burly Mrs Lambert Chambers has reigned. Now, in perfect tennis weather – there is no wind, it is mild – Lambert Chambers is fighting for her tennis life. Lenglen, all over the court, wins the first set 10–8. Lambert Chambers, reined by her corset-cinched waist, stands firmly on the baseline. But that famous forehand wins her the second set, 6–4. Mrs Lambert Chambers has power; Mlle Lenglen power and agility. The third set which goes to 9–7 is as fierce as the first. Lenglen, who has just turned twenty, survives two match points, and many dipped forehands, to beat forty-year-old Dorothea Lambert

Chambers, who would have liked a bit of brandy herself during the match, but refrained, she said, because 'such a thing was not English'.[1]

It was not only the daring clothes and saucy manners which distinguished Suzanne Lenglen. Her speed on court, her pyrotechnics, her grace, her lithe movement, were without precedent. She eschewed the sedate baseline game of English womanhood. She ran to the net. And in so doing, she revolutionized women's tennis and heralded a revolution in women's sport.

In Nice, in the South of France, Lenglen's father, who was the Svengali of her career, had watched the visiting leisured English on court. Papa attributed his daughter's success – albeit not quite in these words – to the androgyny of her play. Instead of the well-placed drives of the ladies' game, hit coolly from the baseline, he had taught his daughter to run, to play fast, aggressively, to use the whole court. He had taught her to play like a man.

Not that anyone was ever ungallant enough to notice. 'If lawn tennis was this Atalanta's recreation,' *The Times* swooned, 'running is her forte ... if run is not too strenuous a word for her fluent motion – and there she was, where she wanted to be, at the net.'

Lenglen, the vivid, charismatic new-comer, the first foreign-born female Wimbledon singles champion, was playing an entirely new game. The years that followed established her as the finest player of her time. After her first startling Wimbledon victory, Lenglen won four more Wimbledon singles and doubles titles in a row. Too ill to play the whole tournament in 1924, she scratched. She won both titles again in 1925. That year she also won the singles, doubles, and mixed doubles at the first French Open – where she did it again in 1926. There were plenty of other triumphs. In the eight years of her amateur career, Suzanne Lenglen lost only three sets and no matches.

Crowds flocked to see her. Wimbledon moved to bigger quarters in 1922. There was still a 'Leng-Len Trail a-Winding'. Even Bill Tilden, 'Mr Tennis', who won both Wimbledon and the US Open that year, and who definitely was not a fan of Lenglen – he once said she combined the characteristics of a prima donna and a street walker – had to admit she was a bigger draw than he was.[2] She loved the crowd. 'The bigger the better,' she often said. And perhaps she played to it. It was her huge histrionic personality, as much as the quality of her playing, which was superb, that made her the biggest draw in tennis, the sport's first female superstar.

She carried a lucky monkey's paw mascot; she wore a fur coat and a lucky gold bracelet; she bloodied her feet, so hard did she run during play.

No one knows though if she would have been up to Chris Evert or Martina Navratilova or to the young West German Steffi Graf, on a good day when her big toe isn't in plaster. Kitty McKane Godfree, one of the generation of English players who was glad to see the back of La Suzanne, was probably right when she said: 'What I sincerely believe is that if Suzanne were twenty today, and she had all the modern coaching and training, the new type of racket, the new type of balls, the change in the foot-fault rule, and the huge incentive to become a millionaire in two or three years' time, I think that she would have done it.' She didn't have any of that. 'We played the game for fun, and the biggest [mentions] from the newspapers.'[3]

Ah, newspapers. Not to mention magazines.

> She was *the* player for the Jazz age, gay, brittle, and brilliant. She had style and such glamour that the white rabbit fur coat she wore was always called ermine in the newspapers.
> Virginia Wade, *Ladies of the Court*, 1984

In the art of manipulating stardom, Suzanne Lenglen was a pioneer too. She both understood, and used, the media as no female sportswoman had ever done before. Her 'shocking' attire at Wimbledon was not just for ease of play. It did not just bespeak her ease with her body. It was not simply a liberated decision to put her own comfort and the standards of play ahead of decorum. It was all of these. It was also calculated to hit the headlines.

In 1920, a year after Lenglen had débuted at Wimbledon in scandalous 'near nakedness' and a soft hat, women won suffrage in America and Lenglen won two Olympic gold medals at tennis. She returned to Wimbledon centre court with bobbed hair, a flapper, wearing the soon-to-be-famed Lenglen Bandeau. This was a headband of coloured silk chiffon, several yards of it, which she wrapped around her hair before play. It was glamorous. It kept your hair out of your eyes. It mopped up that supposedly non-existent entity, a woman's sweat. And it was eye-catching. Other players began to don bandeaux.

Then – and this is the sort of thing that hadn't happened to a sports star before – the Lenglen bandeau, which was extensively commented upon in the press, became international high-street chic. People had been shocked by the Lenglen Look when she first wore it on the court, but Lenglen continued to dress that way, on court and off. By the mid-1920s, when Lenglen's clothes were designed by Patou, women

5

everywhere were wearing copies of her one-piece frocks, her pleated skirts, her long cardigans.

When Suzanne Lenglen began to build her legend, celebrities were still admired from a respectful distance, though it was not such a distance as it used to be. Everybody knew that stars could not know everybody, but everybody could know the stars. The tabloids made sure of that. *The Times* was no slouch either, though the ultimate tabloid, television, had not yet made reportage pores-on-the-face intimate.

Fur coats, glitzy dresses, eye make-up, were the tools of the celebrity's trade; a way of encoding stardom in titillating mystery. Lenglen used them. Tennis rackets did not yet signify stardom; Suzanne Lenglen forged the link.

But those who come first have trouble. Her pre-eminence and domination of tennis often made her ill.

No one would defeat Lenglen *anywhere*, until she retired in 1926. Once, though, after a dreary ocean crossing that had aggravated her chronic asthma, Lenglen was persuaded to play in the US Championships of 1921, at Forest Hills, even though she had symptoms of bronchitis. It was her one American sojourn. She had come, sponsored by a French charity, to undertake a fund-raising tennis-exhibition tour for the war-sacked villages of France. But Papa had warned her to stay away from the US Championships. Uncharacteristically, Lenglen, aged twenty-two, disobeyed Papa.

At Forest Hills, four days after her ocean voyage, with rain precluding all but a morning's practice, Lenglen faced the American defending champion Molla Mallory, a powerful baseliner, who made no allowances for Lenglen's health. Mallory blasted her 6–2 in the first set, and was leading 2–0 when Lenglen suddenly said, *'Je n'en peux plus! Je suis vraiment trop malade!'* (I can't go on. I'm really too ill.)[4] Then she ran off the court in tears. She did not return.

This was not the American way. From the Atlantic to the Pacific, there was derision for the tennis Queen of Europe. Lenglen sailed home as soon as possible, leaving behind a bankrupt reputation and a hotel bill to be footed by the charity.

At the revenge match – which turned out to be the following year's Wimbledon final, on which Mallory's husband bet $10,000 – Lenglen defeated her, 6–2, 6–0, in just twenty-seven minutes.

In 1924, Lenglen, suffering from a long illness, probably hepatitis, seemed an iffy entry for Wimbledon right up to the end. But the new American prodigy, Helen Wills, was coming for her first attempt at the Wimbledon crown, and there was speculation that Suzanne Lenglen, who had taken to her bed weeks before, was sick with fear. Whatever the cause of her illness, she was jaundiced and weak. There were dark circles under her eyes. Papa and the doctors told Suzanne she would have to scratch from the championships.

'J'irai! J'irai!' (I will go. I will go.), she said, and did.

There were 17,000 ticket holders eager to watch her in the Wimbledon final that year, but it was soon clear she was physically shattered. Even before she was scheduled to play Helen Wills, she nearly lost a match, eventually won it, and scratched from the championship.

Two years later, people were still saying Suzanne Lenglen was scared of Helen Wills, a solemn doctor's daughter from California, who by 1926, at the age of twenty, had won the US Championship three times in a row. Lenglen finally faced her in February 1926, in a much-anticipated, much-hyped, challenge match. Extra grandstands were erected at the Carlton Club; tickets went on sale for $11; but there were only 4,000 seats. Touts were able to sell tickets for five times their face price. One of the two hundred visiting journalists noticed that even so, the Carlton was pulling in half a million francs (about £300,000). How much of it was going to the players? Helen Wills and her mother were living in luxury at the Carlton Hotel. A Paris couturier had outfitted Wills with a £10,000 wardrobe. Was this an under-the-table pay off? Wasn't Lenglen similarly involved in receiving such 'hospitality'? A press conference side-stepped the questions. But this was the first time payments to 'amateurs' had been aired in public.[5]

Rain delayed play for three days. Suzanne's dry cough, which had bothered her so much at Forest Hills, became insistent. At the start of the match she was pale and felt weak. A friend had a glass of champagne waiting for her at the end of every game. The well-known American writer James Thurber covered the match for *The New Yorker*. His panegyric to young Helen was impressive; Lenglen won.

> The participation of girls and women from lower income groups was restricted to informal street games, a few supervised exercise classes, and field days in public schools.
>
> J. J. Coakley, *Sport in Society*, 1986

But Lenglen's amateur career ended with a sour taste. Her last Wimbledon, in 1926, began much as usual. King George's opening day handshake for Suzanne Lenglen got a page one photograph in the *Daily Sketch*; Lenglen, who hoped to be presented at Court, had often been received in the Royal Box. There were big, admiring Wimbledon crowds. There was even sunshine. But suddenly Lenglen found herself in a sea of bitter circumstance. The French Tennis Federation had forced her to break her winning career-long doubles partnership with Elizabeth Ryan, an American. Now Lenglen was partnering a Frenchwoman of dubious standard. Her cough had returned; the dark circles too.

The Wimbledon committee had unaccountably scheduled Lenglen to play both a singles match, and the important doubles match against 'Bunny' Ryan on the same day. Moreover, it was to be her first round doubles match. Lenglen said she would not play both those matches in one day, and left, convinced the timetable would be amended, as quite a few people thought it should be. But apparently the match had been scheduled at the Queen's pleasure.

The next afternoon Queen Mary arrived at centre court. Suzanne Lenglen did not. There was polite pandemonium, which Norah Gordon Cleather, who was to become secretary of the All-England Club, described in *Wimbledon Story*: 'What could be done? What would we tell the Queen? The minutes dragged and dragged. Officials were summoned urgently to the Committee Room.'[6] Lenglen turned up, half an hour late. She always maintained she thought the match had been postponed, but she was berated for rudeness, and stormed off. Her mixed doubles partner, Jean Borotra, was sent to apologize to the Queen.

Helen Wills, who had been waiting to see the match, went into the dressing room. Behind the white door with the gold lettering, 'The Lady Champion', Wills heard Lenglen crying. 'So I quickly left, and that is all I know about the incident, except that people usually have a reason to cry, and the reason must have been a real one because Wimbledon meant much to Mlle Lenglen.'[7] There was talk of awarding the ladies doubles match to Lenglen's opponents by default, but at the insistence of the opponents it was merely postponed.

The press played the incident as a deliberate affront to the Queen. And the Queen of England was a bigger celebrity than the tennis Queen of Europe. The crowds grew unfriendly. Queen Mary passed near Lenglen and gave no smile of recognition. Lenglen was distraught. The Palace maintained there had been no snub; the Queen had not seen her.

With difficulty, Lenglen won her next singles match, against a Mrs G. J. Dewhurst of Ceylon. There was a hostile crowd at the mixed doubles which followed, and a disheartened Lenglen could not play. She and her partner Jean Borotra lost. Lenglen skulked off the court and out of London, refusing to give a single interview and scratching from the rest of the tournament.

Not so surprisingly, a few months later, she joined the fledgling professional tennis tour, which had just been organized by the promoter C. C. Pyle – it was rumoured his initials stood for 'cash and carry'. There would still be champagne and roses, but no need to win at all costs. 'At last, after fifteen years of torture,' she said to reporters, 'I can enjoy my tennis.'[8] Although tennis did not go professional in a big way until 1968, Pyle was able, in 1926, to guarantee Lenglen $50,000, and when he made a profit of $80,000, it is said he gave her $25,000 more.

Part heroine, part exasperating child, part Theda Bara, part brilliant self-publicist, Lenglen was even more graceful than anybody knew. Even while she walloped her every opponent aggressively, even while she let it slip out that winning was everything to her, she projected the fey image of 'Frenchness', of femininity, of Beauty – although, as Norah Cleather put it, Suzanne, no beauty, was 'an ugly flapper'. She was in love with tennis; with a little affection left over for Papa, and a lot for herself. If she was a vamp, she was a chaste one; if she was an athlete – and she was – she was no jolly hockey stick.

> I know that women are strong . . . And I must add that, while I accept utterly that beauty and pleasure are culturally and historically specific, and in no way escape ideology, nonetheless they are beauty and pleasure and I want to hang on to them in some form or other.
>
> Richard Dyer, *Stars*, 1979

Lenglen eluded the usual double-bind of female sportstars – that false paradox – was she a sportstar or a woman? But she didn't do it unscathed. All those illnesses – some of them made up so she could default without scandal, some of them real, most of them psychosomatic – were indications of the cognitive quarrel she was having within herself, the role conflict that has afflicted most successful sportswomen.

Not all would be as successful at the media game as Lenglen. But she was the prototype of the professional – when tennis went open in 1968, and in the years after, we saw it all again. Players who could would create themselves in her image and the PR firms would offer parental guidance.

Just as tennis pros are today, Lenglen was talked about, argued about, admired, imitated: she attained the eminence of a Hollywood star. She had that mixture of ability and flair, and the instinct for self-marketing that is known as star quality. Lenglen had an aura, a particularity; a staged costume-and-cosmetic 'femininity'. She oozed with product identifiability.

Not all future tennis superstars would be as glamorous as she was, but they would all be aware of the image they were projecting. A Paradise of gold-lined centre courts was gained. But Innocence was lost.

Six weeks after her thirty-ninth birthday, La Prototype died, in 1938, of leukaemia. The fairy tale had not ended happily. Real life fairy tales rarely do. Her most useful legacy, the one that was crucial to the emergence of women in sport, had been handed on nearly two decades before she died. It had been delivered at Wimbledon when Suzanne Lenglen stepped out of her constricting underwear, that corset and the petticoats, when she rolled down her stockings to the knee.

> All women tennis players should go on their knees in thankfulness to Suzanne for delivering them from the tyranny of corsets.
> Elizabeth 'Bunny' Ryan, winner of nineteen
> Wimbledon doubles titles, 1914–1934

Prior to that, fashion had hampered women's tennis for years. Every stricture society could design for womanhood had been translated into fashion, and women attempting to play tennis fought a war of attrition which, even after a century, they still have not quite won.

Tight corsets made it hard to breathe let alone lob in the 1880s. The first Wimbledon singles champion, Maud Watson, who held the title for two consecutive years, in 1884 and 1885, played in a long-sleeved, ankle-length, flouncy full-skirted dress, which finished with an elaborate draped apron at the stomach, and a bustle at the back. She wore ankle boots and a stiff, brimmed 'boater'.

Laugh, but not at Maud Watson. Blanche Bingley (later Hillyard), who took the title from her, was, so far as clothing went, virtually Watson's twin.

Bit by bit women broke free. Tennis's first prodigy, big-boned, sturdy 'Lottie' Dod, was a law unto herself. In 1887, on her way to the first of her five Wimbledon titles, Lottie, then only fifteen, defiantly hiked up her skirt to calf length. Might being right, when she insisted ever after on nine inches of daylight between her skirt and the ground, she got away with it – on the grounds that she was still a girl. Eighteen years later, May Sutton rolled up her sleeves.

Skirts, though, remained for the most part at the ankle till the First World War. Those knife-like steel-boned corsets persisted too. Outer garments, however, were 'predominantly white'. White stockings, of course. And the ladies wore neckties.

Fashion prudishness lessened after the war; in fact women were a little freer in all spheres. Hence, eventual acceptance of Lenglen's naked thighs and upper arms. Sleeveless shirts on occasion too. Lenglen's English contemporary, Kitty McKane Godfree, played sleeveless. But she wore white stockings.

It is hard to believe that as recently as 1927 a player was angrily booed for appearing at Wimbledon without *stockings*. Propriety was outraged and let it be known. 'That is how I played on our farm back home,' said Billie Tapscott, a tanned South African. 'I never dreamed it would cause such a sensation.'

There is disagreement about who was the first woman to wear shorts. The Spaniard, Lili de Alvarez, who was as much a fashion-plate as Lenglen but not so good a player, appeared on centre court at Wimbledon on 23 June 1931, wearing short trousers which she had designed herself. They gave her the advantage of freedom of movement, but most observers thought they wouldn't catch on because they were 'unbecoming'. In 1934, Helen Jacobs and Dorothy Round contested the Wimbledon final in culottes.

At last socks, neatly turned down at the ankle, were beginning to replace stockings. In 1939, the year the great American player Alice Marble hammered Kay Stammers, 6–2, 6–0 in a superbly played, vintage Wimbledon final, both players wore short-sleeved shirts and no-nonsense culottes, and those by then standard little bobby socks.

In the 1950s, after another war, women worldwide were subject to the feminine mystique. Players made a big show of cooking their husband's roast beef and two veg, and not only were tennis skirts mini minis, but frilly 'underthings' came into view. The TV cameras, which had been on court experimentally since 1937, couldn't take their eyes off them.

In his anecdotal social history of celebrity-mongering, *Common Fame*, Richard Schickel, long *Time* Magazine's film critic, dates the concept of celebrity from the first widely circulated tabloid, Lord Northcliffe's *Daily Mirror*, which began in London, in 1903, as a newspaper for women. By 1909, the paper was selling a million copies as a sensational 'half-penny illustrated'. In the old days, royals, Franz Liszt, and singing stars like Jenny Lind had their swooners, but always from a respectful distance. Press photographers changed everything.

One who was sent to take pictures of Queen Marie of Romania

disembarking from an ocean liner is said to have shouted: 'A little more leg, Queenie.' And thus was born the 'photo opportunity'.

Stepping on the toes of the 'big shots' – or looking up their skirts – was justified because newspapers were building an ever better-informed populace. This democratic ideal often got drowned in the flood of trivial information. Too much in too many editions. Sometimes, though, democratizing worked. All those photos of La Lenglen speeded the changes in women's fashion, which until then had been such a constraint.

The history of fashion will tell you that sport is the most important influence on women's clothing in the twentieth century. The women who joined the first ladies' cricketers' club in 1890, or played in the first ladies' international hockey match, were not among those who had been ridiculing 'bloomers'. Tennis was the first sport to be played widely by ordinary middle-class women. Motoring was affordable only to aristocrats, and bicycling, which gained adherents among women of all social classes, was not always technically practised enough for sport. Getting out of corsets and into trousers and shorts was not only important to all of these women, it was important to all of those who would come after. Loose sports clothing freed women to move.

Teddy Tinling, the fashion designer, has claimed to be 'the first specialist in clothes for movement'. He was responsible for many of the recidivist excesses in tennis clothing. As a boy, he hid behind potted plants to get a glimpse of Suzanne Lenglen, whose diva style he says he idolized. He hung around the Grand Hotel at the Nice Club on the Rivieria and was soon refereeing her matches. At Wimbledon he was the MC at centre court matches. Off-season, he says, he would gaze at the pictures of her that lined his bedroom walls: Teddy Tinling was effectively the first male groupie. Suzanne Lenglen was his Marlene Dietrich.

Unfortunately, he didn't leave it there. He had camp, superannuated notions of what a woman was. It was he who perpetrated the lace-trimmed panties, the eye-catching 'feminine' underpants, on 'Gorgeous Gussy' Moran at Wimbledon 1949. Two hundred press photographers lay on their backs at courtside, with their camera lenses aimed up Moran's skirt.

In 1952, another American, 'Little Mo', Maureen Connolly, the second youngest Wimbledon champion and the darling of the crowds, took the first of her three consecutive titles in style, in tailored but short, often sleeveless, tennis dresses. Shorts reappeared in the 1960s, but they didn't take for long. Skirts – sometimes pleated, always short – and tennis dresses had won the day. There was a long and from time to time ardent flirtation with colour.

In 1973, Virginia Wade, Evonne Goolagong, Rosie Casals, and Billie Jean King posed wearing Tinling's new line – unconstricting, tailored, sleeveless 'dacron' tennis dresses. There were smiles on their faces. By then, though, one would never know for sure if these were smiles of approval at the new uniform, or bought-and-paid-for publicity shots.

Watch them practise when they are not on screen and you have trouble finding anyone who is not in shorts or in a warm-up suit. Even Gabriela Sabatini, the Argentinian who is known more for her face and figure than for her forehand, which is good, avoids those mini-skirts and mini-dresses when she is practising.

She never ever put on a skirt at Eastbourne, in 1986, except to play an *official* match. There was practice every morning and afternoon of that stately 'ladies' championship, and on court one saw Sabatini, just like the rest of them, in shorts or, if it was cold, in a navy blue track suit.

Martina Navratilova, Hana Mandlikova, Jo Durie, Virginia Wade, Helena Sukova, Kathy Jordan, Zina Garrison – this list could continue, perhaps to include the entire roster – none of them wore a skirt or a tennis dress for practice. Why not take a look some time in Oakland or Adelaide or Stockholm? Why, after struggling for the right to wear them, have the pros allowed shorts to become a thing of the recent past?

We all know the answer. Far more important than ease of movement, or comfort, or personal preference – the freedom to play one's game as one wants – is, so it seems, being comfortable with one's image. Or rather, one's sponsor being comfortable with one's image. So, before the women of tennis go on court to do battle, they don those little skirts that show their underwear.

The women's pro tour today is woman-run. It is what Hemingway, who got some things right, would call a moveable feast, a banquet of sport that travels from country to country and lasts eleven months of the year. The female pros have become a nomad tribe of highly skilled and ridiculously highly paid Amazons. But they are nervous and make many such concessions because the media, and some of the paying sponsors, still think that to gain their eminence they have, like the ancient Amazons, cut off a breast.

English Roses

The silver-grey head nearly touched the peroxide blonde one, as ninety-year-old Kitty McKane Godfree leaned forward to press the famous silver plate into Martina Navratilova's big hands. They muttered a few words – which once would have been called girl talk but now, in 1986, was regarded benignly as the murmur of sporting history.

The Czech who wore glasses had just won her fifth consecutive Wimbledon title, becoming the first player to match the more than half-century-old record of the temperamental Suzanne Lenglen. Kitty McKane Godfree had also been there when Suzanne Lenglen achieved her fifth straight win in 1923. And Godfree had been there in 1924, when La Grande Suzanne scratched. It was the Englishwoman Godfree who stepped into the record books that year in Lenglen's place.

> I still want an all-time Wimbledon singles record, which means winning it nine times at least.
> Martina Navratilova, in 1985, 1986, 1987

Now Godfree's role had changed: it was to bear witness to tennis history. She was the oldest champion on the tennis circuit. Martina Navratilova quipped that she wouldn't at all mind hitting some balls with Godfree, who, even after a hip operation, played doubles with her friends.

Godfree was born a bony, wiry woman, not a curve on her;s he had never ever been a dolly girl. But training with weights to build strength and, by the by, a bit of muscle had not been the fashion in Godfree's era. Navratilova, like the rest of today's female champions in most sports, uses weights. And she plays as many matches in a season as Godfree and Lenglen would have played in five years. You could see

14

that the new champion's calf muscles bulged, and the old one's calf, just visible beneath the hem of her soft blue dress, was straight as a willow, as it had been even in her prime.

Kitty McKane Godfree's entry into tennis history occurred before she married. In 1924, still Kitty McKane, and already twenty-seven – the age at which Suzanne Lenglen retired – she was England's 'young hope'. The crowd loved McKane's stubborn, purse-lipped expression on court, and the dogged tenacity of her play. Her chief weapon was her stamina, and she didn't mind running either. She wore the now usual Lenglen-inspired 'bandeau' headband, and a large, jaunty neckerchief to mop up any unladylike perspiration.

In the Wimbledon final of the year before, Kitty McKane had been defeated by Lenglen, but was hailed anyway as the first Englishwoman finalist in three years. Now, here she was again, facing the solemn prodigy from California, Helen Wills, who at eighteen was already the American champion, and who was making her Wimbledon début. Wills, in her schoolgirl midi blouse, shapeless white skirt, and business-like green-visored eye-shade, was the only serious challenger to glamorous Suzanne Lenglen. That French prima donna, who had had things her own way in women's tennis for so long, had scratched from Wimbledon after nearly losing a match because she was ill. This was the first time since the First World War that the Wimbledon final was played without Suzanne Lenglen. What a pity, the British fans thought, that with the French Goliath gone, an American David should turn up.

Without much hope, Kitty McKane went on to the court, patting her bandeau. She had lost to Wills at their one previous meeting, the season before, at Forest Hills, in the very first Wightman Cup.

Helen Wills, annoyed at having to wear white stockings because Queen Mary hated bare legs, pulled her green eye-shade down over her eyes. She strode on to centre court. In California and South Africa you could play bare-legged. The match began: the dogged, experienced English rose versus the stolid American schoolgirl, who was a genius at the sport. Ignoring her own pessimism about the outcome, McKane stubbornly kept those grey eyes on the ball. She served and volleyed consistently, and after four games, she led 3–1.

> The crowds never really liked Helen Wills and in all her years at Wimbledon there was not one time when they were really on her side. They always wanted her opponent to win.
>
> Virginia Wade, *Ladies of the Court*, 1984

The crowd roared, and Wills evidently woke up. Her countenance never changed, but with powerful shots rather than fancy spins, Wills barraged first one flank of the court, then the other, taking nine of the next eleven games. Kitty McKane despaired: 'I was getting her drives back but never really attacking myself, and I decided that I wasn't any good at all.'

But Helen Wills showed no emotion. No matter what happened on court, no matter how many points she won, or lost, like Björn Borg so many decades later, Helen Wills gave no sign. Her cool manner began to annoy the press and the crowd. With that eye-shade shadowing her brow, you couldn't clearly see her face. But it was assumed she felt nothing. She was wooden, cold, an Ice Maiden. At that Wimbledon, she would earn the nickname 'Little Poker Face', which as time went on became Miss Poker Face. It was not a compliment.

'There is no proof,' Wills said in explanation – imagine having to apologize for *not* losing your composure – 'that people do not become more calm at difficult moments than more nervous.' Because she was conventionally pretty and, as she grew up, very elegantly pretty, they found another way to call her unfeminine, unwomanly. Even her intellectual interests, her disciplined talent for drawing portraits, were a sign of it – of frigidity, unfeminine self-control. She was hardly a woman; she was made of ice.

Decades later another American, Chris Evert, was derided on both sides of the Atlantic as the 'Ice Maiden'. She was the Beast. But by Chrissie's time image-making had become a paid professional art. Evert was transformed to 'American Beauty'. Yet she never changed her style of play; her cool, methodical, merciless, baseline game. Not much was done to her manner either.

One honest cliché applies here: beauty is in the eye of the beholder. The Evert camp had done its best to melt the Ice Maiden image, and the sports writers had by then been gifted with Navratilova. And, dear girl, she got engaged. The beholders in the media didn't exactly change their story-line – they simply changed lenses and focussed on a different aspect of her character. Why? Partly because Evert had learned a few tricks of media management, partly because novelty is nearly everything in journalism and the Ice Maiden bit was getting tatty, mostly because they needed a Beauty as they had a new Beast.

Helen Wills, schoolgirl, however, knew little of this as she pounded the ball across the net. Helen Wills now led 6–4, 4–1, but there was nothing but that opaque face. In the second set, she came within a point of making it 5–1 four times.

But suddenly, Kitty McKane couldn't put a stroke wrong. She had found the sweet spot in her racket. She saved those four points and won that game and the next four to take the second set. Wills was tiring. McKane's stamina prevailed; she won, 4–6, 6–4, 6–4.

Years later, Helen Wills called that match 'the most grueling' she had ever played. After her defeat, she wept in the dressing room. There would be many tennis players crying their eyes out at Wimbledon over the next half-century, but not Helen Wills. That was her only defeat at singles in nine Wimbledons.

Kitty McKane had become the first Englishwoman to win the title in a decade. Then she married, changing her name in the record books, and in this chapter, to Godfree. If this seems awkward to the reader, think how it must have been to the player, having instantly to change not only her private identity but her public one – the name she read in the headlines. Think how awkward it is to tot up great achievements – or even to notice them. In the history of sport women vanish suddenly from the record books because they marry and their name changes – even today, when actresses and writers, and other women who make names for themselves before they marry, often don't relinquish their maiden names.

The man McKane married, Leslie Godfree, once Wimbledon men's doubles champion, is less important to tennis than she has turned out to be. Leslie Godfree's most important moment in tennis history had come in 1922, when he hit the first ball on the centre court of the new Wimbledon ground. He kept the ball. For two decades, Kitty kept it dusted.

The 1926 Queen's-Jubilee-year Wimbledon was supposed to be a celebration. But Lenglen, having 'insulted Royalty', withdrew in a huff, Helen Wills had appendicitis, and reliable Elizabeth Ryan had a horrible cold. Kitty McKane Godfree found herself in the final again, facing another under-trained natural with daring, sensational shots, that dark-eyed, Spanish fashion-plate, Lili de Alvarez, who could hit 'wonder' half-volleys with power and speed from losing positions on court, but who couldn't run. Unlike Kitty McKane Godfree, de Alvarez had not been schooled at one of the English physical training colleges for women. Godfree was fit; Lili de Alvarez was brilliant.

In the first set, Godfree hit hard ones from the baseline and won, 6–2. Then, with an elegant shrug of an elegant shoulder, Lili de Alvarez began to slam shot after beautiful shot. Godfree lost the second set, 4–6. In the third set, Godfree was just one harrowing point from going down 1–4, when de Alvarez began missing easy shots. Godfree took five games in a row, to win the set and the match. Queen Mary awarded the prize, a five-pound voucher to the jewellers Mappin & Webb.

And so Kitty McKane Godfree became the prototype of British tennis's favourite sort of heroine. She was a stubborn plugger who put herself and her audiences through agonies as, occasionally, she tardily pulled victory out of defeat, to conquer bolder, more flamboyant heroines.

Godfree triumphed on an occasion of national yearning, Queen Mary's Jubilee Wimbledon, just as Virginia Wade was to do fifty-one years later at the Wimbledon Centennial, the hundredth anniversary of the oldest lawn tennis championships, which coincided with Queen Elizabeth's Silver Jubilee. There are celebrations at Wimbledon whenever possible and Kitty Godfree has often been there, a symbol of continuity in the game that revolutionized women's sport.

It would not have been amusing to see Virginia Wade's face on Sunday morning, when she read the *Observer*'s ruminations on what had made her, a week before her thirty-second birthday, the 1977 Wimbledon champion. The lengthy opinion piece, the only one on the event reprinted in the British *Sporting Year* annual, became the accepted version. What had changed 'the woman named Virginia Wade who had disappointed us so often?' What had happened was this: 'a prickly, complex cocoon' – Virginia Wade's psyche – had opened. After her startling victory in the US Open at the age of twenty-three, Wade had taken nearly a decade to fulfil her promise, although in the three years before that magical Wimbledon, she had found a niche among the world's top five.

The secret of her ability to climb the summit of tennis, to win Wimbledon – the one Wimbledon that really mattered most to the British public and to the Queen – was, said the *Observer*'s Christopher Brasher, Virginia Wade's exposure to the 'American way of life'.

But was he right?

Evidence was cited: in the year of her triumph, Wade had put in more hours on the tennis court than ever before, driving herself hard all season, because she had been on the road with one of the then American league teams, the Apples. She was, as the American idiom goes, in the fast lane: four world-class matches a week in different cities, travelling constantly, practising two to three hours a day in between. Wade had seen her team-mate, 'the ultimate professional', Billie Jean King, at work, seen her 'train like a mad thing' as another English player had put it. There was also the matter of believing in oneself: American-style positive thinking.

> Women's assertion and the feminine sex-role stereotype are related in at least two ways: (1) women tend to show deficits in negative assertion and social initiation, consistent with the stereotype, and (2) some people act negatively to people whose behaviour does not fit the stereotype.
> Charlene L. Muehlenhard, *The Stereotyping of Women*, 1983

'The sheer professionalism of Billie Jean dripping on her like a tap,' Brasher said, coupled with 'the philosophy of her friend Mary-Lou Mellace (with whom she shared her New York flat) that ambition can be achieved by guts and determination' had turned Wade into a winner.

Five years earlier, she had told him: 'I hate people who work too hard. I think laziness the absolute end, but it is overwork I really despise.' That he now called 'a typically amateur English attitude. It has all gone now,' he said, 'replaced by a hard-working professionalism.'[1]

It sounded like the brutal truth. It left out, though, two things.

First, although born in Bournemouth, she had grown up in South Africa, and so was not thoroughly imbued with the British love of defeat. Second, she had linked herself to women who win. 'Really it was because I had changed my life,' she has said, 'that I won.'

The gospel according to Brasher emphasized the get-up-and-go American qualities which had rubbed off on Wade. Surely, though, the crucial factor was not American personality itself but the fact that these influences, these two role models, were women; nor was Wade a passive beneficiary. She had *chosen* to immerse herself in a world of women who had no ambivalence about winning. She had become part of pro tennis's new-girls' network.

Near midnight, Annabel Croft brought the wildly cheering Royal Albert Hall crowd to its feet. There was a noisy explosion of delight – whistles, applause – the admiration of British tennisdom. Champagne corks popped, the fans in dinner jackets clinked glasses. Annabel Croft, the baby of the team, had won her 1984 Wightman Cup match with a strong, wristy, unreturnable forehand.

'After it was all over, I felt so high,' Annabel Croft remembers. The match itself, though, all two and a half hours of it, was relentless torture. The Albert Hall is an unnerving venue. Even Chris Evert, who has won every Wightman singles match she has played since 1971, feels hemmed in by the Albert's tiers of ornate boxes, her dignity assaulted by the echoing clatter of forks and knives.

For Annabel Croft, then eighteen, the youngest British player to play at Wimbledon for fifty years, there had been immense pressure. 'The pressure was so intense I got a splitting headache in the second set.' She lost the set. The headache didn't go away. She played on. 'It was very hot too. I thought I would be sick on the court.' The captain of the British team, Virginia Wade, urged her to go on. 'She calmed me down a bit. She was soothing. She managed to give me confidence and lessen the tension somewhat. Virginia was terrific. But I was quite pressurized.'

The pressure, of course, would never let up; it was a concomitant of the high-stake, high-tension women's circuit. Added to that, was the media spotlight when, at nineteen, Croft superseded Jo Durie as the British number one, becoming the youngest player to head the British women's list since the start of open tennis in 1968, two years after she was born.

But just as they had for Jo Durie, things went from good to bad to worse without ever quite having been wonderful. Croft dropped behind Durie and then behind the tall but not hugely successful Sara Gomer. Croft admitted she didn't like the tennis life. Annabel Croft – it was wildly and not so wildly rumoured – was contemplating retiring.

That old giveaway – body language – showed her lack of confidence: she wasn't, in 1987, the perky Annabel she had been when she first joined the tour. And you could see on the lineaments of her body, the ambivalence of her commitment to pro tennis. Watching her practice at Eastbourne, the previous summer, with the bright pink headband holding her blonde hair in place, a circle of sweat on the back of her shirt, one saw Annabel Croft animated and playful and breathless, like any pretty teenager. But there was much too much puppy fat for an athlete; compared to Martina Navratilova or Hana Mandlikova or even young Beauty, the Argentinian Gabriela Sabatini, who doesn't herself move that exquisitely, Annabel Croft looked out of shape. It was a week before Wimbledon. After the first-round disaster of the US Open, that September, Croft gave the game away: 'Too many chocolates,' she said ruefully.

It was American junk food that had nearly been Navratilova's nemesis. She triumphed anyway eventually; but Navratilova, the lonely defector, had no option but to get back to her tennis. Croft, the girl who grew up with a tennis court in the back yard, had too many other tempting possible life scenarios.

And Annabel Croft's attempt at excellence has been blocked at every turn by the British way of life. When she was nine, her local tennis club in Farnborough refused her membership because she was too young.

When Croft's parents were contemplating sending her to a new school five years later, her mother explained that Annabel would need extra tennis coaching outside school. 'No, she won't,' said the headmistress. 'Our teachers are perfectly adequate.' By that age, American hopefuls had already learned to 'kill, kill, kill' at a good tennis academy.

> Being the best in Britain still means going against the grain. It's a question both of money and attitude. Behaving well often counts for more in British clubs, where tennis has traditionally been more of a recreation than a sport.
>
> Anne Spackman, *Sunday Times*, 1986

Annabel Croft turned professional at fifteen. This was young for a Briton; a sign, many thought, of being inelegantly 'keen'. As the British number one, Croft attempted to buy the unused land separating her local private tennis club from a golf club, her intention being to develop a bustling American-style country club. Planning permission was not forthcoming. No one doubted the need for more indoor facilities. The Sports Council and tennis establishment's £20 million project launched in 1986 was not expected to obliterate the unfavourable comparative statistics – European countries had ten to thirty-five times the number of indoor courts as there were in Britain.

Croft concluded that the Brits she was talking to didn't want the intrusion of fuss or change or near-by paying-players of the wrong sort. 'The land is overgrown, but they won't let me buy it,' Croft complained. 'They say it's for rent only and I can't build on it. It's really insane. It's a typically British attitude.'

Strangers

Harlem is only fifteen miles from Forest Hills. But Harlem and Forest Hills, the original home of the US Open, have always been worlds apart. Forest Hills, in its heyday, acknowledged only one near neighbour. That was Wimbledon, which believed in 'fair play' and crisp tennis whites.

Harlem is black. Tennis still tends to be whitest of white. Little white lies in tandem with big, brutal white lies have kept black players out. Polite bigotry is still enshrined in the sociology of the game. But in 1950, tennis apartheid was ended, when the player they called the 'Black Bombshell', Althea Gibson, cracked the colour bar in tennis.

Tall, tough, rough, from the Harlem slums, Althea Gibson played her first tennis outside her family's tenement apartment on New York's 143rd Street. She is the sport's first Cinderella. And as in the original fairy tale, Althea Gibson's Cinderella story, in which a handful of black princes and a golden-haired, white fairy Godmother appear, did not change the structure of the kingdom. The wicked step-sisters needed no favours from princes, no waving magic wands. They had tickets to the ball.

The staid, tiny black American middle class sustained Althea Gibson throughout the 1940s – partly for her own sake, partly in hopes that she would make a place for blacks in world tennis. Her talent was the one necessary ingredient. But it was the unexpected and unlikely tennis-racket-wielding, white fairy Godmother from Hollywood who effected Althea Gibson's entry into the snobbish bastions of world tennis. There is surely a lesson in *realpolitik* there.

By sheer chance, 143rd was one of Harlem's least mean streets. During the daytime, policemen put up wooden barriers at the ends of the street, closing it to traffic, so children could use it as a playground. It was a Police Athletic League play street. The winos, drug-pedlars, and pimps kept their distance.

All summer long, Althea Gibson played paddle tennis on the baking city streets. Gut-strung rackets weren't sufficiently vandal-proof, so the Police League played paddle tennis, in which you hit the tennis ball with a wooden paddle. The 'court', which was marked out on the asphalt street, was about a quarter of the size of a standard tennis-court. She was learning the wrong game.

Soon, though, Althea Gibson was champion of the block, and won quite a few medals representing 143rd Street in competition with other Harlem play streets. In 1942, when she was fifteen, she won the New York City Parks Department tournament. The soon-to-be-very-famous black bandleader, Buddy Walker, who already had a reputation as a musician but who was still short of cash, was working during the summer off-season as a children's play leader. Impressed when he saw Althea play other children, he took her to the Harlem River Tennis Courts at 150th Street and Seventh Avenue, and had her play a couple of sets with one of his friends.

Althea never forgot the occasion: 'A lot of the other players on the courts stopped their games to watch me play. It was very exciting; it was a competitive sport and I am a competitive sort of person.' Even if she wasn't before that exhibition match, she most assuredly was after it.

A black schoolteacher who had been at 150th Street arranged for her to play at the Cosmopolitan Tennis Club, to which he belonged. In those days it was, Althea Gibson recalled, *'the* ritzy tennis club in Harlem'.

The Cosmopolitan's membership had rigid ideas of social propriety. Gibson was, by her own admission, 'living pretty wild'. She recalls: 'They were undoubtedly more strict than white people of similar position, for the obvious reason that they felt they had to be doubly careful in order to overcome the prejudiced attitude that all Negroes lived eight to a room in dirty houses and drank gin all day and settled all their arguments with knives.

'I really wasn't the tennis type. I had trouble as a competitor because I kept wanting to fight the other player every time I started losing a match . . .' she says.[1]

She had played truant often and left school at the earliest opportunity. She was mostly 'on welfare', the public dole. As she wasn't at all interested in the menial work that was open to her, she wasn't even looking for a job. Her friends of her own age were not exactly paragons of propriety, nor was she. But the Cosmopolites put up with her and she put up with them.

Gradually she gave in to propriety: 'The polite manners of the game that seemed so silly to me at first, gradually began to appeal to me. So did the pretty white clothes.' Black, in the 1940s, was not yet beautiful.

'After a while I began to understand that you could walk out on the court like a lady, all dressed up in immaculate white, be polite to everybody, and still play like a tiger and beat the liver and lights out of the ball.'

Soon, losing was no longer the problem.

It was not difficult to dominate black girls' tennis; there were few opponents in a game that was usually played in private clubs; it was too easy; it was frustratingly boring. Gibson began to hang around pool rooms; there were, in Harlem, many destructive distractions.

She was brawny, she liked sport more than she liked make-up. Her father, an underpaid garage mechanic, had wanted her to be a boxer until he realized it was 'unsuitable' for a girl, but by then he had taught her to fight. It was only later that she worried that she would be a failure as a woman because she was an athlete, and a failure as an athlete because she was the wrong colour for her sport.

Like any teenager, she could be rebellious, troublesome, particularly when she was 'acting out'. On an afternoon when the boxing champion Sugar Ray Robinson was doing a Harlem walkabout, Althea Gibson pushed to the head of the crowd, and said aggressively: 'You're Sugar Ray. Well, I can beat you.'

He took her home to meet his wife Edna Mae, who saw at once that Gibson, now a gangling teenager who was nearly five-foot-eleven, was very unhappy. Sugar Ray, who was *the* role model for athletic black kids of his era, did indirectly help change Althea Gibson's life, but it was Edna Mae who took a direct interest. 'She had a gaunt build and felt she was the least good-looking girl she knew,' Edna Mae Robinson remembered. 'She had insecurity and went into herself. She used to talk wild. I tried to make her feel she could be something.'

The worlds of white and black tennis rarely intersected, but a white woman from California, Alice Marble, the 1939 Wimbledon and the four-times US singles champion (1936, 1938–1940), played an exhibition match at the Cosmopolitan. She had played baseball happily and well until, at age fifteen, she gave in to the pressure to play something that was more feminine. She had a powerful tennis game. It was Alice Marble who invented the woman's serve-and-volley game, the tactics of which were serve hard, come to the net, attack. This was, by the late 1930s, regarded as the 'typically American' game.

'Until I saw her,' Gibson said, 'I'd always had eyes only for the good men players. But her effectiveness of strike, and the power that she had, impressed me terrifically. Basically, of course, it was the aggressiveness behind her game that I liked. Watching her smack that effortless serve, and then follow it in to the net and put the ball away with an overhead as good as any man's, I saw possibilities in the game of tennis that I had never seen before.'

Althea Gibson was big, lean, wiry: that added up to strong. She too was capable of a big game. Her triumphs so far had been confined to the small world of black tennis. She was Negro girls' singles champion of New York State. Then she took the national title. Her coach was the one-armed tennis pro Fred Johnson.

Now the black-run American Tennis Association, which had always been separate from the US Lawn Tennis Association, but which of course had never been equal, put on a New York State Open Championship, at the Cosmopolitan Club. She won it. 'What mostly made me feel good was that the girl I beat in the finals, Nina Irwin, was a white girl. . . . I was not only as good as she was, I was better.'[2]

The strict discipline which would make her the best tennis player in America began in August 1946, when Althea Gibson, just turning twenty, left New York City. She was to live in North Carolina in the household of a black, tennis-playing doctor during the school year so that she could return to high school and prepare for college. The doctor had a tennis court in his backyard. In the summer, she moved to Virginia. A second doctor took her in his car to play the tournament circuit.

Life in the South was precarious for an uppity New Yorker. The paint might be peeling in the slums of Harlem, where there was crime and racism, but when she got on the bus in North Carolina she was galled to see: 'White in front, Colored in rear'. There was no difference, however, in the price of the fare. She took a seat as near the front as she could get away with. The black girls she went to school with had Southern belle notions – well, they did in comparison with her. She didn't have much time to flirt with the boys; she didn't seem to have much interest in anything but sport. And so they relegated her socially to the back of the bus.

Three years later she graduated from high school and went deeper South, to Florida Agricultural and Mechanical College, where she had an athletics scholarship. She had won the black women's national title every year since 1947. (She would eventually win it ten times in a row.) She was now thought to be as good as the leading white players.

Sport is, in theory, an arena for anti-racism because individual performances are subject to objective measurement. Evaluations of blacks are less likely to be influenced by racial prejudices than they would be in situations where evaluations are more subjective. But first you have to be allowed to play. The fabled Eastern tournaments, which were the necessary stepping stone to the national championships at Forest Hills, were by invitation only, and none were sent to blacks.

Now Alice Marble, the most undersung heroine in women's tennis, was to figure in Gibson's life again. Memories are short in sport, but Alice Marble's name was writ large; they still respected her at Forest Hills, where she had won the last of her four singles and seven doubles titles in 1940, before going professional the next year. She had won all of her titles *after* contracting tuberculosis – the diagnosis had come when she collapsed on court at the 1934 French Open. TB was a killer then, and a scandal because it was thought to be an 'unclean' disease. Doctors told Marble her career was over. Marble returned to win at Wimbledon and Forest Hills.

In 1950, ten years after her last glorious tennis, she was a hard-smoking battler with a cough. Now she took on the monolithic US Lawn Tennis Association, charging, in *American Lawn Tennis* magazine, that the USLTA had a definite, though unwritten, policy of excluding blacks from tournaments.

'I can't honestly say that I believe Miss Gibson to be a potential champion, I don't know,' Marble said. Althea Gibson's groundstrokes could knock your head off; the serve was fast. But her 'bold game', with its 'lovely strokes', she wrote, often relied on power rather than finesse. And many players failed to live up to their promise. But if Gibson was not given a chance, Marble herself 'would be bitterly ashamed' of tennis. The newspapers picked up the story. Amid raging controversy, the USLTA was forced to change its ways to quell the bad publicity.

> If she can do it, a proud new chapter will have been added to the history of tennis. If she cannot, we will have seen nothing more and nothing less than one more youngster who failed to live up to her promise. But if she is refused a chance to succeed or to fail, then there is an uneradicable mark against a game to which I have devoted most of my life, and I would be bitterly ashamed.
>
> Alice Marble, *American Lawn Tennis Magazine*, 1950

When Althea Gibson stepped on to the green court of the West Side Tennis Club, at Forest Hills, she made history. She was the first black of either sex ever to play in the national championships. At twenty-four, she had shattered the colour bar in American tennis.

Surely it was too much to expect that she would also win the championship? She whirled through her first match victorious. When Gibson, with her rough-and-tumble game, was listed to play Louise Brough, the thrice and reigning Wimbledon champion, the Forest Hills crowd snorted. They knew a thing about tennis. Brough, whose every shot was sliced, whose play was carved and cut, and who made fewer service faults than any player since Suzanne Lenglen, would walk away with the match. In Harlem, though, the bookmakers were working overtime.

Louise Brough took the first set, 6–1.

Unfazed, in the second set Gibson trounced her soundly, 6–3.

Now it was getting interesting. Even the least colour-blind of sports-writers sighed. What a story it would be if the 'Black Bomber' were to defeat the champion.

The third set was a slugging match. It was anybody's match and neither player was giving it away. As the score rose and rose and rose, the crowd held its breath. The sports-writers scratched at their pads. At 7–6 in Brough's favour, the pressure was immense, the atmosphere electric.

Byron and Shelley would have understood what happened next: the heavens split. The rain stopped all play for the day. Had the tension in the stadium been communicated to the clouds? Or was it banal coincidence? It was left to the poets to speculate; the bookmakers – and not just in Harlem – got cracking. That day the press earned their living too. The players winced and watched the skies.

By morning, when play was resumed, Althea Gibson had had too much time to think about the awe of the occasion, the possible upset victory; she was a nervous wreck. Louise Brough won the match 6–1, 3–6, 9–7.

But Althea Gibson had won national acclaim. Wimbledon would come next.

There had been great black tennis players before her, but because they had not been allowed to play against white, they had not achieved any reputation outside the black tennis ghetto. It was Catch–22. Sports achievements were not valued unless there were whites involved to make them significant enough to record. In 1917, Lucy Slowe had become the first US singles champion on the black circuit. Her victory, at the Monumental Tennis Club in Baltimore, Maryland, had not been page one news in the nationals.

Ora Washington held on to the black ATA women's singles title for twelve years, from 1924 to 1936. Because the renowned champion, Helen Wills, now Mrs Freddie Moody, had declined a challenge match,

Ora Washington had stayed out of the annals and out of the national newspapers.

England, in the summer of 1951, welcomed the arrival of the 'first Negress' ever to 'climb the heights of amateur tennis'. She would play in Manchester, then at Wimbledon. The press reported that there had, of course, never been a colour bar in England. Even so, they felt obliged to print intimate details about this exotic new species of tennis player: Althea Gibson, it was noted, took a bath every afternoon.

The novelty of being the first black player began to wear thin a few years after that first Wimbledon, in which she had reached the quarter-finals. Her national ranking dropped from seventh to twelfth. Money was tight. In Harlem people grew up early. At twenty-eight, she felt she wasn't getting anywhere, and that she had been a child for too long. In frustration, she put in an application to join the US Army; it would be a steady career and would make a woman of her – and, she felt, high time. Sport was well recognized as a way up for exceptionally gifted black Americans; it looked as if, as in most cases, it wasn't going to take her far enough. Since the Second World War, the armed services were the other recognized way out of mean poverty for blacks.

In the autumn of 1955, before her application had been accepted – in fact, just in the nick of time – the US State Department intervened, inviting her to make a 'goodwill' tennis-playing tour of South-East Asia. Because the 1954 Supreme Court decision that schools should be racially integrated had led to internationally reported riots and lynchings in the South, America badly needed a black goodwill ambassador. Gibson agreed to go.

That tour changed everything. 'At the time, I was champion of nothing and unlikely ever to be.' The knowledge that the US government thought she was 'a somebody' did wonders. She won the Indian singles title and then went on to the European circuit, where she won fifteen consecutive tournaments, reached the Wimbledon quarter-finals, and went to the final at Forest Hills. In Asia, she had found her game.

On the brick-red clay of the Roland Garros Stadium, in Auteuil, Paris, she demonstrated it. In May 1956, Gibson was battling in the sun against the defending champion Angela Mortimer for the French championship. The first set went to Gibson, 6–0. There was a hush: was history about to be made?

But the second set seemed likely to go on to eternity as the score mounted slowly: 6–all, 8–all, 10–all, with rallies of twenty, even thirty strokes, played for each point. Both women's play was stupendous: stamina would have to be the deciding factor. And the tall, tough, slum kid had it. Gibson finally took the marathon set 12–10. She was the new champion of France, and the first black woman to win one of the world's four major Grand Slam singles titles.

Queen Elizabeth II was there on the scorching Saturday of the 1957 Wimbledon final. In the luncheon room, ice blocks were put in front of the electric fans so that the VIPs would enjoy the meal. From time to time, someone alluded to the unusual, er, backgrounds, of the two finalists. Sadly, neither was English, and both were the wrong kind of American.

Althea Gibson was big and black. In two months, she would be thirty years old. Her opponent, pony-tailed Darlene Hard, who was Gibson's doubles partner, was small-boned, blonde, to all appearances a golden girl, but she came from a blue-collar Mid-western family and had been a waitress to finance her tennis career. The match was announced, and the middle-class, even upper class, tennis sorority and fraternity sat down in seats surrounding the centre court to watch two working-class Americans slug it out. The Queen was in the Royal Box, behind the baseline.

On court, the temperature was close to 100 degrees Fahrenheit. There was no breeze at all; it was suffocating. Perhaps all those childhood summers playing on the baking Harlem streets helped. Gibson was quick and alert on the court and less inclined to be erratic than usual. Today, her game was pure, aggressive Alice Marble: Gibson's tactics being to try to win all points off service or volleys from the net. It was a classic serve-and-volley game.

Darlene Hard's delicate drop shots were no match. Gibson decimated Hard, 6–3, 6–2 in an unusually one-sided final. It had taken her thirty years and forty-nine minutes to win the most coveted title in tennis.

'When I had won, they tell me I kept saying, "At last! At last!"' Gibson recalled in her memoirs. All she can remember doing is running to the net and shaking hands with Darlene Hard and uttering the usual cliché, 'I was lucky.'

Then she talked to the Queen.

Elizabeth reportedly said, 'It was a very enjoyable match, but you must have been very hot on the court.' Gibson's reply: 'I hope it wasn't as hot in the Royal Box.' The tennis was better than the conversation; at Wimbledon it always is.

At the Wimbledon Ball that night, at the Dorchester, Gibson, in her floor-length dress, sat at the head table between the Duke of Kent and the men's singles winner, the Australian Lew Hoad. She and Hoad danced the first dance together. When it came to the lady champion's thank you speech, she rattled off a long list of names – social workers, teachers, friends, the doctors, cousins – the people she had known before she became somebody. More than one of the well-mannered, well-dressed guests found the speech boring; but it was heart-felt; and it did go on and on.

Then, breaking custom further, she serenaded the other dinner guests, singing 'Around the World', and 'If I Loved You'. Many people have mentioned that the distance from the slums of Harlem to the Wimbledon Ball is rather more than around the world. No one seems even to have considered that she might have been hinting that she didn't entirely love the white tennis Establishment, who were so belatedly accepting her only because she was champion.

Gibson went home, to a heroine's welcome: a New York ticker-tape parade. There were crowds lining the streets, and from the open windows of buildings came a summer snowfall of white ticker-tape, torn up newspapers, shredded telephone books, confetti.

Only three people had seen her off at Idlewild Airport when she left for Wimbledon. Now she was besieged by would-be friends. Politicians got in on the euphoria that surrounded her new fame. She was 'a credit to her race'. Many people thought she might also become a credit to their bank accounts. Or at least an asset with their voters. But nothing could deter her from the tennis.

At Forest Hills, two months later, in the final of the American championship, the player who had knocked Gibson out of her first Forest Hills, Louise Brough, fell to her 6–2, 6–3. A dozen black men – but no other women – played that tournament. The black doctors and her success had paved their way. Gibson was named Associated Press Woman Athlete of the Year.

And the next year at Wimbledon and Forest Hills she did it again.

If it is a heavy burden being the top-ranked black woman on the international circuit, Texan Zina Garrison doesn't show it. In 1984, at the age of nineteen, Garrison, the youngest of seven children, won the European Indoor title in Zurich, becoming the first black woman to win a major event since Leslie Allen had won the Avon Championships in Detroit, in 1981. That was the year Zina Garrison won the Wimbledon and US Open junior titles. In 1985, Zina Garrison defeated Chris Evert in straight sets to win the Amelia Island Plantation championship. Garrison, who has ranked fifth in the world, is the best black player since Althea Gibson.

Garrison was, even in her teens, a role model for many black children. Not just in her home city of Houston, where she learned her tennis in the municipal parks programme for youngsters. Not just in New York City, where she put on tennis demonstrations for ten and eleven year olds.

The American city parks programmes – of which Billie Jean King is also a graduate – are the best alternative to being free, white, and upper middle-class if you want to be a serious tennis player. (There are precious few working-class Brits in tennis – white, black, or otherwise.)

There are still few blacks in tennis, however. A 1969 study of 265 American black athletes found that eighty per cent were involved in track, but many would rather have been playing tennis, or other socially more prestigious sports like gymnastics and badminton. 'Limited opportunities', not 'individual preference' had guided them to track. Ten years later the figure in track was still eighty per cent. A paper presented at the American National Black Women in Sport Conference, in Washington DC in 1980, spoke of 'an under-representation' of black women in swimming, golf, gymnastics, synchronized swimming, fencing, and tennis. There has not been much change. Building a tennis career costs money, which most blacks in Britain, Europe and the US don't have. Few young black players are fortunate enough to find princes and fairy Godmothers. Sports sociologist Doris Corbett says, 'Black women face all the discrimination that all women face plus there is the additional burden of racism. This is especially true in sports.'[3]

Zina Garrison says that she never encounters prejudice in tennis. 'I'm insulated,' she says. She has her equivalent of the black doctors. Wherever young black players are growing up and scanning the tennis magazines or watching the TV sports programmes they are looking for Zina Garrison – and finding her play reported far less than that of players with whiter glamour.

Althea Gibson's fairy Godmother Alice Marble, the great pre-war champion, had come from California, from a world far removed from Harlem. She knew Clark Cable. The actress Carole Lombard had encouraged her recovery from TB. Alice Marble became 'Hollywood's favourite tennis player'. The enormity of her courage in taking on the tennis establishment, in peaceable 1950, smack in the middle of the age of conformity, is hard to overstate. What has gone entirely unnoticed is her other egalitarian achievement, which occurred undramatically, little by little.

Alice Marble perhaps did not realize it at the time, but she was starting an old girls' network in tennis. *What was so magnificent was that it even welcomed new girls.* Nine years after storming the barricades on behalf of Althea Gibson, Marble helped out another young woman who had been born into the wrong social class for tennis. Billie Jean Moffitt, later King, a lower-middle-class WASP from California, was the chubby daughter of a fireman and a part-time Tupperware saleswoman.

Alice Marble became her coach. 'I got to hit with her when I was fifteen,' says Billie Jean King. Every week-end Alice Marble tore apart and put back together – improved – the teenage Billie Jean's game. Pleurisy and heavy smoking and a rasping cough didn't prevent Marble from being an effective coach. 'With her help and being around her, I really learned and observed a champion's mentality. The positive thinking,' King says. 'I think she saw a little bit of herself in me.'[4]

One evening, Billie Jean confided she wanted to be the best player in the world, better even than Alice Marble, and Marble, who hadn't quite mastered the psychology of supersedence that makes the best teachers and coaches, got furious. The lessons were over.

King went on to win a record twenty Wimbledon titles. Long after she, too, had been superseded as a player – on the windy, celebratory, September 1986 day of the 100th US Championship final at Flushing Meadow – Alice Marble, at the age of seventy-three, handed the victor's trophy to Martina Navratilova and the 19,000 people seated around the centre court applauded and whistled and shouted and stamped their feet. If anyone amid the vulgar fanfare and the fine tennis of that centennial regarded Marble as a symbol of continuity, it was an error. Make no mistake, she was not a decrepit Old Dear. Alice Marble was an embodiment of transition. Change. She brought in the new girls, she argued against racism; she didn't carry on business as usual.

Her young charge Billie Jean followed in her footsteps.

Hype and Circumstance

Mother's Day 1973 started badly for Margaret Court.

The big-boned Australian who hit the hardest ball in the women's game was the most famous mother in tennis. On this foggy 13 May California morning, the day of the televised 'Battle of the Sexes', which pitted her against the American professed male chauvinist, Bobby Riggs, Margaret Court's fourteen-month-old son Danny woke early and tossed her favourite pair of tennis shoes into the toilet.

The day would get worse.

Billie Jean King, the biggest name in women's tennis, had refused Riggs's challenge, considering it beneath contempt. Thirty-year-old Margaret Court agreed to play him because the money – $10,000 guaranteed by TV, plus $10,000 more to the winner – was so enticing. Although she had won *everything* in tennis, Court had peaked before million-dollar money entered the game. Despite her three previous US Open singles titles (1962, 1965, 1969) and her two previous Wimbledon singles championships (1963 and 1965), in 1970, her *annus mirabilis* – the year she won the four top tournaments, capturing the Grand Slam – Margaret Court earned somewhere between $15,000 and $60,000 – depending on which estimate you accept. During the next two years her income plummeted. Pregnant, she played little, concentrating on having the baby, and won only the 1971 Australian singles championship. She won no major singles title at all in 1972. 1973 was her comeback year.

Riggs saw the Battle of the Sexes as a come-back vehicle too. He was fifty-five, a former Wimbledon and US Open champion, currently ranked number one in the men's fifty-and-over bracket. He was a proud and loud male chauvinist. Women belonged in the kitchen, he said, and in the bedroom, not on the tennis-court. They played badly. 'Since women don't play tennis as well as men do,' he said, 'they don't deserve to be paid as much as men.'

They weren't. But he was annoyed that Billie Jean King had become the first woman athlete in any sport to earn more than $100,000 in a single season. Tennis had only recently begun to go professional. King was the prime fighter for equal pay, which hadn't happened yet. But women were taking control of the circuit with their own pro tour, and the big money was starting to come in. In 1971, the first full year of the new Virginia Slims women's pro tour, King dominated the game, winning $117,400 in prize money. It was at the time a fortune – for a woman. Rod Laver made $292,000 on the men's tour the same year.

That sort of money was not yet being spread around. Riggs was earning what he considered nearly nothing, and now that he was a 'senior', his matches were not happening on centre court. Women 'were raking in the loot – and getting all the glory,' he complained. He was sure he 'could beat any woman player in the world'.

As soon as Margaret Court, who had the most aggressive, the most powerful – the 'manliest' – game in women's tennis, agreed to the televised challenge match, Riggs began to boast that he would beat her and that that would put women in their proper place, which wasn't on a tennis-court. He said it on television and to sports reporters and to Margaret Court herself – as often as possible. It wasn't idle boasting; it was a calculated ploy.

Margaret Court was known to choke when the pressure was on. Virginia Wade calls her 'the nervous champion'. Court played a daring serve-and-volley game. She took more chances, staked more on being able to make the first volley than any woman up to her time, and she was right to – she was, by far, the most able player on the circuit. But at tense moments, she often fluffed. If not for her temperament, Margaret Court could conceivably have doubled her impressive match win record.

Court may have been particularly nervous about competing against men. She was a heavily-built woman, with a long jaw. Not very dainty. She was unhappy with her nice big shoulders. At times she may have envied the delicate little Brazilian Maria Bueno, to whom she had lost her Wimbledon title in 1964.

When Margaret Court won her first Wimbledon championship – as Margaret Smith – she spoke of her lack of womanly fulfilment in the role of tennis champion. Too eminent for comfort, she retired, opening a boutique in Perth, Australia. She returned to tennis only after her marriage. Now, in the spring of 1973, with no recent string of victories to bolster her ego, how could she *not* feel a conflict about how her femininity would fare in the match with Riggs? She was, many thought, 'psyched out'.

Riggs's pre-match strategy had been to bring the psychological temperature to the boil. 'I knew about her tendency to cave in under the pressure of big matches. I determined to do what I could to build up the pressure on Margaret in all of my press conferences by emphasizing the importance of the match,' he admitted, with absolutely no contrition, in his memoir *Court Hustler*. 'In my comments I tried to give the impression that the pressure was all on Margaret. I insisted she had everything to lose, as the woman's champion upholding the reputation of her sex, while I had nothing to lose,' he said.[1]

Originally, Riggs had mooted it as a 'fun match', but he trained with desperate seriousness. Every day, he downed 415 pills prescribed by the Hollywood nutritionist who had rejuvenated Liberace and Lawrence Welk, the two old-timers with the most virile audience ratings on American television. Riggs, a talented huckster, worked to build Riggs vs. Court to huge notoriety. 'I called it the Match of the Century, and this caught on.'

'My nineteen-year-old daughter, Dolly, who came out to California from school in the east to see the match, was torn by it. She encouraged me, but she did say, "If you weren't my father, I'd be rooting for Margaret Court." '[2]

And so a hokey, trumped-up non-match, which had been dreamed up to return a has-been to the limelight, was billed as the 'Match of the Century'. By the time it was played in California on Mother's Day before an audience of sixty million television viewers – in the United States, Australia, Canada, and Mexico – it had become an archetypal Battle of the Sexes.

Riggs arrived for the match with his tennis racket and an armful of red roses, a Mother's Day bouquet. There was a note too. It said, 'For one of the all-time greats in tennis who is just as great a mother.' Court curtsied her 'thanks'.

There was a shorter than usual knock-up; TV couldn't be kept waiting. Then play began, Court hitting them fast and hard, Riggs playing soft and slow. He could never have beaten her at her own game, and he didn't try. He says she hadn't expected him 'to play like a woman' – by which he means the limited range of his shots, not the rich psychological strategy or the technical finesse. In fifty-seven minutes it was over, 6–2, 6–1. Court had choked and lost. Someone called it the Mother's Day Massacre. The label stuck.

Billie Jean King was getting on a plane from Japan to Honolulu when she heard the result on the radio. She had lost to Margaret Court in two dramatic Wimbledon finals. But at the age of twenty-nine, five-foot-four-inch Billie Jean King was the Wimbledon, the US, and the French singles champion, and she was the star of the burgeoning Virginia Slims pro tour, which she and Gladys Heldman, the tennis magazine publisher turned promoter, had founded, in 1970. Nine female players had joined together to play their own women's tour when they became outraged at the huge disparity in the prize money being offered to male and female tennis pros. Now Billie Jean King was viewed as a 'women's libber'. On the issue of equal pay for women, King was, to say the least, outspoken. In the face of the Court Fiasco, she agreed to take Riggs's challenge, and the money might have had something to do with it. The opponents of women's liberation hoped her defeat would polish off the American women's movement.

The match was hyped for all it was worth – $200,000 in television and other rights, with an extra $100,000 for the winner. In the four months between the two challenge matches, the $10,000 Court had risked so much for – and lost – had become a mess of pottage.

In America, money has always talked. Now it lectured. The same entrepreneur who promoted Muhammad Ali vs. Joe Frazier into a twenty-million-dollar media boxing spectacular, took on King–Riggs. At the press conference in New York, called simply to announce that King had accepted the challenge and would play some time, some place, the promoter, Jerry Perenchio, declared, 'The Ali–Frazier fight was "the Fight". This is "the Match".'

This was balderdash, but it suited everyone. Big stories make big bylines and a temporary small increase in circulation. One grateful journalist even called Riggs 'the white Muhammad Ali'.

Riggs's pre-match strategy was the same as the one he used on Margaret Court. 'I intended to put the pressure on her from the very beginning and keep building it up,' he said. 'This is the Libber versus the Lobber,' he told the press. 'We said we had the Match of the Century the last time. But obviously we had the wrong girl. We should have had the Women's Lib leader, Billie Jean.'[3]

Billie Jean King's reply: 'You do your hustling off the court. I'll do my hustling on the court.'

Women tennis players can't stand the pressure of playing against men. Girls are brought up from the time they are six to read books, eat candy, and go to dancing class. They can't compete against men, can't stand the strain.

Gene Scott, quoted in *Court Hustler*, 1973

Bets were rife too, with Bobby Riggs 5–2 favourite to win when the match eventually took place on 20 September 1973, in the Houston Astrodome. Riggs says that Nora Ephron, who was covering the match for the American men's magazine *Esquire*, insisted on Jimmy the Greek's slightly more favourable Las Vegas odds when she bet five hundred dollars on King. It was a kitty collected from all the women journalists.

'I won't play,' Billie Jean King says.

'She just won't,' Larry King says.

The lights are being set up at the Houston Astrodome for the Riggs vs. King match, which is to take place in two days' time. Thirty thousand, four hundred and seventy-two people are intending to be there, an all-time record for a tennis match. One thousand seats are reserved for celebrities who have paid $100 each. The eighty-piece band from the University of Houston has had its red uniforms dry-cleaned, and the majorettes, frantically practising, are bathed in sweat. There are forty-eight million Americans expecting to slouch in front of their television sets to watch the Battle of the Sexes, even though the movie *Bonnie and Clyde* is getting its first televised showing on another channel. In Europe and Australia and in the Orient, millions of people are planning to watch via satellite.

'I just won't play,' Billie Jean King tells Roone Arledge, who is the head of ABC-TV Sports. Unless the well-known player-promoter Jack Kramer is barred from the commentators' booth, the chunky woman with the short, fat legs that carry her so quickly over a tennis-court is intending to baulk. 'I have fought Kramer and what he stands for – opposition to women's tennis – all my life,' she says. 'I didn't care if the whole human race had bet on that match,' she would explain later, 'I was not going to play if Kramer was up there with Howard Cossell.'[4]

Sportscaster Howard Cossell was not exactly God's gift to women, but Jack Kramer, she felt, was their dedicated opponent. His pigheadedness, in 1970, had led to the start of the women's tour. When he refused to allot any more than one-twelfth of the prize money to women at his Pacific Southwest Tournament, nine female tennis players, led by Billie Jean King, boycotted the tournament. Instead, they played their own tournament in Houston, Texas, for a purse of $7,500. The sponsor was the Philip P. Morris tobacco company, manufacturers of Virginia Slims. By the following year, total prize money on the Virginia Slims women's tour had gushed to $500,000. Billie Jean King didn't like the idea of Jack Kramer there, in the ABC-TV booth, poisoning the minds of millions, and cashing in on her success.

She has told this to the TV sports people, including Roone Arledge, for weeks, and they have regarded it as a joke. Now, Roone Arledge says, 'You're not really serious, are you?'

And that's when Larry King, her business manager and husband, says, 'Roone, Billie Jean won't play. She just won't. I know her. Don't force her to make that decision. Believe me.'

Arledge does believe Larry King.

A man's word is his bond. Even in 1973, a woman's word is still a whim.

Paradoxically, that Catch-22 of femininity is at this moment finally working in Billie Jean's favour. Women, it is believed, are by nature unreasonable; and it is unreasonable for her to baulk now, with so many dollars and cents riding on the match, and so many eyes at the ready.

Maybe this is the one time they shouldn't have believed her – or rather Larry. Who knows, maybe she would have given in if Arledge had dug in his heels, but he didn't, too risky, *prime time*, 8 to 10 p.m. And for Kramer, a big man in tennis, as his colleagues at the network know, this is just one spot appearance. But if she refuses to play, and it comes out she warned them, *weeks* ago, no one at the network wants to follow that thought to its logical conclusion. Instead, Kramer is out.

So, Billie Jean King picks up her racket ready to play, with one victory for equality in women's tennis already chalked up. But things don't look good. Aside from the pressure, which is white hot, and the odds, which are against her in every bookmakers in the world, there is the fact that the match is to be the best of five sets, even though the rules limit the women's game to the best of three. She has never played the best of five in competition. But the TV network slot for the match is two hours of richly sponsored time – and there has got to be enough tennis to balance out the commercials. So King must beat Riggs at his own game.

He makes his entrance at the Astrodome in a rickshaw. She is delivered on a golden divan, born aloft by four beefy football players. She accepts the kiss and the candy Sugar-Daddy sucker he has brought her, one of his sponsor's products. Her gift for him, the male chauvinist pig, is a piglet.

There are smiles, cheers, music, applause. Fanfare. Then she stalks out on to the Sportsface carpet, and wipes the court with him. Her speed, her backhand, his double-faults. It is a straight set victory, 6–4, 6–3, 6–3.

For reasons which can be analysed, but which are, at their core, irrational, this defeat of Bobby Riggs, aged fifty-five, by a woman player in her prime, convinced the world that women's tennis was worth paying for. This absurd match became for women's tennis the drop shot and volley heard round the world.

It was, quintessentially, a media event.

It was designed for television which, like the tabloids of the past, and indeed like most newspapers of the present, likes to keep things simple. Good vs. evil, man vs. woman; nice clean polarities. Television crews look for what Richard Schickel, in *Common Fame*, calls 'simplifying symbols – usually people, sometimes objects – that crystallize and personify an issue, an ideal, a longing'. This is one way of making abstract issues accessible. What matter if ideas get a little *lumpen* on the way to transmission? For every ideology or event there is a spokesperson, an emblem. Mailer = literature. Walesa = dissidence. A gaunt Ethiopian = famine. 'These are the movie stars of the world of (simplified) ideas.' In this way, Billie Jean King came to = women's liberation.

She also, for many people, came to equal tennis, even though by now Chris Evert was warming up in the wings. Crusty fathers-in-law knew who you meant when you said Billie Jean. Or even BJK.

There is no doubt Billie Jean's victory was a big one for the women's movement – and for all women. One guy said to me after the match: 'This set my marriage back ten years – and I've only been married two.'

Bobby Riggs, *Court Hustler*, 1973

Myth has an imperative, buttonholing character: stemming from an historical concept, directly springing from contingency (a Latin class, a threatened Empire), it is *I* whom it has come to seek.

Roland Barthes, *Mythologies*, 1972

American loners pull the trigger on celebrities to get a spot on the evening news, to make history instantly. This is because they realize more than most of us do how influential celebrities have become. They sell products, they sell ideas, they sell political candidates. If it is true, as Richard Schickel says, that celebrities now are 'the chief agents of moral change in the United States', may God have mercy on our souls. On

20 September 1973, however, when King trounced Riggs, and which she still speaks of as the match in which she aced the most stress, even after winning a record twenty Wimbledon titles, God was on our side. The match was seen as a Battle of the Sexes which women had won. It was a sign of women's liberation. Or was it a signifier? In any event, it had more than avenged the Mother's Day Massacre.

> In 1967 I won all three titles at Wimbledon – singles, doubles and mixed – and I came back to my country, and there was no one to meet me, no one at all. And barely six years later, there I was in the Houston Astrodome, playing prime time to the world in what amounted to the Roman Colosseum, with everyone in civilization chanting my name, hating me or loving me . . . and people were throwing money at me or grabbing at me or calling me a symbol or a leader or a radical feminist.
>
> Billie Jean King

Lottie Dod, of course, had done it all before. The Battle of the Sexes on the tennis-court had been won way back in 1888, when the teenage girl from Cheshire, England, defeated the reigning Wimbledon champion, Ernest Renshaw. There is a telling photograph (see plates) of them sitting together on a park bench. She in a hat and long skirt, with her feet flat on the ground, a tennis racket in her left hand and a grin on her chubby, soft-featured face. He has his legs crossed, his cap pulled down, and is glowering. No one knows whether or not this photograph was taken before or after their exhibition match at Exmouth, but it looks like after.

Dod won her first Wimbledon when she was three months shy of sixteen and is still the youngest winner in the more than a century of the championships. As a schoolgirl, she was allowed to wear slightly shorter skirts than her older opponents, which meant it was easier for her to run. Dod was a natural: strong, fast, and exquisitely co-ordinated. Virginia Wade, who is a student of the history of her game, believes her to be 'the first player to approach the fitness and athleticism of the men'.

Black-haired, opinionated Dod was the women's Wimbledon singles champion when she faced Renshaw, who had been a singles finalist three times. He was a top player and in his prime. She lost her first exhibition match, but took him to three sets. As was the custom, he had a handicap – she started with a score of 30 in each game. So did she –

those long skirts and corsets. Later that year, she beat him. At a time when women had so little encouragement or opportunity to develop their muscle, it was an extraordinary achievement. It didn't, however, make Lottie Dod rich.

After winning Wimbledon five times, Dod retired at the age of twenty-one. It is tempting to see that as the first occurrence of what would be a very common syndrome a century later: had Lottie started too young and burned out? No other woman could beat her. None was even putting up an interesting fight: 'Ladies would find (if they tried) that many a ball, seemingly out of reach, could be returned with ease,' she said archly. 'Instead of running they go a few steps and exclaim, "Oh, I can't" and stop.' She got bored with winning Wimbledon, and went on to become a golf champion, and to compete in the Olympics in archery. Tennis was not a career then, there was no pressure on Lottie Dod to win, or even to compete – one year she and her sister went boating in the Hebrides instead of playing Wimbledon.

In May, not long before Mother's Day 1981, Billie Jean King found herself the target of another media blitz. This time it was hard to be a winner.

Marilyn Barnett, who had been her lover, filed suit for 'galimony'. Billie Jean King learned of the lawsuit in Florida, pondered it in New York, and flew to Los Angeles for the press conference, where she said: 'Yes, I had an affair while I was married, and it was with a woman.'

The lesbian taint had long shadowed tennis and golf, indeed sport itself. As one woman tennis pro said at the time, 'Reporters don't ask Arthur Ashe who the gay men on the circuit are. But they ask the women players which players are gay.'

There *were* lesbians on the tennis circuit. There are lesbians everywhere. Even in the staid 1950s, twenty-eight per cent of women interviewed admitted to Kinsey researchers that they had sexual responses to other women and thirteen per cent had had sex to the point of orgasm. Thirty years of openness towards sexuality had been going on since then.

> If I had been caught making love to a male movie star at high noon in Times Square, it wouldn't even have made the six o'clock news. But Billie Jean and a woman . . .
>
> Billie Jean King, *The Autobiography*, 1982

There may even be more lesbians in sport than is proportional to the population; it took a certain amount of guts for a woman to admit to homosexual feeling – a certain amount of disregard for convention – and it was still unconventional for a woman to put her body on the line at élite sport. Moreover, as the American sportswriter Jane Kaplan observed, the fear of being thought homosexual has kept some heterosexual women out of sport.[5]

Somewhere in a village in France or maybe in Huizen, Holland, or in a small town in Derbyshire, there is a woman in frilly underwear who, if she had dared to compete seriously at tennis, could have knocked the bejesus out of Chris Evert or even King or Navratilova or young Steffi Graf.

Sport has always been, and still is to a very large extent, viewed as masculine and masculizing territory. You had to be a lesbian to be interested in it; and if you were not, sport would by some alchemy – the slap of sneakers on the track, the sight of naked breasts in the changing room – transform you. The reason reporters went around looking for lesbians in the changing room was that it seemed *unnatural* to them for women to play sport.

But because sport was an affirmation of manhood, no one saw any particular reason to doubt a sportsman's heterosexuality. The discovery that Big Bill Tilden, the Mr Tennis of the 1920s, was gay, and the more recent revelations by American football players, did not make many people regard macho Sportsworld with suspicion.

> Social suspicion of the female athlete is increased when the female is black, from a lower class, lesbian, or necessarily must develop characteristics that are defined as 'masculine', such as strength . . . Mere participation in sport can cast a woman's sexual preference into question, just as participation in ballet can for men.
>
> Mary A. Boutilier and Lucinde SanGiovanni,
> *The Sporting Woman*, 1982

What complicated the whole thing for Billie Jean King was money. King was now raking it in; Barnett, the ex-lover, wanted a share. Ever since tennis had allied itself with a tobacco company, the sport had been wed to commerce. The Women's Tennis Association, a go-getting, PR-conscious players' union, had been formed by King and others in 1973. Its brief had been to make money for the players, and it had. Since

1975, there had been pay parity between the sexes at the US Open. The money in the sport was now enormous.

In the centennial year of the US Open, 1986, the winners, Martina Navratilova and Ivan Lendl, each took home $210,000 (£140,000) in prize money, a twelve per cent increase over the previous year. By then seventeen female players had earned prizes of more than a million dollars each, topped by Natratilova whose purses in that year alone were $1.4 million. King herself would, by the end of her career, have pulled in two million dollars. And none of that counted the biggest booty of all, fees for endorsing products.

When the galimony scandal was about to break, what was worrying Billie Jean King at least as much as what Mrs Jones in Smalltown, Mississippi would think, was the effect the scandal would have on her endorsements. Women were marketed in sport on their *perceived* femininity. You had to be a winner to get an entry, but a petite, soft, well-dressed, pretty, white, ladylike winner was the one who could win in the sponsorship stakes. Often she was the one who got attention on the sports news pages or programmes too.

This is slightly less true than it used to be, particularly in North America. Britain and Italy, for example, have not changed their opinions of women in sport very much. But in the United States and Canada, even in Japan, many more women than used to are participating seriously in sport; if more women have biceps, the commercials have to change – the customer is always right.

With a battery of lawyers, Billie Jean King won the law case in the courts. Her careful presentation of the case to the media and the public, who in America can forgive almost anything if you own up and don't seem terminally embarrassed, helped. Her constituency, her chief fans, were feminists – in the United States that includes most female high school graduates and their mothers. She didn't entirely avoid speaking up for Mom and apple pie (and why not, they're terrific), but she didn't recant entirely either.

Gloria Steinem, who is still the respectable voice of American feminism, wrote to King, expressing sympathy at the fact that she had

---

In those few moments of a lifetime that Marilyn and I shared, she gave me a great deal. She was extremely important to me. And if she hadn't burned me, I would have no regrets. No, not for the love. None.

Billie Jean King, *The Autobiography*, 1982

---

to bare her private life in public: 'It's not fair that you were forced into this position – but now that it's happened, I think some good will come of it.'

King estimates that, in addition to walloping legal fees, the case cost her at least $1.5 million (£1 million) in earnings.

The half-a-million-dollar contract to endorse a new line of tennis clothing with the Wimbledon name on it was 'ninety-five percent finalized', King says. It was cancelled. So was an existing $300,000 contract with Murijani jeans, a $45,000 deal with Charleston Hosiery, and a $90,000 contract with a Japanese clothing firm. Cancelled television commercials, corporate appearances, and coaching and training fees added up to more than half a million dollars more.

NBC kept her on as an announcer for Wimbledon, even though the contract had not yet been signed.[6]

By the time the media got the goods on Martina Navratilova, there was precedent. She lost money; she lost tennis matches; she survived. She had become the finest female tennis player of her time, and in the end she was content, as the title of her autobiography suggested at *Being Myself*.

Cultural lag means that in some countries, in some newspapers, she gets more disparagement than in others. Professional fogeys like journalist Auberon Waugh continue to hawk the old bigotry. In the summer of 1986, in *The Spectator*, he wrote with vitriol of Martina Navratilova:

> Perhaps she would have grasped at least part of the reason [the crowds, allegedly, don't love her] if she had been able to watch herself play against the deliciously pretty Miss Gabriela Sabatini, from Argentina, at Wimbledon on Thursday's television. The sad and beastly truth, for all to see, is that Ms Navratilova, through no fault of her own, is extremely ugly . . . ugly women have to be really exceptionally pleasant to be loved . . . ugly women (like very small men) are often bitter, aggressive and chippy . . . a significant number of these bitter, malevolent women have adopted lesbianism as their cause . . . I wonder if Ms Navratilova's failure to be loved by the crowds has anything to do with her self-proclaimed lesbianism?[7]

The 'sad and beastly truth' is that Waugh knows how to write a polemical essay, but he doesn't know how to sift fact from prejudice. The real truth is that Martina Navratilova attracts huge, admiring crowds, at all her matches, and that autograph books are proffered from every variety of tennis *aficionado* – from schoolgirl to macho stock-broker.

Like La Lenglen and BJK, Navratilova is a less-than-sacred, much-sinned-against, much-admired institution. *The Times,* not as yet a coven of radical feminists, has even reported her pre-Wimbledon dream.

Czechmate

High noon arrived at 2.08 on the clock, on 4 July 1987. In blazing sunlight, Martina Navratilova, pre-eminent, but skittish, and nearing her thirty-first birthday, served the first ball of the Wimbledon final to that strapping, blonde, eighteen-year-old West German, Steffi Graf. Graf won the point.

All season, Graf, the sport's most talented newcomer, had been a giant killer – she had behind her a string of forty-five consecutive victories. Navratilova had fallen to her in the French Open in the spring.

In the weeks before this Wimbledon final, Navratilova, who had not won a single tournament all season, even switched to Graf's racket. Navratilova said she could hit the ball harder with it. To appease her irate sponsers, she stencilled their monogram on the other manufacturer's racket. Now many thought she lacked the confidence to win against Steffi Graf.

But grass was Navratilova's surface. Wimbledon her home. Her serve was still efficient; her will mighty. But so, of course, were Graf's. Would the thirteen-year difference in their ages be the deciding factor? And if so, would it be trained stamina that would win, or youth? Graf surely was the princess of tennis. Was she to be crowned queen at this Wimbledon final? Or would it take a while longer? The thrilling 1987 Wimbledon final, their first meeting on grass, showed that women's tennis was now often more exciting then men's.

The American boxer Sugar Ray Leonard had given Martina Navratilova a miniature tennis racket for luck. She stuffed it into her sock, and went out on to the court. Ignoring the sun in her eyes, Navratilova served and volleyed in her best manner. Graf defended with that powerful forehand, and attacked with aces. But after thirty-nine minutes, Navratilova had won the first set; after sixty-nine minutes, she

46

had won the match. The only time the young pretender was ahead in the entire match was on that very first point.

> Can I have some water please before I die?
> Martina Navratilova, after the 100th Open semi-final

On that windless day, Navratilova equalled the fifty-year-old record of Helen Wills Moody's eight singles titles. She one-upped Suzanne Lenglen's sixty-year-old record of five *consecutive* titles, and became the first woman to match William Renshaw's record of six titles in a row. Navratilova also equalled Bjorn Borg's tally of forty-one consecutive games won at Wimbledon.

She intended to return to Wimbledon to try to better the Wills Moody record. Graf might get in the way of that, but Navratilova had only to win one game on the grass of Wimbledon to surpass Borg in the record books.

At the US Open and in the French and Australian championships, the other Grand Slam events, there were years of catching up with history ahead of her. The challenge of again achieving the Grand Slam itself (winning all four of those championships in the same season) beckoned. Perhaps you had to be a tennis player or a sports lunatic to see the sense in this. But it was sound psychology: she continued to set sequential, attainable goals for herself.

Martina Navratilova, who had ranked number one in the world since 1982 and number one on the money list, was not really after money anymore. More than $11 million in total prize money would pay for more conspicuous consumption than she had time to engage in. How many hamburgers could one hungry woman eat? It was history, those tiny notations in the record books, that she was after now.

Navratilova has striven not only to be the best player in the world, but to be the best she could possibly be. And her obsessive pounding of tennis balls has affected more than just her own game. It has vastly improved the state of play.

At top level, the women's game is now far more interesting than the men's game. It requires more skill. In the women's game, you can see the plot building. It is high drama, not just a pistol whipping.

Increasingly, the men's game is a young man's game. Bam, bam, bam. Too quick to be satisfying. Hard, unreturnable shots – not deftly placed ones.

And it is the women who have been drawing the big crowds at

Wimbledon since – remember? – 1919. Suzanne Lenglen played that final in a hat. But after the match, there was blood on her shoes, she had run so hard. Three years later the Wimbledon championships had to move to a bigger ground to accommodate the crowds who came to see her play. Headlines spoke of the 'Lenglen lines a-winding'. . . .

Women have been drawing crowds ever since. The standard of play goes up and up and will continue to now that it isn't considered entirely *louche* to get a few muscles.

At Wimbledon, in 1987, the winner got a pay increase of sixteen and a half per cent over the previous year. That was £139,500 for the female champion and £155,000 for the male. The difference was £15,500. That is double many a Briton's annual income, but only pence in tennis terms. Why then pay the women less? Wasn't it to make the point that the men's game was the real game? Wasn't it to keep the women in their place?

It is true, though, that women play fewer sets. Why – goes the counter-argument – should they get equal pay for less work? There are two compelling reasons. One is that they give equal value. Three sets of women's tennis is as gripping as five sets of bam, bam, bam.

Secondly, the gentlemen could change the rules. It has been done before. At the Virginia Slims championship, the one women started themselves, the final at Madison Square Garden is played as the best of five sets. No one faints dead away.

At the US Open, even though they still play best of three sets, women have been getting equal pay for years. And the sky hasn't fallen. In fact it rarely rains for the US Open. Wimbledon is plagued with heavy weather. Is someone up there trying to tell us something?

In the interests of that great Wimbledon tradition, fair play, shouldn't the women at last get equal pay? It could be done by raising the women's pay, or by lowering the men's.

There is more money, more cheering, but less tennis history at the US

> I risk nothing, because my life in Prague leads to nothing good . . . . Away from Prague I can gain everything, that is to say, become an independent man at peace with himself, who is employing all his faculties, and as a reward for good and genuine work gets the feeling of really being alive, and a lasting content-ment.
>
> Franz Kafka, 1914, in Max Brod's *Franz Kafka*, 1960

Open. On 5 September 1986 the crowd at Flushing Meadow had patriotically applauded the winner of the centennial US Open, the Czechomerican Navratilova. In the days when America was called the 'melting pot' and the Statue of Liberty waved welcome to the tired, toiling, and poor, several ethnicities appeared, Czech-Americans among them. But the Czechomerican, characterized by several abodes in several states of the union, a big income, and expensive tennis rackets which she (or he – let's not forget Ivan Lendl) has received by the gross, and gratis, is a brand-new, much-welcomed, American ethnicity.

After defecting from Czechoslovakia, Martina Navratilova was granted refugee status in the United States in 1975, becoming an American citizen on 21 July 1981. On the day of her triumph in the 100th Open, she was annoyed when the ladies and gentlemen of the press called her Czech, and she said so: 'Come on, I'm an American. You can't *go* on where we were born. If you do that McEnroe would be German.' John McEnroe was born in a manger in Wiesbaden. He was as American as violence and apple pie, and at that moment, Boris Becker's moment, he wasn't a good enough player to be German.

There are cycles in tennis history, eras, in which players from one nation tend to dominate. Just now it was Czechoslovakia. A Czech, compact Hana Mandlikova, who had two houses in the US and later got a new base in Australia, faced a Czech-American, Martina Navratilova, in the 1985 US Open final. For the first time in world tennis, it had been Czech and Czechmate. The 1986 Wimbledon final saw it happen again. Then the final of the Centennial US Open pitted Martina Navratilova against the tall, grasshopper-thin third Czech, six-foot-two-inch Helena Sukova. Sukova of Prague – whose mother had taught Navratilova so much of what she knows – sliced, dinked, lobbed, and perpetrated a particularly wristy topspin. The Czech era, so long looming, had most certainly arrived. Yet Graf, the young West German, was already there.

It is said that some people at the Women's International Tennis Association, the up-market players' union, which keeps a canny eye on the obscenely well paid image-stakes, have told Graf that she needs a new hair-do. They may be right about that. Not that it ought to matter. But when Martina starts losing regularly enough, if Steffi ain't careful, the tabloid media will select her as the new Beast. No one has any complaints about Steffi's forehand, although Gabriela Sabatini, the Argentinian who is Beauty, says she sees a chink in it.

If Steffi gets a new hair style, will they then advise a new nose? A pretty boyfriend (that's what made the media stop the Iron Maiden sniggers about Chris)? Will they suggest that she wear mascara on court? It will be interesting to see if Steffi does get packaged for the sponsors. Will her words start coming out frozen, pre-pared. And when she really starts winning, when she becomes the best, will she become the player the sportswriters most love to hate? This is a syndrome that doesn't happen to men. There were always admirers of Superbrat. Even those who criticized him deplored what he did – not who he was or what he looked like.

When she was the Queen of world tennis, Chris Evert swapped double-fisted backhanders with fourteen-year-old Tracy Austin, who had pig-tails and braces on her teeth. Ten years later, it was Mary Jo Fernandez, also fourteen, with the same braces and backhand. Watching their match was like watching the same player at each end of the court. 'She's my idol,' Mary Jo said. 'My game is pretty much modelled on hers.'

At thirty-one, Chris Evert had found her harder work than Tracy had been. 'She's physically stronger than Tracy was when she was fourteen. And in ten years' time you'll be seeing even stronger fourteen-year-olds.' Maybe. But would they be American or European?

No nation is sacred and unique . . . Providence has not set America apart from lesser breeds. We too are part of history's seamless web.
    Arthur M. Schlesinger, Jr, *The Cycles of American History*,
                                       1986

The failure of the next generation of Americans was partly due to the fact that for the most part their game had been modelled on the narrow baseline play of Evert herself. Thus do role models function, for good and evil.

When Billie Jean King was pre-eminent, every girl's game, if at all possible, was serve and volley. Indeed, that had been the American way of tennis since the late 1930s, when that talented Californian Alice Marble wowed Wimbledon. But when 'Chrissie' arrived in the early 1970s, coaches began to tell their girls to hug the baseline. Now that she was adding some lunges for the net to her own game would the next generation open their minds? Athletic Navratilova was difficult to copy, and anyway many were stuck psychologically on Chrissie's limited example. Graf, thankfully, was an original.

It is possible to make sportstars say almost anything. You feed them the line. 'That must have been one of your most disappointing moments.' 'Yes, it was.' They may even repeat your phrases. But even if they don't, in the paper it comes out, 'It was one of my most disappointing. . . .'

In tennis, though, it is much harder to put words in anyone's mouth. The Women's International Tennis Association (WITA) is run like a multi-national corporation; it is savvy. Its PR rep sits in on many press tent interviews. (This means you have to scurry courtside in all weathers.) The top players may also have connections with the big sports PR organizations who advise them on media matters. These tennis Amazons have for years been the focus of media attention; they are experienced at the media game; they have their own tactics.

In an American tennis magazine, there was a report of one of the many mind games Hana Mandlikova uses to increase her ability to concentrate. She stares at a watch for a minute, then imagines the hands moving for a minute. The game is supposed to teach her to make her play more consistent. Mandlikova's coach is Betty Stove, the Dutch player whom Wade defeated to win her 1977 Jubilee Wimbledon title. Stove reads the sports psychology books to find mind games, which all the players now use. Watching Hana practise, on the eve of Wimbledon, I ask Stove to tell me another mind game.

'That is the one we give out,' she says.

Mandlikova has the best timing, the greatest flair, the most gorgeous style of any player on the circuit. But the label that has stuck, the epithet, is 'erratic Hana'. The timing, the speed, she is supposed to have inherited from her father, who was an Olympic sprinter. The stylish shots she picked up in the Czech tennis schools, which are the clean little secret of Czechoslovakia's tennis success. The ability to put those shots they taught her into play so prettily is something all Hana Mandlikova's own.

At the age of twenty-three, in 1985, she won the US Open, having defeated both Chris Evert and Martina Navratilova. That made Mandlikova the first player since Tracy Austin, four years earlier, to defeat both players in the same event. Mandlikova's first victory over Evert had been in 1981. But she does have her off days.

I now put it to Stove. 'Why is Hana erratic?'

Betty Stove looks dismayed.

'Is there any answer you give out?'

'She's very playful,' Stove says. 'That's how she is. She doesn't want to play the most effective shot. She wants to play the most beautiful.'

That is the quintessential manufactured reply. But perhaps one can work with it. 'That must break your heart.'

'Yes, it does.'

In the press tent, Mandlikova sits down for an interview. The hennaed WITA PR rep is there. So is my friend the photographer. Mandlikova explains why, in her view, the Czechs are dominating world tennis: 'The players have determination because tennis is the only sport where they can travel and they know they can keep their money. They try so hard because they know it is the only way to be free.'

This is not exactly a socialist analysis. One wonders what the Czech Federation thinks whenever she comes out with it. It is also more proof that tennis is a special case in being one of the few sports controlled by the women themselves. Mandlikova can sound off about the lack of freedom in Czechoslovakia with impunity. If she were an Olympic

---

I ran past the first watchman. Then I was horrified, ran back again and said to the watchman: 'I ran through here while you were looking the other way.' The watchman gazed ahead of him and said nothing. 'I suppose I really oughtn't to have done it,' I said. The watchman said nothing. 'Does your silence indicate permission to pass?'

Franz Kafka, *Parables and Paradoxes*, 1931

---

champion instead, reins would be pulled – and not just in Eastern Europe.

But why is she so erratic as a tennis player?

'I don't think I am erratic at all. It's just that the press always try to get something on the player. Nobody is perfect so they give me this label that I am erratic. So I just have to live with it. But I think being number three in the world for three years – I don't find it erratic at all.'

If she disagrees with being erratic, does she disagree, too, with having the most beautiful game?

'It's up to other people to judge, not me.'

Does she work at making it beautiful rather than powerful?

'NO.'

'Betty said to me that sometimes you don't win a match because you go for the most beautiful shot rather than the most powerful.'

'I would be surprised,' there is an edge to Mandlikova's voice, 'if she said that.'

Mandlikova's lips tighten, the softness of her expression goes, the delicate features of her face go hard. Angry, she is, in effect, calling me a liar. But all I had wanted was a gloss on Stove's PR-intended quote; an extra fillip, a confirmation. Mandlikova's anger is entirely unexpected; it is interesting.

'I have it on the tape. She really did. She said you were a little playful sometimes.'

'That's maybe the word,' hisses Mandlikova, standing up peremptorily. She is cutting short the interview. 'I am playful. But *it doesn't mean I am playing for the crowd*. Thank you,' she says, in a tone that makes it sound more like go to hell. Her head tosses, those icy blue eyes glare, and out she goes.

Mandlikova was annoyed at me, but I was now enthralled by her. Most tennis players will tell you they are entertainers – even Olympic athletes tell you that these days – supposedly that's why they merit all that money. It is a debased notion of sport, however. The gladiator keeping the Roman crowd's mind off the dire state of the Empire; a circus of athletes instead of caged lions. You know those clichés.

Mandlikova, though, meant that she was entertaining herself when she was being playful; although she is as interested in money as the rest of them – sport is an apogee of greed – her pride is in her craft, in her game. Was that old-fashioned attitude part of the secret of the Czech success?

'No secret training camps, magical coaching methods or any kind of strange phenomena unknown to outsiders whatsoever,' were found in Czechoslovakia, when *Tennis* magazine went and had a look. 'Just sheer basic common sense, hard work, good organization and a selfless devotion to the true spirit of the game unhindered by snobbery or power politics.'[1]

And the Czechs didn't have to pay for fancy private training like the Western players did. The nineteen million Czechs had the benefit of 3,000 public tennis clubs, each with a trained coach, or two, or three. In all, these clubs had 60,000 members, with an expectable rise of 2,500 each year. So it is not entirely surprising that, although Navratilova has not yet gone over the hill into defeat, Mandlikova and Sukova and a manicured handful of other Czechs are there ready and nearly able to send her scurrying home to Fort Worth, Texas.

How ironic it would be, though, if that sensible Czech system were defeated by one naturally gifted, strategically placed *Wunderfrau*. Steffi Graf, the prodigy, the powerhouse, has pyrotechnic skills. Her father Peter, who has run a tennis school, runs her career; her mother played till a back injury put her out of the game. Steffi Graf started playing at the age of four.

2

Passion and Defiance

The Long Run

As Grete Waitz pinned up her braids so they wouldn't slap her in the eye as she ran, the morning fog began to burn off. The first ever women's Olympic marathon was about to begin, and on this 5 August 1984 California morning, Grete Waitz feared that the day would be blisteringly hot. The Norwegian, who had been the trail-blazer in women's distance running, was one of the favourites. But she had trained for the twenty-six-mile, 385-yard race in the relative cool of Norway until just before the Games. Now she was wondering if that had been a mistake.

The wafer-thin form of the blonde-haired ex-schoolteacher Grete Waitz was known to millions of people worldwide. 'Grete the Great', whose coach was her schoolteacher husband, had become the first female international marathon star. In Oslo, her statue stood outside the Bislett Stadium – a rare honour for an active athlete anywhere. And she was still only thirty. She was no longer the world record holder, but Waitz was the world marathon champion, and on the great occasions she was usually at her best.

The Norwegian had trained for a tactical race: slow and steady from the start line, with a well-judged finale of speed. Waitz had it in her to kick over the last 10,000 metres, to cap twenty miles of running with a six-mile burst – if it wasn't too hot. She was afraid of the heat over the last six miles, when the sun would be high and they would have left the beaches and the cooling sea breezes, to run down the cordoned Marina Freeway into the cauldron of the Los Angeles Coliseum.

Waitz's most dangerous challenger, five-foot-two-inch, leggy Joan Benoit, had almost missed the Olympics. The dark-haired, 27-year-old American from Maine was the world record holder, but just seventeen days before the Olympic trials, in May, Benoit had had surgery on her right knee. It had been touch and go whether it would heal in time. 'I don't know how I am here today,' she said.

Quite unlike Grete Waitz, Joan Benoit was no tactician. She was a slogger: steady to the end, with no dazzling kick. Her even pace and her stamina were her weapons, and she had sharpened them with ever-faster weekly twenty-mile runs in the torpor of heat-struck Maine. Today it wasn't the weather she was thinking about.

Benoit, who had found to her cost that pinned numbers irritated, now checked that her race number was taped securely to her shirt. Just before the 8 a.m. start, she pulled on a white cotton painter's cap, to keep the dark hair fringing her forehead from bouncing. She wore the cap back to front so it wouldn't obstruct her view.

The race began at a slow, cautious pace, with the field running in a pack. But after just three miles, Joan Benoit noticed she was leading by twenty yards. 'I thought, this is the Olympic marathon, and you're going to look like a showboat leading for halfway and then having everyone pass you.' The sensible thing was to slow down. But the 5-minute-40-second-mile pace, not particularly fast for the distance, felt right.

At five miles she led by thirteen seconds. The leaders of the pack were Waitz, Rosa Mota, the Portuguese European champion, whose every marathon was getting faster, and that other Norwegian, Ingrid Kristiansen, a rising star. With them was the Briton Priscilla Welch, who had slipped off her wedding-ring and watch to lighten her load. Priscilla Welch was thirty-nine, a dozen years older than Joan Benoit, who was still at the front. At the halfway mark, she led by more than ninety seconds.

The pack of runners and the TV commentators were sure Benoit was going too fast too soon. Her pace had increased to 5-minute-20-second miles, and her awkward, slightly splayed stride was an ungainly sight. 'We thought,' Ingrid Kristiansen said, 'Benoit will break down, and we'll take her.'

At nineteen miles, her shirt soaked with sweat, Benoit had a two-minute lead. It was humid now, and eighty degrees Fahrenheit. Hot. Nearly two hours into the race, Benoit, tuned to her own steady rhythm, was thinking her own apparently calm thoughts. 'I just was praying that my knee would not give way.'

Grete Waitz, a little ahead of her planned schedule, desperately switched on the speed. Benoit, seemingly oblivious, kept on running, still at her own pace. But Waitz was getting closer. Second by second, ignoring the smog and the heat, her wan face showing the strain, Grete Waitz closed the gap.

'But I knew I couldn't catch her,' Waitz said. She sliced an impressive thirty seconds off Benoit's lead, but she had left it fifty-six seconds too late. 'I could perhaps have run faster,' Waitz said, but because of that heat, 'I was afraid of dying.'

The 77,000 people in Los Angeles Coliseum who had been following Joan Benoit's 2-hour-24:52-minute front run on the huge stadium television had begun cheering miles back. Now she entered the stadium. 'Their welcome, jarring in its intensity,' *Sports Illustrated* observed, 'showed that she, and her event, had more than reached emotional parity with any other in the Olympics.' Joan Benoit waved her cap in the air as she lapped the Coliseum.

Her Olympic triumph crowned her with fame and no small fortune. That year alone, Joan Benoit earned $402,000. The history of women in the marathon until then had been an utterly different one. It is a story of lonely, solitary triumphs, in which women have not only had to fight to endure the distance, they have had to fight off officials who wanted to bar them from the competition 'for their own good'.

'This win is a triumph for women's athletics,' Joan Benoit told the press who crowded around her. 'Now that we have proved that we can stand the conditions of the marathon, maybe they will include the 5,000 and 10,000 metres in the Olympics in the future.' The Norwegians and the others heartily endorsed that. Rosa Mota had come third, Kristiansen fourth. An elated Priscilla Welch had finished sixth for a new British record. Now, she was getting ready to put on her wedding-ring.

The loneliness of the long distance runner is perhaps impossible to imagine today, when Olympic marathons get TV coverage, when 20,000 people may run in London, New York, Tokyo, or Paris in marathons down city streets where crowds – sometimes numbering well over a million – cheer, and club runners and their children hand out tiny paper cups of mineral-spiked water.

Moreover the mooted loneliness of the male runner is historically a lie, literature's contribution to the mythology of sport. Even in the early days of the marathon, a male athlete never ever faced his ordeal alone. His friends or patrons monitored his training. And during the race he had a back-up team to dose him with strychnine and egg; to sponge his brow with water; to refuse him – for his own good, as it was thought – even a drop to drink. At the 1904 Olympiad in St Louis, the British-born American Thomas J. Hicks, who had received all that help, was lucky to finish alive. He won the race he had led, and he was wildly cheered. It would be more than three-quarters of a century before a female Olympic marathoner was applauded.

In 1896, when the Olympics were reborn in Athens, the Olympic ideal did not include women. There were 311 athletes from thirteen countries; among them, no women. There were forty-three events in ten different sports. None was deemed suitable for women. A Greek woman named for the Muse of Tragedy, Melpomene, who wanted to enter the marathon was refused permission. It is said she ran anyway, alone, starting behind the men and finishing in four and a half hours, having run the final lap around the outside of the stadium. There is no mention in the annals, but Melpomene's run is inscribed in Olympic legend.[1]

Marathons run unofficially – often illegally – would be the only ones 'open' to women for the next three-quarters of a century. Thirty years after the rebirth of the Olympics, on 3 October 1926, Violet Piercy stubbornly ran the first recorded woman's marathon. Running through the London suburb of Chiswick, she covered the gruelling 26-mile 385-yard distance in three hours 40:22 minutes. The modern Olympic marathon distance had been standardized at the London Olympics of 1908, where the course from Windsor Castle to London's White City stadium measured twenty-six miles, but runners were required to cover an additional 385 yards of the track to finish in front of the Royal Box. At that all-male marathon, even the losers were cheered wildly.

Because the marathon distance was thought to be dangerous for 'the weaker sex', no woman tried to better Violet Piercy's time for another thirty-seven years. In December 1963, an American, Mary Lepper, clipped the record by three minutes twenty-two seconds in Culver City. By then, the world marathon boom had quietly begun to build, and women were insisting on running the long race. Came the spring, and Dale Greig not only brought the record back to Britain, but she also shattered the psychological three-and-a-half-hour barrier. She achieved her 3-hour-27:45-minute record, running unofficially in a marathon on the Isle of Wight.

In 1966, Roberta Gibb sneaked into the then premier event in the United States, the Boston Marathon. No one particularly noticed the runner without a number. She did it again in 1967.

That was the year Katherine Switzer, who had been training with the men of the University of Syracuse track team, used the nineteenth century feminist ruse to get an official entry. Switzer applied for a place in the marathon as K. Switzer – exactly what E.[lizabeth] Blackwell had done to become the first American woman admitted to medical school.

K. Switzer, number 261, arrived on the cold, rainy day of the race in a baggy, hooded sweat-suit. She stuck close to the Syracuse team. As she warmed up and stripped off the sweat-shirt, a startled, and then angry, official noticed the woman in ear-rings and make-up. He attempted to remove her forcibly. One of Switzer's team-mates, a 220-pounder whom she later married and divorced, pushed the official out of the way, but not before a press photographer snapped the scuffle. The story gave women's marathoning headlines across America; Switzer became a heroine of the burgeoning women's movement.

But officials of the Amateur Athletic Union suspended her from their roster, and reaffirmed that women were not allowed to run more than one and a half miles. 'It was unbelievable,' Kate Switzer, who was to become a TV commentator at the 1984 Women's Olympic Marathon, says. 'Here I had just done something which they were saying was impossible, and they wouldn't change their minds about it.'

Neither would Kate Switzer. She kept turning up at races, in neon green trainers, with matching ribbons for her hair. The glare of publicity meant that change would have to happen eventually. But it was not until five years later, in 1972, that Boston officially opened the marathon to women.

The cold statistical facts show the phenomenal improvement that women now made worldwide. Although few women, compared with men, were running the marathon, and those who were were still training in an amateurish and *ad hoc* manner (to some extent that is still true), huge improvements were made to the world record.

On 31 August 1971, the Australian Adrienne Beames crashed through the psychological three-hour marathon barrier, with a run of two hours 46:30 minutes. In Spain, in the spring of 1977, the five-foot-one-inch Frenchwoman, Chantal Langlace, became the first woman to run faster than six minutes per mile for the distance.

That skinny, fair-haired Norwegian schoolteacher, Grete Waitz, was the first to capture the world's attention. In 1978, she finished the Big Race in the Big Apple – the New York Marathon – in a woman's world record time of two hours 32:29.8 minutes. She was 104th overall, with 999 women and 10,000 men behind her. Her time was over two minutes faster than any woman who had yet run the distance, and thirty years earlier it would have won the men's Olympic marathon.

The next year, amid much speculation as to whether she could run another record-splintering marathon, Grete Waitz returned to New York, and did it again – and more. A track-nurtured runner, she also broke world records at the middle distances of 3,000 and 10,000 metres (about six miles). This required speed more than stamina. Waitz now chopped five minutes off the world marathon record.[2] In the process, she smashed the psychological 2-hour-30-minute barrier, with a run of 2 hours 27:33 minutes.

The New York Marathon was perhaps the largest and certainly the most hyped marathon in the world. American television carried the marathon live – but no mention at all was made of Grete Waitz during nearly two and a half hours of TV coverage.

> Without so much as a syllable about Waitz, [TV] signed off at 2.27:00 into the race. Astute tube watchers were able to see a world record being set during the closing credits.
> *New York Running News*, 1980

'Everyone lining the streets, every writer, every journalist – everyone was waiting to see what Waitz would do,' one incredulous eyewitness said. 'Everyone, that is, except television. TV signed off.' There were some red faces at the network on the morning after. Waitz's triumph was the first widely noted instance of TV's blindness to the interest the public now had in women's sport. Not for the last time, TV coverage of women's sport lagged behind the public and even behind the press.

The rise of the marathon was the sport story of the decade – and the women's marathon plainly was where the action was. Not a millisecond was pared from the men's marathon in the decade of the 1970s, whereas the women's record, cut into ten times, was whittled down by more than half an hour. Men were running as hard as ever; women were running for the first time.

By 1980, the United States alone had 8,000 female marathoners – and sixty-six of them had performances under two hours fifty-five minutes. Yet running the marathon was still odd for a woman – the future world record holder and Olympic marathon champion Joan Benoit would later admit that at first she had been loath to tell anyone that she did marathon training.

In 1980, for the third consecutive year Grete Waitz won in New York, this time slimming the record by another two minutes. In 1981, Joyce Smith of England, who had not started to run marathons until she was forty-one, peeled back the record twice. What, it was wondered, would she have accomplished if she had run the event earlier?

It was Grete Waitz, though, who that year won the first London Marathon.

In Manhattan, in the autumn of 1981, when Grete Waitz had to pull out of the New York Marathon at fifteen miles with sore shins, the long-haired, long-limbed, conventionally gorgeous New Zealander Allison Roe won, and in the process landed what male sports writers considered to be 'the biggest blow yet for women's marathon running'.[3] She finished four places ahead of America's Mr Marathon, Frank

> When I first started running I was so embarrassed I'd walk when cars passed me. I'd pretend I was looking at the flowers.
>
> Joan Benoit, Olympic marathon champion
> in Los Angeles, 1984

Shorter, who was the 1972 Olympic marathon champion and the star of the much-reported men's marathon boom.

Now the jokes about women runners became less frequent, but they were perhaps a little more bitter. From 1969 to the end of 1986, the women's record had improved by forty-six minutes; the men's record not even by a minute and a half. Less than fourteen minutes separated the sexes; a difference of under ten per cent. The women's marathon record was improving at a much faster rate than the men's. Optimists predicted women would overtake men by 1990 or the year 2000.[4]

If women just kept increasing their marathon record at the same rate, they would catch up. And many fewer women were running than men, so when the pool widened and a larger percentage of talented women ran, at their optimal age, women would be bound to overtake the men. So the argument went. The counter-argument came: the women's record would begin to increase more slowly as, like the men's, it reached a higher standard and 'hardened'. There is truth in that. But there are plenty of indications that women will continue to get better for a long time. What marathoner Allison Roe said after her 1981 New York victory still has validity: 'Provided women are prepared to put in the sort of training that men do, I don't think there need be any limitations to what can be achieved, particularly in big city marathons where spectators are so helpful with their encouragement and enthusiasm.'

But women have yet to 'put in that sort of training'. Scientific studies show that few women had begun to train for sport with the same degree of intensity as men, even by the mid-1980s. (See the chapter 'Is Anatomy Destiny?')

It even appears that women have some physical advantages in the marathon. They may, on average, feel more comfortable than men in the final stages of a marathon. The harrowing stage for male marathoners is usually between eighteen and twenty-two miles when they may suddenly find they cannot run any more – they have 'hit the wall'. The body stalls because it has run out of energy and because it is dehydrated. Because women sweat less, they become less dehydrated. Because of their metabolism, women seem to be less prone to slam into the marathoners' wall.[5]

Women faster than men in the marathon? Does it matter? Probably not. Is it possible? To answer that one, we will surely have to wait until a generation of women grows up without embarrassment about running and are offered the same opportunities and rewards as the men. It seems we have seen nothing from women yet.

Slicing world records is a different discipline from winning races. To win a race you go only as fast as is comfortable and necessary to get ahead of the pack. You play a 'safe' so that if you don't come first, you are sure of second or third. To break a world record you may have to go at a faster pace than you are sure you can keep up. That could be embarrassing for a runner of note. 'If you go for the record,' Ingrid Kristiansen says, 'you can break down and maybe finish fifth or sixth.' She says she is not afraid of that.

The hollow-cheeked Norwegian, who for so long lived in Grete Waitz's shadow, has matured into unprecedented eminence, becoming the only athlete in history to hold the 5,000 metres, 10,000 metres and marathon world records simultaneously. In the spring of 1987 she added the world half marathon.

The Mistake
of the Century?

The Times sports writer David Miller has wondered in print if it isn't time for women to have their own track and field athletics championships so that they can get the full attention of the media, instead of being reported as an adjunct or afterthought of men's athletics.[1] It is a good question, but one which ultimately will be answered by economics. Is there money for two sets of world championships? Two sets of American and European championships? Even perhaps two sets of Olympic Games? Is there a Billie Jean King and a Gladys Heldman to mobilize women to take economic control of their sport?

It seems there may also be a legal dissuader. In 1986, a man filed suit against a woman-only Boston ten-kilometre race on the grounds that it discriminated against men. He won. This ruling could conceivably lead to the outlawing of all women-only events and put an end to equal prize money in mixed races, if the female winner finishes behind the man.[2]

The irony is that women have had to fight hard and well to become – auxiliaries. The entire history of women's track and field events in the Olympics – not just in the marathon – has been one of elbowing in. But women had been doing rather well on their own. Was joining the Olympic movement the mistake of the century?

The First World War had convinced women that they could hammer nails and, if they had to, the heads of enemy soldiers; they had the stamina, the strength, the guts to outlast hunger and hardship; they could manage farms, money, and their own lives. In most countries of the world, however, they could not vote.

Enter flappers in short skirts. Enter Suzanne Lenglen, who had débuted at Wimbledon *sans* garter-belt in 1919, and was now eminently visible as La Prototype. Enter a second formidable French woman, Alice Milliat, who used reason and perhaps even wiles to urge women's track and field events into the Olympic Games. Although women, all six of them, had played graceful tennis and golf at the 1900 Olympics, and in

1912 the female form had adorned the swimming pool, vigorous track and field, which caused a lady to perspire rather than glow (and suggested she might get somewhere on her own two feet?) had been resisted.

The French Baron Pierre de Coubertin who had resurrected the Olympics in 1896 had long since made his view known: 'Women have but one task, that of crowning the winner with garlands.'[3] He was still the major-domo of the Olympics.

Alice Milliat got to work on her counter-plan. Because the International Amateur Athletics Federation (IAAF) had refused to have any truck with women, Milliat founded her own organization.

In March 1921, 100 sweaty female athletes gathered together in chic Monte Carlo to take part in the first women's international track and field meeting. Women came from France, Britain, Switzerland, Italy, and Norway to high jump, hurl the javelin, put the shot; of the six running events, the longest was the then daring, long-for-a-woman, two-lap 800 metres.

The newly-formed international sporting union, the Fédération Sportive Feminine Internationale (FSFI), whose baby the Monte Carlo event was, had had its first success. The United States and Czechoslovakia also became members of the Federation, which had been founded to formulate rules, ratify world records, and encourage international competition.

Now, after Monte Carlo I, the woman-run Federation could have thumbed its nose at the all-male IAAF, but no, it kept sipping pernod with the enemy. The women still wanted in to the Olympics. The shortest distance to the Olympic arena, it was now clear to these women, was not going to be a straight line. They would have to do some running round their own arenas first.

Three hundred females turned up at Monte Carlo II the following April for the second international meeting. They came from seven countries to jump, throw, and sprint. Encouraged, the Federation decided to stage another big athletics meeting that very same year, the Women's Olympics.

At last, the men took some notice – they pressurized the female organizers to call their event something, anything, else. So, Paris hosted women from five nations at the hastily organized Women's World Games. It was good athletics, but the Games failed in their main purpose – to persuade men to let women's athletics into the 1924 Olympics.

In 1926, Gothenburg in Sweden welcomed women from nine European countries and one woman from Japan, competing in thirteen events at the second Women's World Games. One of the victors was the eighteen-year-old Japanese runner, Kinue Hitomi.

In the five years since the inception of the women's Federation, athletics had swollen from piddling local and national events to a river of muscle and adrenalin that flowed through Europe, North America, and the Commonwealth.

The goal of the Federation had always been to join the Olympic movement, and at last the men accepted them – up to a point. At the 1928 Olympics in Amsterdam – only thirty-two years late – women were indulged. But they were limited to a mere five events – high jump, discus, and 100 metre, 4 × 100 metre relay, and 800 metre races.

The 1928 Olympic début of the 800 metres was besieged by controversy even before the start. The women had insisted on running the event, two laps of the track. But many Olympic officials deplored the 'dangerous' decision to let them run it, as God had intended runs of such wearying distance only for men. It was a perilous distance for women to run – more than two minutes of jiggling of the insides, you know.

The winner of that first Olympic 800 metres, Lina Radke of Germany, certainly didn't think so. Radke ran this event, which was so arduously masculine, only twenty-six seconds slower than the Frenchman who won the men's 800 metre race. Undertrained, inexperienced, with no explosive start, she nonetheless zipped to the finish in two minutes 16.8 seconds, with Kinue Hitomi, the only Japanese woman at the Olympics, right behind her for silver.The top six finished within ten seconds of each other, the first three bettering the world record. Some of the runners collapsed with exhaustion and/or disappointment toward the end of the race or just beyond the finish – a not unusual sight today after an Olympic middle distance final. Nor was it anything compared to the gore witnessed in men's distance racing at the time. But the sight of ladies in distress offended conventional propriety. There was uproar.

A *Road Runners Club* report, many years later, put it exactly right: 'Isn't the point of racing to reach one's limit at the finish line? When male runners collapsed *en route* in the marathon, it was called drama, but when women reached this physiological level, it was labelled "frightful" and officials from several countries jumped on the IAAF to cancel the "frightful episode" from future Olympic Games.'[4]

Count Baillet-Latour, who had become president of the International Olympic Committee, went even further. He named four 'aesthetical' sports which were the only ones, in his view, suitable for women. His list – gymnastics, swimming, skating, and tennis – did not include athletics. But the women weren't about to go.

The 800 metres, however, was struck from the Olympic programme, and did not return until 1960.

'The 800 metres was a scene of a very limited amount of distress among the defeated competitors,' recalls the Olympic champion sprinter Harold Abrahams. 'Somewhat sensational writing by many of the journalists present resulted in that event being omitted.'[5]

Lord Noel-Baker, who was deputy commissioner of the British contingent, would say later, 'The trouble with this 800 metres was that the competitors had not been properly trained.'[6] No. The 'trouble' was surely that the women wanted badly to win.

Even as recently as 1978, the all-male International Olympic Committee decided against allowing the 3,000 metres at the 1980 Moscow Olympics because it was 'a little too strenuous for women'. The 3,000 metres and the marathon did not gain admission until the 1984 Los Angeles Olympics. The 5,000 and 10,000 metres had to wait until the 1988 Seoul Olympics.

But let's not get ahead of this salutary story. The inclination of the men was to 'protect' the weaker sex out of long events lest they do themselves physical damage. After the 1928 Olympics a block of American women lobbied to oust women entirely from the 1932 Olympics lest they damage themselves further, physically – *and morally*. Arguing that the competitive and commercial Olympic spirit was corrupting, they offered to put on their own more playful, more cooperative games with singing and dancing (probably, some snickered, daisy garlands too). This was the first onslaught against the competitive male model.

If women had taken this direction, what a different world sport would be.

Los Angeles 1932 boasted the first ever specially built Olympic Village. It was only for men. The women were put up in a hotel. In track and field, they had two new events – the 80 metres hurdles and the javelin – to be thankful for, but as the 800 metres race had been dropped, there was only one more event than there had been in 1928. The weather was balmy; the Depression was on; but the Olympic organizers had gone in for plenty of razzmatazz, and would, like their counterparts half a century later at Los Angeles 1984, make a huge profit. Practically every Olympic record was broken

Because LA was the other side of the world from Europe, there were less than half the number of male and female participants than at the previous Olympics: 127 women, 1,281 men. The women were outnumbered about ten to one.

The female star of these games was the down-to-earth, loudmouthed, eighteen-year-old Texan 'Babe' Didrikson. Her legs were long and lean, with muscles that rippled. As it happened, she was the first well-known 'shamateur' in athletics.

Hers is an interesting story, which begins on a Houston basketball court. One rainy January night in 1930, Babe Didrikson, shooting baskets for her Texas high school girl's team, was spotted by a scout. Immediately after the match, he rushed into the changing room to offer the sixteen-year-old Mildred Didrikson a job – $900 a year to become a stenographer at an insurance company. Her real job would be to play 'amateur' basketball for the company's team, the 'Dallas Cyclones', which got its and the insurance company's name in the papers often enough to warrant the high salary. At the time, a typist got $624 and a coal miner $723, and the Depression was on. When offered this job, Mildred Didrikson, who came from a large, financially strapped family, threw a spitball out of the changing room window and told the scout she would let him know.

Her decision, a few days later, to become a basketball-playing Dallas Cyclone was to be an historic event in Olympic athletics. Her basketball coach soon realized that his star player was an exceptional all-round athlete. On 16 July 1932, the insurance company, Employers Casualty of Texas, sent Didrikson to Illinois, as a one-woman team at the American Olympic trials. Winning five events in the space of two and a half hours, she set new world records in the javelin and high jump and scored thirty points. The runner-up was Illinois Women's Athletics Club, which had twenty-two women on the team.

Two weeks later, Didrikson arrived in Los Angeles for the Olympics. Athletics had its first star. And business had its grip on woman's amateur sport. This would characterize the modern era. Didrikson's appearance at the Olympics, which were supposed to be for amateurs, was one sign of what those American women who had wanted women to shun the Olympics had predicted – corrupting commercial influence. 'Babe' Didrikson was the first woman to get under-the-table and not-so-under-the-table payments for women's Olympic sport.

Mildred Didrikson liked to be called 'Babe' after her hero, the famous baseball player Babe Ruth. Didrikson had the braggadocio of a Norse hero or, her more likely role model, a Texas redneck. Her Norwegian immigrant father, who believed ardently in physical exercise, had been a better influence. He built exercise equipment in the backyard for his seven children. His daughter Mildred's secret, aside from a great natural gift, was that she was exceptionally well exercised. She even lifted weights: lifting flat-irons tied to either end of a broomstick had done wonders for her biceps.

Like Suzanne Lenglen, with whom she had nothing else in common – except an enormous gift for sport – Babe Didrikson understood the press instinctively. She kept it simple: was always quotable and always herself. 'I came out here to beat everybody in sight,' she said, 'and that is exactly what I'm going to do.' Her middle-class opponents were as appalled by her manners as they were by her sporting ability. They said she had no social graces. This was not quite true. Her social graces were down-home honesty and unselfconsciousness, straightforward cracker-barrel humour, and rough, manly talk. The press could not get enough of her. She was – and despite themselves they loved her for it – one of the boys. Although she later married a wrestler and played golf with the President, she never lost that redneck allure. No one would ever call her feminine – no one would dare to.

And this Didrikson was as good as her word. She began to win everything they would let her enter.

There was a crowd of 60,000 in the stadium on Sunday, 31 July, to see her hurl the javelin. They had come to see a giantess, but the short-haired ex-basketball player was six inches under six feet, and weighed in at 120 pounds. She was lean and compact with, by the standards of the 30s, plenty of muscle.

Unperturbed by her début in the international arena, she won the gold medal and set a new Olympic record in the javelin. Four days later came the 80 metres hurdles. She was away with the gun, her left leg leading over the eight hurdles, sprinting nicely on the flat. Gold again and a new world record.

The high jump, on the last day of the Games, ended in a bizarre decision by the judges. Didrikson made a record leap of five feet five inches. So did her opponent, also American, Jean Shiley. Neither could jump any higher. The judges broke the deadlock by awarding Didrikson the silver medal and the joint world record, but they ruled her jump, which was a kind of dive over the bar, illegal. Jeanie with the long lightbrown hair got the gold. This was an illogical decision. Didrikson had jumped in the same manner throughout the competition. An illegal jump ought to be disqualified, not awarded a world record; and the problem ought to be pointed out early in the competition, not at the end. Not for the last time, as it turned out, the Solomons broke their own rules.

Although unfairly denied that gold medal, Babe Didrikson became the only Olympic athlete of either sex to have won medals for running, throwing, and jumping events.

The Women's World Games persisted, despite entry into the Olympic Games.

In 1930, they had been held successfully in Prague. That time Kinue Hitomi brought five women with her from Japan. Now came the nineteen-nation-strong fourth World Games in London in 1934. Plans were being made for the fifth Games in 1938.

These women's games were seen as a thorn in the side of the Olympics – even though the Olympics really didn't welcome women. Alice Milliat's women's Federation, which ran the World Games and kept tabs on women's world records, found itself in a bargaining position at last. The fact that Didrikson had attracted crowds to the stadium in Los Angeles had helped. Now the all-woman Federation offered to cancel the 1938 Women's World Games and wind itself up if the all-male IAAF would accept women, recognize their world records, and ensure that there was an enlarged women's athletics programme in the 1936 Olympics.

All this was agreed; the women's Federation and their Games were disbanded; but the boys welched on the deal.

As the social biologist and historian Kenneth Dyer says in his book, *Catching Up the Men*, it is 'a rather unpleasant story'.[7] The IAAF failed to recognize all the women's records – the 400 metres, the 1,000 metres, and others not standard for men or not deemed suitable, were not recognized for years; some still aren't. This means that women holding the records have never received official recognition. As the record was all the reward that was going, it was particularly galling. More important to women's sport as a whole, though, is the fact that the empty columns in the record books made it look as though there were hardly any women athletes in the early days.

This had two immediate effects: young women with an interest in athletics believed certain distances simply weren't run by women, were unsuitable, and turned their interest to others; hence they had less scope for their talent than they should have had. Secondly, the absence of official evidence of achievement kept the numbers of women's events down at the Olympics and at other IAAF competitions because, as in wage increases, or with bank interest rates, improvements were relative. The less you had, the less you got.

A third effect was to create the myth that women's athletics was the frail sister of men's athletics; simply the second sex of the Olympics. And it wiped out most of the evidence of the Women's World Games, which rarely get even a footnote in the history of athletics.

As for the gentlemen's agreement to provide more Olympic events for women athletes, that they felt unable even to recommend until *after* the

1936 Berlin Olympics. There were no new athletics events for women in 1936, and at the first Olympics after the War, in 1948, only three more events were added.

But you just couldn't keep women down. Women were still outnumbered nearly ten to one at the 1948 London Olympics, but the greatest athletic achievement of these Games was accomplished by a woman.

FASTEST WOMAN IN THE WORLD IS AN EXPERT COOK.
Daily Graphic headline, London, 5 August 1948

The *Daily Graphic*'s headline and report of Fanny Blankers-Koen's Olympic victory is a master period piece. After the first bold-face headline came the smaller one, 'I shall train my two children to be athletes as well.'

Fanny Blankers-Koen won an unprecedented four medals at the Games. The piece in the *Graphic* appeared after she had won the first two. It began:

> This amazing Dutch athlete, who holds the world record for the high jump, long jump and the 100 metres, has thus gained an Olympic double, the first woman ever to achieve the feat.
>
> But at home she is just an ordinary housewife. She is an expert cook and darns socks with artistry . . . Her greatest love next to racing is housework.

After the Second World War, in which women had driven ambulances and aeroplanes, made bandages and bombs, and run factories, the men were back; the feminine mystique was looming.

Blankers-Koen, at the age of thirty – past her prime, her peak years lost to the war – was the outstanding sports champion of the 1948 London Olympiad. But the newspapers did not quite report it like that. They did as they always have, and probably always will: they slanted the story. The subtext of the *Graphic*'s headline and article doesn't take much decoding. The Dutch housewife heroine was not as desirable as a British male sprinter would have been to the newspaper lads from Fleet Street. But they worked with it.

At least, though, racing was named as Blankers-Koen's first priority. Maureen Gardner, the nineteen-year-old from Oxford who had so nearly won that she was also credited with the world record, was stereotyped even more thoroughly. 'Maureen Gardner, shyest girl at the

> 1924 was Nurmi's year; 1936 will always belong to Jesse Owens, and 1948 to Fanny Blankers-Koen.
>
> Harold Abrahams, *The Olympic Games Book*, 1956

Games, who most people thought had beaten the Dutch wonder girl, is more excited about 11 September than about her record-breaking run. It is her wedding day.'

Blankers-Koen took her third gold medal in the new 200 metres race. And on Saturday, 7 August, the last day of competition, she again broke the tape on the finish line, giving the Dutch team victory in the relay and earning her fourth gold medal. She set three Olympic records and one world record. Even her coach, whom she had married in 1940, had been wrong. He had said: 'You're too old, Fanny.'

On her return from the Games, Blankers-Koen was hailed in Amsterdam, and conducted in a carriage to the town hall to be congratulated by the mayor. Her neighbours, so the story goes, collected enough money to give her a present: a bicycle, so she could rest her feet. There is a wry humour there, but also perhaps a subliminal message to stop running, to slow down, to conform.

It is hard to know if distinguished athletes like Babe Didrikson and Fanny Blankers-Koen would have received the worldwide attention they did, had they performed at a woman-run, women-only Olympics. Would Babe Didrikson have been so severely stereotyped as a tomboy? Would Blankers-Koen have become the housewife *extraordinaire*?

It is certainly clear, though, that women's athletics lost ground when it entered the male-run Olympics. In 1921, at that first, hastily organized, women's international meeting in Monte Carlo there were ten track and field events. In 1948, after two decades within the Olympics, there were only eight. At the Olympic Games as a whole, women were still outnumbered ten to one. Putting women's athletics under the control of men set back the development of the women's sport.

The Olympic début of women's track and field in 1928, which seemed initially to be a giant sprint for womankind, became instead a historical sprained ankle. Women lost control of their sport. They not only became vulnerable to the whims of men. They became vulnerable to the whims of governments.

Our Medals
vs. Their Medals

Washington DC, April 1980. Midnight. At the Lincoln Memorial the Harvard-educated New Yorker, Hendrik Hertzberg, who is a speech-writer for the American President from Georgia, shakes a shock of lank brown hair out of his eyes and insists that the official reason for US withdrawal from the 1980 summer Olympics, in Moscow, is not just words: it is a fitting symbolic gesture.

Rather than get into a shooting war over the Russian invasion of Afghanistan, the United States had decided to shoot down the Moscow Olympics. The on-the-record reason for sacrificing the athletes, who spent four years of their lives preparing for these Olympics, is, he says, the true one. It is not because they are a small, economically powerless group, who can't answer back, but because withdrawing from the Olympics is a necessary moral sacrifice – understandable, as sport has symbolic value. Most particularly do the Olympics, which have always been viewed as a showcase for national aspiration. 'No, the President is not mix-matching sport and politics – sport has always been tied up with politics. Our medals vs. their medals – you know.'

Eugene, Oregon, a mecca for American runners. Mid-afternoon, two days later. The dog-eared Russian phrase-book on the living-room bookshelf tells the story obliquely, but Mary Decker, America's top woman runner, wants to make it perfectly clear: 'I was eighteen for the last Presidential election, but I didn't vote because I didn't feel I knew enough about politics. I still don't feel like I'm an authority. But this time I'll vote – because I do know that I don't want Jimmy Carter to be President again.'

Like most Americans who had serious Olympic prospects, Decker, the filmstar-thin Madonna of the middle distances, pre-eminent at the mile, feels she has been betrayed. She has four world and North American records, is fit, and has been looking forward to achieving the

74

fastest times of her life in Moscow. 'I'm angry – we're all angry, because we're raised in a country where the Olympics is IT – the ultimate.'

Decker had opposed the President's decision as loudly and irately as had the top male athletes; sometimes more so. It was the first time that Mary had been publicly quite contrary. Not everybody thought such aggressive behaviour was suitable for a woman. And Mary Decker herself was eager to give this visiting journalist her recipe for carrot cake – to balance the unfeminine harsh words she had to say about the President of the United States. She also advised journalists to drink orange juice before a morning run. But her public fury was a sign that women's sport was coming of age. She felt free enough to be an athlete not a lady, albeit with homely disclaimers thrown in.

Indeed, women's athletics had become extremely serious business; just how serious is encapsulated in Mary Decker Slaney's extraordinary career. Decker had had her body restructured with a scalpel to practise her sport; and not just four years, but going on ten years of her life, had gone to preparing for the 1980 Olympics. In 1980 her rage was not at losing a race, but at losing the chance to run it. The much-misunderstood open aggression that came at the 1984 Los Angeles Olympics in the clash with Zola Budd was as a result of the same frustration.

Of the fastest women in the world, those with global fame – the American Mary Decker Slaney, the South African Briton Zola Budd, the East Germans Marita Koch and Marlies Göhr, the Czech Jarmila Kratochvilova – have all been regarded by their governments as cold warriors. (Some runners, as we will see, are more welcome as warriors than others.)

In 1972, at Munich, when the 1,500 metres made its tardy Olympic début, the Russian middle-distance ace, Lyudmila Bragina, beat her own world record. Four years later, Bragina changed her event to the 3,000 metres and smashed the world record. That same year, another lean Russian, Tatyana Kazankina, only five foot three, took over the 1,500 metres world record, becoming, at the age of twenty-five, the first woman to run the distance in less than four minutes. She broke the record twice more and captured the Olympic title twice. Kazankina, who took time off in the 1980s to have two children, returned in 1984, aged thirty-three, to capture the world 3,000 metres record. Pregnancy, it was beginning to be noticed, was nature's own aerobic conditioner. Both Russians had enviable lungs and long, muscular legs. They had achieved great sporting feats.

But no promoter has ever wanted to give either of them secret payments for winning world records; no multi-national corporation wanted to lobby to have the rules changed so they could advertise their product. The Russians and other East European runners and discus throwers and hurdlers dominated world athletics. But their image in the West was steeped in paranoia. The press portrayed them as unlovely masculine semi-robot products of sports engineering by totalitarian regimes.

What was needed was a Western Golden Girl. Perhaps an all-American girl, in pigtails, who would grow up to be an all-American sweetheart; a woman who would know enough to run in ear-rings and gold trinkets but who would still – because of her natural talent – run the mile faster than any other woman in the world. And, after a little surgery and a lot of training, along came Mary.

In the summer of 1973 she became, at the age of fourteen years 224 days, the youngest ever American track international; before her fifteenth birthday she defeated the Russians at 800 metres in their own town of Minsk. She was a cold warrior, all right. Pigtailed and pert, she was known as 'little Mary'.

Too young for Munich, she was widely regarded as a good prospect for the 1976 Olympics, but she never made it to Montreal because she developed leg pains which made it impossible to train. She spent the next three years in retirement from running, in search of a cure. 'I saw so many doctors.' Even the thought makes her frown.

She had first suffered serious injuries, to her ankles and heels, in 1972 when she spent the summer with plaster casts on both feet. Decker had spent more time in casts and on crutches than most people who play non-contact sports do in a lifetime.

Then a conjunction of geography and personality occurred. New Zealander Dick Quax, the 1976 Olympic 5,000 metre silver medallist, who later became Decker's lover and coach, arrived in Boulder, Colorado, for some high-altitude training. Decker, a 'has-been' at seventeen, was enrolled there at the university. Quax had had similar problems with his legs, and had been cured by surgery. The operation was fairly common in New Zealand, whereas in the United States it had been limited mostly to football players. 'In less than three months I was able to run up to 100 miles weekly,' Quax recalls.

What had happened to Quax and to Decker, and, indeed, to many runners who trained hard while young, was that their muscles had grown too large. While running, blood rushed into their muscles causing considerable pain because the muscle sheaths couldn't expand sufficiently. The surgeon slit the sheaths which encased the shin muscle, so that the muscles would have more room in which to grow.

In 1977, Decker underwent this operation on both legs. Two weeks after the operation she jogged half a mile gingerly. The following year, after four years off the track, she set a world indoor record for 1,000 yards. 'It was wonderful. I was so happy. For the first time in three years that awful pain was gone.'

But the pain came back, and in August of 1978 she had a second operation, this time only on her left leg. Decker limited her running to thirteen miles a day, training in the morning and late in the afternoon, and began to have many fewer injuries.

In 1979, she moved to Eugene to join Athletics West, a 'club' run by Nike, the shoe manufacturers, for world-class athletes. Sport had not yet gone open: Nike employed her as a 'saleswoman' and provided a psychologist, a physiologist, a masseur, who gave the athletes hour-long massages twice a week, coaching as required, and shoes and sports clothing. The athletes lived together companionably, in groups of four or five, in large, rambling houses, where there was always plenty of muesli in the cupboard, and usually a row of muddy running shoes lined up near the door. The athletes Decker shared with were all male. Of the twenty-nine Athletics West club members in 1980, Mary Decker was the only woman.

That didn't surprise her either. Fair was by no means fair in women's athletics; parity was utterly unknown. That year, when she broke another world record, she was paid, she said proudly – though not for publication then, as it was still illegal – an under-the-table bonus of $3,000 (£2,000). Whereas Henry Rono's fee for setting world records, Decker volunteered, was $6,000. (Five years later, when payments had become legal, she was paid $75,000 for a non-record run.)

In a running career that had been racked with pain, missing the 1980 Olympics was a new sort of pain altogether. Decker tried to focus her anger and disappointment on President Carter, who was the cause of it. She was not entirely successful. In April 1980, as America's Olympic hopes collapsed, so did Decker's rare ten-month spell free from injury. By inattention, she allowed herself to strain an Achilles tendon, which she knew to be sensitive, and which she also knew how to keep in working order.

This meant time on crutches again.

Decker's disappointment had been a calculated cost of the Cold War. All over the United States and in the sixty-odd other nations that boycotted, and in Britain which had put pressure on athletes not to compete, athletes felt the same rage. Life went on: Decker extended her range. In six weeks of summer during 1982, she set world records at 5,000 and

10,000 metres and reset her own world record in the mile. The following year, at the first World Athletics Championships in Helsinki, Mary Decker put in some fierce front running to win the 3,000 metres race. Tatyana Kazankina had nearly outkicked her at the end of the race.

Then, four days later, came the extraordinary 1,500 metres world championship race. The closest metric distance to the mile, the 1,500 metres, about four minutes on the track, was nerve-wrackingly touch and go. Only the two Russians were capable of beating Mary Decker. Zamira Zaitseva, the European silver medallist, had the fastest personal best at the distance. Yekaterina Podkopayeva was one of the Soviet Union's many fine middle-distance runners, and would have been British number one had she been born in the UK, but she had not been considered good enough to win Olympic selection for the Moscow Games.

The contestants shot forward at the start. The first lap of the 400-metre track was run in 64.04 seconds – faster than the men's final. Decker, in the lead, was setting the pace. She held the lead as they passed 800 metres, then 1,200. Zaitseva was at Decker's elbow all the way, the other Russian well behind. Along the back straight, Zaitseva spurted forward, passing Decker with just 200 metres and about thirty seconds to go. Around the turn she opened up a five-metre lead.

Decker had done the work of the race; now the Russian, with a faster finish, looked set to benefit. With just 100 metres, about fifteen seconds, left in the race, Mary Decker began to close the gap. But could she do it quickly enough? Ten metres from the finish, as Decker swept past, Zaitseva dived for the finish line and crossed it on the ground, in second place. Decker had run the last four hundred metre lap in 60.2 seconds, even faster than the first. The second-placed Russian was followed by her team-mate, Mary Podkopayeva, who had spurted from behind to take third place. It was marvellous athletics. It was viewed, too, as a great American victory. Decker was now the pre-eminent middle-distance runner in the world.

No one could beat her. Could they?

Stellenbosch, South Africa, 5 January 1984. Running barefoot and from the front, seventeen-year-old Zola Budd sheared six seconds off Mary Decker's 5,000 metres world record.[1] As the slightly built runner ran the final lap, the crowd began to chant 'Zo-La, Zo-La, Zo-La'. To some it sounded like an African tribal chant, the chant of the white African tribe.

Three months later, Zola Budd was a British citizen.

Laatlammethie – that was what Budd's parents called her, in Afrikaans it means late lamb – had applied for citizenship four days after arriving in London. It had been granted just ten days later – on the personal instructions of the Home Secretary. In a country where thousands of immigrants routinely waited for years to have their applications acted upon, where it was said black South Africans need not apply, this white South African, who had no quarrel with apartheid, had been rushed to the head of the queue in the hope that she might win Olympic gold for Britain. But even those who were outraged were really not surprised.

The House of Commons was told that 'failure to give her priority would have been unreasonable'. Although Zola Budd's maternal fore-bears were Afrikaner *Voortrekkers*, Budd's father's father had been born in London. As her parents were maintaining the charade of settling in England, she could be granted citizenship as a dependant child until her eighteenth birthday, 26 May. Later, it would take years longer to obtain. The Olympics would have come and gone. A talented runner would have been denied an opportunity to run. A 'British' chance at victory would have been lost.

When he was no longer in office, the then Minister for Sport, Neil Macfarlane, said the government had been 'swept along'. But that was simply not so. They had willingly colluded with the *Daily Mail* newspaper, which had brought Budd to England, in an attempt to subvert the boycott of South African sport. South African teams were barred from major sporting events, including the Olympics. A number of the country's sports figures had emigrated to be eligible for interna-tional competition. Sidney Maree, a black South African, had become an American citizen; but his naturalization had taken the statutory four years. Some said that Budd's defection would further undermine South African sport.

Neil Macfarlane had known all along that that was double-talk: 'I had no doubts that if she were to run for Britain in Los Angeles and if she were to win a gold medal, when she stood on the rostrum, with the national anthem echoing round the stadium, people would identify her as a South African running for this country.'[2] Surely, it was obvious her victory could benefit only South Africa and the circulation of the *Daily Mail*, which offered exclusive inside information on her whereabouts, her training programme, her fealty. 'Zola Budd will become a great British athlete . . . her heart lies here.'

To be sure, it would have been sad for Budd herself if her application had been denied; but it would have been politically responsible. Hype and political circumstance had made her a special case. That a page-one sporting controversy of this sort could centre on a teenage girl runner was an extraordinary development, though, in world athletics. Governmental mountains had been moved for a sports*woman*.

Los Angeles, 10 August 1984. Decker vs. Budd in the Olympic 3,000 metre final. Midway in the race, Decker and Budd, both front runners, were ankle to ankle in the lead, running in established positions in the same inside lane. Then for some thirty or forty yards they ran with Budd in the lead by two or three feet – half a stride. Decker twice tried to regain the lead. As they came off the bend into the straight with just over three laps to go, Budd edged in, to block Decker at the very moment that Decker again spurted forward to catch up. Decker's right foot spiked Budd's left leg; Budd lost her stride; Decker her balance. She crashed to the ground, with Zola Budd's racing number in her fist.

Budd had stumbled, but she stayed in the race. The blonde-haired dark horse, Maricica Puica, took the lead.

The crowed booed the distraught Budd to a seventh-place finish. Decker, in tears, was carried from the Coliseum with an injured hip. In the tunnel of the stadium, she bitterly rebuffed Budd's attempt to console her. To the press, Decker said – and there was as much venom as pain in her voice – 'I hold Zola responsible for what happened.'

Budd was disqualified for obstruction. But the winner of the race, Maricica Puica of Romania, said, 'It was Mary's fault. She was the girl behind and should have seen the way forward.' Videos of the race taken from six different angles and examined frame by frame showed that Puica was right. Officially, Budd had not obstructed Decker; Budd was reinstated. Mary Decker had not been tripped; she had fallen. Another Olympic chance had eluded her: she could not believe it was her own fault. It had to be Zola Budd's.

Jim Ryun, an American runner who had fallen at the 1972 Olympics, but who was less famous than Decker, was among the millions who saw the angry press conference. 'As I saw her on television, I was thankful for one thing: I hadn't had a press conference immediately afterwards. It gave me a little time to gain some composure.' That was to be the most forgiving assessment Mary Decker would get.

Poor Mary.

She not only lost a medal, she lost her role as America's sweetheart. True, she *had* been a bad sport. But they are all too common in the 1980s. John McEnroe leads a cast of thousands – which includes football hooligans on and off the field. American newspapers frequently report *high school* teams and coaches in various sports disqualified for cheating or other unsportsmanlike conduct.

Sculpture of a girl athlete running (530 BC), from muscular Sparta where men were men and women could be strong without eliciting snide remarks

This fourth-century BC Greek vase depicts Atalanta outwrestling the hero Peleus. No medieval maiden ever stripped to wrestle with a knight

Roman mosaic from Piazza Armerina, Sicily, showing a female gymnast or dancer in something very like a bikini

The Nadia Syndrome: Olympic perfection at fourteen; anorexia at seventeen. Nadia Comaneci on the balance beam at Wembley, 1977

(*Above*) That well-known golfer, Mary Queen of Scots, playing at St Andrews, 1563

(*Left*) One of the first women on record to die for sport: Sophie Armant Blanchard crash-landed in Paris, 1819, when her gas-powered balloon caught fire, after fourteen years of successful ascents

The bicycle: first an instrument of freedom, then of sport. Victorian lady enjoying a country ride

Gertrude Ederle, the first woman to swim the Channel, arriving in England after her 14 hour 39 minute swim, in August, 1926

The young Princess Elizabeth life-saving at the Bath Club, London, June, 1939

Originally a test of gentlemen-soldiers, the three-day event is now firmly in female
hands. Virginia Holgate Leng, the world champion, jumping at Badminton, 1986

No sweat mars the brow of Lancelot Glasson's *The Young Rower* which was Picture of the Year at the Royal Academy in 1932

The partisan crowd at the Olympic Coliseum had booed Budd at their own volition; it looked from their seats exactly as it looked to Decker on the track – like obstruction. They had felt the anger and frustration, even if they did not themselves experience the physical pain. There had been bitter feeling in America against Budd.

ABC-TV, whose commentator had blamed Budd and *The New York Times* would later apologize for America's lack of sportspersonship.

Decker didn't quite. But within twenty-four hours she had moderated her irate stance. She didn't take the blame, but she tried to put the anger and the nastiness behind her.

Six weeks after the event, with her hip still sore, Mary Decker said, 'My coach talked to her coach and we feel it's time to put all of this behind us. Who was at fault is irrelevant now. It was an unfortunate incident. Now I look forward to running aginst Zola again.' But the fans would ever after blame Mary, the victim, for the lapse.

Human nature is not a machine to be built after a model, and set to do exactly the work prescribed for it, but a tree, which requires to grow and develop itself on all sides, according to the tendency of the inward forces which make it a living thing.

John Stuart Mill, *On Liberty*, 1859

Society in general, and the press in particular, judged that her all-too-human reaction was not acceptable behaviour from America's sweetheart. If one looks deeper into this attitude, what was being said is that it is not acceptable for her, a woman, to have these emotions.

Kay Porter and Judy Foster, *The Mental Athlete*, 1986

Poor Zola.

After that Olympic trauma, Zola Budd too seemed to lose heart. Death threats, anti-apartheid demonstrations, classic wet, cold British midsummer weather. It was rumoured that she missed her dog Fraaier, her cat Stompie, her parents, the sun, – she was thinking of giving up athletics and going home. The South African *Star* wrote, 'We hope she chooses wisely,' and nudged her back into the world arena. Laatlammethie, the British runner, was now an Afrikaner golden girl. She was an important symbol of white South African sport.

Correction. Rich Mary. Rich Zola.

There was, it turned out, money in Olympic controversy.

Suddenly, the next summer, an unscheduled second night was added to the Peugeot-Talbot Games at the Crystal Palace on the outskirts of London, and Decker and Budd had their revenge match.

Mary Decker Slaney, married now to a Briton, and double world champion, was paid £56,000. Budd – with neither an Olympic nor a world championship title to her name – was paid £90,000. That was for less than ten minutes on the track. It was said to be four or five times the amount that had ever been paid to an *Olympic* champion for just one race. The discrepancy in fees was explained this way: Decker Slaney (who won) was given what she asked; so was Budd.

The money was paid by the Southern Counties Amateur Athletic Association. Their source was a £250,000 bonanza from London Weekend Television, acting as an intermediary for Britain's ITV Sport which already held world rights to British athletics, and technically need not have paid more. But they weren't worried: their funds had been topped up by America's ABC-TV and South African Television.

The fastest event in running is the explosive 100-metre dash. Ten and three-quarter seconds on the track. Barely time enough for three gulps of air. In the decade from 1977, the East German sprinter Marlies Göhr and the American Evelyn Ashford, both five-foot-five, Göhr slightly heavier, engaged in a leg to leg battle over the distance. The record fell five times; thrice in a row to Göhr, then twice to Ashford. To put it another way, Evelyn Ashford, the Olympic champion, staved off one of East Germany's very finest runners. And in 1986, at the first Goodwill Games, she defeated Heike Dreschler, the sprinter who has been readying herself to take Göhr's place. Evelyn Ashford was quite literally the fastest woman in the world. But unlike Zola Budd or Mary Decker Slaney or Grete Waitz, Evelyn Ashford's is not an international household name. Army brat Ashford is said to be shy, but she was gutsy enough to ask to join the boys' track team at her California high school. Roseville High didn't have a girls' team. Wyomia Tyus, the other outstanding American sprinter, didn't get her due acclaim either. Could it be because Ashford and Tyus are black? Black men are supposed to be sports stars. Black women are supposed to fade into the woodwork. Or better still, to dust it.

Wyomia Tyus won the Olympic title in Tokyo in 1964, the year Martin Luther King announced in Washington DC, 'I have a dream.' She won it again in the pouring rain at the 1968 Mexico Olympics, in 11.8, a new world record. No one had ever won the Olympic 100-metre Championship twice in a row. Her family had wanted her to retire after her 1964 victory because they thought athletics unfeminine. Now, after ten years in track, *she* was thinking of retiring. Where else to go out but at the top? The entire American women's running team had had a marvellous Olympics – three gold medals and one of silver. *Every* medal winner on the US women's team was black. How many of their names come to mind? Or is that an uncharitable way to look at the star-makers – the white men who run the world's marketing departments, ad agencies and sports pages?

The American sociologist Harry Edwards predicts a 'continued decline in the media coverage and visibility' given to blacks. By 1992 'the American sports establishment,' he believes, will have taken 'steps to reduce the black presence, pre-eminence and/or visibility in major professional sports . . . in order to cope with the inevitable increase in cultural, political, and economic liabilities associated with increasing black domination of the sports institution in America – a predominately white and *white-dominated* society.'[3] Such trends tend to follow within the decade in Britain and Europe.

The first of the great black woman runners, Wilma Rudolph, had been impossible to ignore. Human interest was rife in her personal story: she was the twentieth of twenty-two children: 'I had to be fast, otherwise there was nothing left to eat on the table,' Wilma Rudolph told the journalists who crowded around when she won three Olympic gold medals in 1960. Illness had forced her to wear a brace on her right leg until she was twelve. But nothing had stunted Wilma Rudolph's growth; she was a fine-boned, long-legged, elegant gazelle, unusually beautiful. It may not have been entirely what the civil rights activists had in mind, but Rudolph was what the tabloids meant on the few occasions they said black was beautiful.

In Eastern Europe, the round-faced, white psychology student Marlies Göhr, the first woman to crack eleven seconds for the 100 metres, is a legend. Even in the West, there is grudging respect. She embarked on the 1987 world-championship-year season, at age twenty-eight, with twenty-four major titles already racked up (the other East German, Marita Koch, queen of the 200 and 400 metres, had twenty-six). Marlies Göhr, who is exactly the same height as heel-flicking Evelyn Ashford and of the same medium build, runs with an efficient, short pattering stride which brought her to the attention of the East German 'system' early. By age thirteen she was already clocking times that brought the junior teams credit, and getting ready to take over from the then pre-eminent Renate Stecher, a massive, big-boned, heavy-footed woman. In a nation noted for its 'system' two utterly different 100 metre runners had been found to lead the world.[4]

What exactly is the East German system? Is it inexorable and inhumane? Do they pump their athletes full of anabolic steroids to turn them into *Wunderfrauen*? Is there another secret?

Like the Soviets, the East Germans see no shame in admitting that 'The main concern of sports medicine . . . is to study the conditions to which the human organism is subjected during intensive training.' They hope to be able, eventually, to pre-measure the woman of the future.

At the present state of the art, 'It is not possible for a medical specialist to predict an athletic career for an infant child, but he is well-qualified to judge a young person's suitability for competitive sport. Without such a careful appraisal by a sports medical officer no one can become a top-level athlete.'[5]

The East Germans start them young. PE and sports club teachers spot the stars of the future, who can then go to boarding or day schools which specialize in their sport. Marlies Göhr was born in Gera, a small town near the sporting stronghold of Jena. There, she began her career, becoming the most famous member of the Motor Jena Sports Club, whose other illustrious members include her heiress apparent, 100 and 200 metres runner and long jumper, muscular Heike Dreschler.

In a population of 17 million, over 3.5 million people are members through their sports of the national sports union – and of these 73,000 are under six years old. Children up to eighteen pay a monthly membership fee of 20 Pfennigs – the price of a tram ticket. The country has 329 stadiums, 9,918 sports grounds and playing fields, 5,397 sports halls, and 194 indoor swimming pools. All children aged from seven to ten are taught to swim. This adds up to a huge reservoir of talent to choose from – which is one reason why the GDR women's team won all fifteen events at the European Championships in Rome, an astonishing performance that is becoming typical.

Some people think it is masculizing anabolic steroids that have made them victorious. Surely, these drugs do figure, as they do in the lives of many of the world's top athletes. (See chapter 'When in Rome Do as the Romans'.) But anabolic steroids don't work of themselves; they must be combined with hard training along enlightened lines. The American researcher Bruce Bennett came up with another answer to the East Europeans: 'Communist superiority has been due to giving their female athletes the same access as the men to excellent facilities, first-class coaching and extensive competition.'[6] This is so.

The East Germans insist that attending 'centres of excellence' is entirely voluntary – parents are consulted as well as children. We have no proof that it is otherwise. And frankly, how many athletically gifted children in any country of the world would insist that they would prefer to be brain surgeons or pigeon breeders? Göhr, like the others, was shepherded through the system.

The East Germans, proud of their achievements on the track, early on published the book *Track and Field*, which candidly revealed their sophisticated and entirely fair methods. It was leapt upon in the West as evidence of their evil tampering with God's ways. Say 'East Germans', and what came to the mind of the Westerner was male hormones and satanic science. Their science was better than our science; therefore their athletes were better than our athletes. But ours were 'normal'. Nor, so the story went, were ours subject to totalitarian 'regimentation' or 'relentless driving'. The great runner Sebastian Coe recently said, 'If a national selection policy means regimentation, and country-wide coaching schemes mean relentless driving, then it is high time the Western countries grabbed some of it for the Olympic prospects of their own women.'[7]

The East Germans, following the Russian lead, realized early what impact could be made by giving their women a fair chance. Could it be that their female athletes were better than ours because they were encouraged more, because they were positively reinforced, because they got no double messages about femininity vs. athletics – because they got a better deal?

Western nations now have national coaches and squad schemes in women's Olympic sports, and not just in running; but they meet infrequently and suffer from under-funding and under-staffing, particularly in comparison to male teams. And Western female athletes are only now beginning to be encouraged to train at the same intensity as male athletes. The example of the Eastern Europeans has spurred Western nations to give a little time to their women.

But the way forward for athletics is not going to be a state-run system. What is being created is a professional circuit. Athletics is, though, still about where tennis was when Billie Jean King and Gladys Heldman thought up the women's pro tour in 1970. No female runner, no female entrepreneur, has yet taken control in athletics. No female Olympic athlete yet has the cachet – or the cash – of a tennis star. Martina Navratilova started the 1987 season with 11 million dollars of acknowledged earnings. There are not many such golden girls in athletics. Yet.

The grand prix running circuit is booming; more races, more venues, more money every season. The odd *ad hoc* special, like Decker Slaney vs. Budd – the rerun of the Olympic fiasco – at Crystal Palace, will bring in even more money and some autonomy. So far, however, it has also brought plenty of hostility. There was no crucial title to be won at Crystal Palace; the two women were simply running for the money. There was money in it because the public wanted to see them run. The big pay-cheques that Decker Slaney and Budd got for their less than ten minutes on track were, however, called 'the unacceptable face of the new era of athletics' by a British journalist. An American sportswriter spoke of heroines in the dragon-lady *Dynasty* soap opera mould.

There was much nostalgia for the gentlemanly era of athletics that was long gone, and which in fact had barely existed at all. Unequal opportunity and money had been there from the start. Commercial interests had backed runners – including women – since at least the 1930s, probably earlier. Now that payments weren't entirely under-the-table they were larger. And surprise, surprise, that development disturbed the press less when applied to Sebastian Coe than when the loot was going to Fatima Whitbread or Budd or Decker Slaney. As Andy Norman, head of the British Athletics Promotions Unit, said, summing it up nicely, 'The sports correspondents are jealous. It's not so bad if a talented male athlete makes more money than they do. But they can't stand it if it's a woman!'

3

The Worm in the Apple

The Celebration
of Heroines

The worm in the sporting apple goes back a long way. It is Atalanta who first epitomized the female athlete. She grew up in the wilderness, wild and strong and swift – a runner faster than Mary Decker Slaney, with more endurance than the marathoner Grete Waitz. Atalanta was not eager to marry. No fool she. Freedom, she surmised, would wither away as she washed the ambrosia off the plates. But marriage was destiny in those days, and there was not a lot Atalanta could do about it. She did what she could: she refused to marry any man she could outrun. Even today there is a satisfying turning-their-masculinity-back-upon-them aspect to her logic.

Another version of the story says that as a baby she had been abandoned in the Arcadian hills by her father, who had wanted a son. Suckled by a maternal female bear, she grew up to be a famous heroine – at which point her father claimed his paternal rights to choose her husband and, perhaps because she fussed, he limited the field to men who could outrun her. Any who were defeated when they ran against Atalanta would be killed. So compelling was Atalanta's lithe beauty – and perhaps there was also money in it – that many ran and lost and died.

Then, one sneaky so-and-so went for help to the notoriously carnal goddess Aphrodite. (Her affair with Adonis was not the only one that was common knowledge.) She gave Atalanta's suitor some golden apples.

And then the race was on. They were running, not quite shoulder to shoulder, certainly not cheek to cheek, when he rolled a golden apple across Atalanta's path. She stooped to pick it up and then ran on. Twice more he rolled these golden apples, and twice she picked them up. He won the race by guile – now known as tactics – and married the fleet-footed heroine.

The double message of the myth – acclaim for the female athlete, but a strong yearning to frame her prowess within marriage, within a feminine perspective – persists. Women in sport then as now were admired. Today, they are admired more than ever. But they are still admired ambivalently.

That damned Aristotle is the one to blame. Plato had seen nothing wrong with active women. In the *Republic* he argues that women have the same aptitudes as men, and ought therefore to learn music, the art of war, horsemanship, and gymnastics, like men do. 'Not long ago the Greeks thought it ridiculous and improper for men to be seen naked in the gymnasium . . . This is still the opinion of barbarians, but a new attitude has been adopted by Greeks, and it will be the same once women are given equal access to physical education.'

> . . . And as for the man who laughs at naked women exercising their bodies from the best of motives, in his laughter he is plucking 'a fruit of unripe wisdom'.
>
> Plato (427 BC–347 BC), *Republic*

Even with men present in the public exercise space, the palaestra, there is, in Plato's view, no reason why women cannot strip naked, as men do, and join in the exercise: 'virtue will be their robe'. Nor does he scorn worn, wrinkled female bodies: 'not only the young, but even the older'. Women thus educated – in the same manner – as men would become doctors, philosophers, states*women*. The only certain biological difference between the sexes, Plato says, is that the male begets and the female bears.

Unfortunately, it was Plato's ambitious student Aristotle whose philosophy so erroneously influenced later social thought. Aristotle decided that woman is innately inferior to man after considering the functions she performed and the qualities she demonstrated in male-dominated Athenian society, where women were socially dis-advantaged.

> The courage of a man is shown in commanding, of a woman in obeying.
>
> Aristotle (384 BC–322 BC), *Politics*

Not only did Aristotle mistake the social reality of his day for universal biological truth, but he illogically declared that nature had created women to reproduce men but did *not* argue the corollary, that nature created men to beget women. For centuries thereafter women would have to avoid sport to guard their reproductive organs. As the *coup de grâce*, Aristotle announced that men were the active principle, women the passive – even though in reality and in ancient Greek mythology, women had been active since way before his own time.

In Greek mythology, it wasn't just Atalanta who was active. Nymphs, other heroines and goddesses swam, raced, rode, wrestled – and were admired. The god Apollo was smitten when he saw Cyrene wrestling with a lion. Atalanta herself had out-wrestled a hero named Peleus. A great many Greek vases depicted their match, partly perhaps because such wrestling, even then, had a sexual aura. This same Peleus wrestled the goddess Thetis – and defeated her – winning the right to marry her and beget their son, who grew up to be the great hero Achilles.

The macho Spartans inferred from this sort of story that athletic women would give birth to heroes, and prescribed the same physical exercise for girls as for boys. In this militaristic Greek city-state, where men were men, women could be athletic without anyone feeling they were unwomanly. Spartan girls of six to thirteen underwent the same physical training as boys – plenty of rough games. The ancient historian Plutarch says they threw the javelin and the discus, ran, and wrestled along the banks of the Eurotas river. Plutarch may have exaggerated the athletic attainments of Spartan women just a bit, as a way of ridiculing them – a joke on a par with, and about as amusing as, today's jibes at East German he-women and other female jocks. Girls' races were held and girls certainly wrestled too, perhaps even with men – but this may be an ancient libel.

In more effete Athens, mortal women were expected to comport themselves more demurely. Upper-class women were quite secluded, but women's lives in the Attic countryside must have been very different. In all of Greece, however, girls, women – and men – knew the ancient stories which celebrated the able, autonomous, muscular women.

The playwright Euripides routinely lauded Artemis, the goddess who hunted with a bow and arrow: 'Swift as the whirlwind they rushed after her, Artemis, with her arrows, and in her armour with the Gorgon's face.' Athena with her spear had long since been chosen as the patron goddess of Athens. Nor was female ability limited to land: the Naiads were mermaids; the fifty Nereids water-nymphs.

Atalanta outran all opposition, she hunted well with bows and arrows, she had little trouble making her javelin soar. She killed two Centaurs, monsters who tried to attack her, and she hunted the much-feared Calydonian boar. Her arrow is said to have been the first to wound the boar and the man who finished it off was so smitten by Atalanta's bravery, that he gave her the boar's hide and tusks. Many jealous men tried to steal her trophies. Then Atalanta may or may not have rowed with Jason and the Argonauts. After her marriage, achieved by hook and by crook, she and her husband became so lustful that they failed to make certain religious observances, and so were turned into lions.

Like male heroes, Atalanta is depicted accomplishing her great feats on Greek pottery. The black-figure style François Vase (560 BC) shows her on the boar hunt, dressed in a short tunic, with arms and legs bare. A later red-figure drinking cup (520 BC) shows the wrestling match, in which the hero is naked, as was customary, and a near-naked Atalanta wears only shorts and a cap, to keep her ears and hair from being grabbed. Three-quarters of a century later, she wears the cap, the shorts, and a brassière. And a quarter of a century later still, on a red-figure mixing bowl, the brassière is more prominent.

Such pottery is analogous to today's commemorative mugs and plates and T-shirts celebrating great sporting occasions and sportstars. All Greece knew, and celebrated, the story of Atalanta. Like the stories of the athletic goddesses Athena and Artemis, the feats of fabled powerful women were real to the Greeks in mythology; they were in a sense realer than real. Atalanta was an honoured heroine; a female Hercules.

The story of the warlike female tribe of Amazons, on the other hand, appears to have been regarded by the Greeks as a cautionary tale: they were considered too liberated, and they were allies of Troy in the long, bitter war. Weird and unwomanly – said by some to have cut off one breast, the better to shoot with bow and arrow, and to have killed their boy babies – they may be the ancient equivalent of the tabloids' scary fantasy feminists whose favourite sport is rumoured to be bra burning. The American classicist Mary R. Lefkowitz even argues that 'the idea that Amazons were breastless is based on a popular but totally erroneous etymology of their name, as if it came from *a*– (un) and *mazos* (breast), whereas in reality it is a non-Greek proper name'.[1] It is just possible that the audacious Amazons were created by the Simone de Beauvoir of her day, the tale was told by mothers to their daughters, and was such a good story that it was appropriated by male writers – who played it for laughs.

Whatever they meant to the Greeks, the stories of Atalanta and the Amazons tell us that way back men knew that women were not necessarily 'frail vessels', and women knew it too. Hence they ran and wrestled.

As Charles Seltman says in *Women in Antiquity*:

> The important point is that you only evolve, embroider, and recite legends about an imaginary athlete-heroine because your civilization affords some scope for young females to be athletic. No medieval maiden ever stripped to wrestle with a troubadour; no virgin martyr ever raced in the Hippodrome against a saintly deacon; no houri ever left a harem to hunt a wild boar on foot. . . . Where there is legend there is, somewhere, scope.[2]

Mary Lefkowitz concurs: 'No, the Amazons and Atalanta never existed, though the fact that they were described in myth suggests that the Greeks imagined that women could potentially be athletes and fighters before marriage.'[3]

There were, in fact, all-female Herean Games. Less well known today than the ancient Olympics, the Herean Games would have been a better model on which to base the modern-day Olympics. The high-minded Olympic ideal which Baron Pierre de Coubertin resurrected in 1896, and which did not include women, was a naive fantasy of the ancient Olympics, which had begun with a single 170-metre (or 186-yard) race and burgeoned into a brutal, often bloody festival of sport, with few rules, no time limits, and much 'shamateurism'. The *sportif* French baron's ideal, though, would have applied to the Herean Games, run by women.

The records of the ancient Olympics go back to 776 BC. One cannot therefore blame Aristotle, who was not born until 384 BC, for their tendency to sexual apartheid, although it ought to be noted that the boys didn't get the big stadium they wanted until 350 BC, when Aristotle was in his prime. Before that, the games were played in a sort of natural sand-box, an open stretch of level ground. The Herean Games, also held at Olympia, continued throughout the period.

In Olympia, one thousand years before Christ, you would have seen this: women gathering, the young ones tying their hair back, breathing deeply, preparing to run. Someone scratches a fresh line in the dust. They start from the scratch. They run bare-shouldered, with their hair unbound. They wear short, loose dresses and sandals, or no shoes at all. The ground is warm beneath the soles of their feet. It is hot. There are dozens of young women running the 160-yard course. It is noisy and hot and dusty, and there are flies. The feet of the runners make the dust swirl, and some of the women watching and cheering the race cough and spit. Some of the competitors huff and puff at the steepest part of the course. And then, one of the runners has won.

Someone brings a clay vessel filled with water. The runners sit now, anywhere out of the sun. At the top of the hill there are pine trees. Below, there are olive trees and vines, flowering shrubs, plane trees, white poplars. The runners breathe heavily and look down at the rest of Olympia. The most dominating natural landmark is the high hill of Kronus. It is here that the Herean Games take place every four years.

Now women are lining up for the next race. The women in this race are a bit older, those older still would run next.

A few of the women – athletes and spectators – had arrived for the Herean Games by boat. Olympia was fifteen miles inland from the sea, on the north bank of the Alpheios River. Most had walked down from the foothills of adjoining Elis mountain. They were from nearby Elis. Every four years, sixteen Elisian women organized the Games.

They saw to it that each winner – young, older, oldest – was crowned with olive branches. Each winner got a share of the cow sacrificed at the festival, and each had the right to leave a statuette of herself in Hera's shrine. The Temple of Hera and the Altar of Hera were at the foot of Kronus Hill, near where the men's stadium would eventually be built. These prizes were identical to those awarded to the Greek male Olympic athletes.

The goddess Hera, whom the games honoured, was quite a woman in pre-Hellenic mythology. Not only was she the goddess of women and their sexuality, but she ruled the earth. As the daughter of Flesh and Time, she lived through Youth, Maturity, and Old Age. These young women raced in age groups to honour the goddess's three stages. Married women did not compete.

The early, uncorrupted Olympic Games were almost identical to these Herean Games: they staged the same event, a foot race; they were held in a four-year cycle; they were conducted for religious purposes; they awarded the same three prizes; and even the location, Olympia, was the same.

The barring of women at the ancient Olympics, the men's games, appears to have been just a bit exaggerated. Over the 1,000 or so years of the games, there are indications that the laws varied; Victorian male historians stressed what suited them. The ancient historian Pausanias, who is one of the key sources, writing in the second century AD gives contradictory evidence: 'On the road to Olympia, there is a precipitous mountain with lofty cliffs . . . It is a law of Elis that any woman who is discovered at the Olympic Games will be pitched headlong from this mountain.' But elsewhere, he says, 'virgins were not refused admission'.[4] Nor in some eras were whores.

In the early days the games could not be held without one priestess present. Respectable married women, with the exception of a married priestess here and there, seem to be the ones who were kept out of the Olympics on pain of death. Was this because there was something going on that it would be awkward for a wife to see? Were the early Olympics a homo-erotic festival? There is plenty of evidence that this was so – all those men walking around naked, rather like the baths – and it is a commonplace of history that the ancient Greeks thought physical love between men was among the highest of pleasures.

This is a notion of the maleness of sport that deserves to be explored thoroughly . . .

At least one plucky married woman did get into the Olympics and live to tell the tale. Kallipateira's father and her dead husband had been Olympic boxing champions. (Some versions of the story name another sport.) Her brothers were distinguished Olympians too. In 440 BC, or thereabout, she disguised herself as a man, and took her son, whom she had probably trained, to compete at Olympia. She watched the event from the trainer's enclosure, undeterred by the heat, the noise, the dust, the plethora of flies and men.

When her son won, Kallipateira shrieked and leaped excitedly over the barrier, and someone noticed she was female. They let her go without punishment – tradition has it that it was because the men of her family were so distinguished, but it is just as likely that she got away with it because she had been backing a winner. Had her son lost, her fate might have been worse.

Thereafter, a rule was instituted that trainers, like athletes, had to register for the Games naked. This was the first sex test in Olympic sport.

Women could and did enter their horses and chariots in the chariot race. They did not themselves drive the chariot, nor did they attend the games. But like owners today, they knew their horses, and they were awarded the prize. The Spartan princess Kyniska became the first female Olympic champion when her horses won the chariot race in 396 BC.

There are two conflicting ancient reports of her motivation. The historian Plutarch says that Kyniska's brother convinced her to enter one of her notably fine chariots to show that victory in equestrian events was the result of wealth, not skill. Pausanias's opinion that, like any other entrant, she yearned to win at the Olympics, is more convincing in light of the euphoric inscription on the bronze monument that has turned up:

> Sparta's kings were fathers and brothers of mine,
> But since with my chariot and storming horses I, Kyniska,
> Have won the prize, I place my portrait here
> And proudly proclaim
> That of all Grecian women I first bore the crown.[5]

Courage
Above Her Sex

Three thousand years later, the example of invincible Atalanta, running, hunting, hurling her javelin, would inspire an unhappy girl growing up in the East End of London, Fatima Whitbread. Like girls in ancient Greece who learned from the myth of Atalanta that they must marry, but who noticed that in the foot race Atalanta could not be beaten fairly, young Fatima was deeply impressed.

Reared in a children's home, which did not stretch to javelins for the girls, Whitbread – a difficult, parentless teenager – submitted to strict coaching in order to learn the javelin. At the age of twelve, she had read of Atalanta at school: 'They tricked her. They couldn't really beat her,' Whitbread will tell you today. 'Atalanta was a strong woman and a fine athlete. It was something to go for.' Against the odds, Whitbread persevered, and at the age of twenty-five, in 1986 in a stadium in Stuttgart, her javelin soared high enough and far enough to set a new world mark. She became the first woman in the world to throw the javelin more than 250 feet. A happy ending, or even a beginning. Whitbread has years of competion in her yet. It is, though, ironic that in an age when the classics are not on everybody's tongue, young Fatima Whitbread had to look as far back as ancient Greece for a role model in sport.

Women participated in athletics throughout Greece at least until Roman times. They took part in the Olympic Games at Naples, and at Antioch in Syria, and at the Capetoliae founded by Domitian in Rome in 86 AD. In the middle of that century, three athletically gifted sisters from Tralles, in Asia Minor, won foot races, chariot races, and singing competitions at the Pythian Games and the Isthmian and the Nemian Games. An inscription found at Delphi in 1894 records their achievement. But the rot was setting in.

In ancient Greece there had always been admiration for the physical beauty of the muscular women of myth. Atalanta in her skimpy shorts, with or without bra, was not the only athletic female who graced Greek pottery. And in Sicily, at Piazza Armerina, mosaics from Roman times show women gymnasts, wearing something very like bikinis.

The fear of women's bodies can be traced back to the early Christians. St Jerome called woman 'the gate of the devil, the path of wickedness, the sting of the serpent, in a word a perilous object.' St Paul's misogyny was as virulent. Early Christian doctrine emphasized women's physical vulnerability at the same time as it dwelt on their sexual dangerousness. In 320 AD, the Council of Laodicea forbade Christian men to bathe with women at the public baths.

The only gold medal given out to females was for being both a virgin and a mother – and only Mary was capable of winning that. The rest of womanhood was regarded suspiciously as a coven of tempting, tempestuous, potential Eves, dangerous at best; not the sort you would give a javelin to hurl. For the next thousand years life seems to have been too grim for much attempt by women at sport.

Illuminated manuscripts show that it was becoming quite the thing for noblewomen of the thirteenth and fourteenth centuries to hunt with bows and arrows or hawks. Julia Berners, an English nun born in 1388, and an expert hawker, wrote a guide to the subject, in the *Boke of St Albans*. The daughter of an English noblewoman, she grew up at court, and even after she became prioress of Sopwell nunnery, near St Albans, she continued to be interested in hunting. Such agrarian pastimes, along with the skills of war, constituted sport until Victorian days.

By the end of the fourteenth century, well-to-do women took ice skating in their stride, jousted, and played *jeu de paume*, an early indoor version of tennis. Madame Margot of Paris outplayed men in 1424. The old idea of a sound mind in a sound body appealed to the new Renaissance humanists. Isabella, Duchess of Gonzaga, wrote to a friend: 'I hope you will take exercise on foot and on horseback . . . to drive away melancholy and grief.' Paintings and woodcuts depict women of high social rank riding and hunting, dancing and playing 'shuttlecocke' – the forerunner of badminton. Ladies of court, like recreational players today, often found that the fitness they developed through sport had practical physical benefits. Sportive women at the court of Queen Elizabeth I were on occasion observed to have easier labour than the more sedentary types.

There was also for these Renaissance ladies, sport for the joy of it, according to an account by Beatrice d'Este, Duchess of Bari:

I started at ten o'clock this morning with ladies on horseback. We had a fine fishing expedition, and caught a great quantity of pike, trout. Then to make our meal digest the better, we played ball with great vigour and energy . . . and then let fly some of those falcons of mine along the river-side. By this time it was already four o'clock. We rode out to hunt stags, and fawns and after giving chase to twenty-two and killing two stags and two fawns we returned home.

Quite a day, some of which we may owe to the imagination of the Victorian chronicler or to the exaggeration of the lady; but not all.[1]

In 1591, Queen Elizabeth shot three or four deer with a crossbow. Anne of France was good with a lance. All-female hunting parties took place; and women often sat astride rather than side-saddle. The sportive countrywoman of rank continues up to the present day, when princesses ride and ski and learn to fly aeroplanes for sport.

The women of the working classes did plenty of heavy physical work in their houses and in the fields, scything all day at harvest time and, on occasion, riding horses bareback. But they were far too busy for sport qua sport then, as indeed, statistically, they remain today. One medi eval exception was that of female acrobats in the troupes of wandering minstrels and tumblers who went from castle to castle performing, stopping on the way to play at village fairs. These women were known as gleemaidens; perhaps partly for their *off*-stage acrobatics.

As cities grew up, women who lived in them had little opportunity for sport, which was a country pastime. With great lawns at her disposal, Mary Queen of Scots was, in the sixteenth century, one of the first golfers; indeed she was criticized for playing too soon after the funeral of her husband. By the next century, many ordinary people had become Puritans, rejecting sport for all on the grounds that it was insufficiently repressive, insufficiently rigid; sport was too physical; too pleasant. Life was meant to be a vale of tears.

Women were 'the weaker vessel' anyway, weaker than men in mind, spirit, and body. And courage was not deemed to be a feminine characteristic. But queens and great ladies rode and hunted if they so desired, and farm women and servants were tacitly exempted from the mystique of feminine *physical* weakness. And war in Europe and America gave great ladies and ordinary women much opportunity to demonstrate what was spoken of nervously as 'courage above their sex'.

In 1620, the Pilgrim Mothers, accompanied by the Pilgrim Fathers, set off to settle America – back-breaking work. In Massachusetts, the most noteworthy sport was to be witch-hunting. Back in England, a series of wars created a new role for women: the crop-haired 'Gallant She-Soldiers' of ballad (and reality) who, disguised as men, rode horseback, wielded sword, musket, and sixteen-foot-long pikes (rather like scything with a pitchfork, they thought). Such military skills are perhaps the origin of sport. Like the first-century warrior Queen, Boudicca, who was no mean charioteer, ladies of the seventeenth century were by no means squeamish either. Libelled as a better soldier than her husband, Charlotte de la Trémoille, Countess of Derby, a Royalist, was a 'virago' who had stolen 'the Earl's breeches'.

> One can detect a certain masculine desperation in the repeated claims that the heroines of the wars acted out their martial role with the greatest reluctance . . . not a few of the 'Great [female] Heroicks' accepted their unusual destiny with zest.
>
> Antonia Fraser, *The Weaker Vessel: Woman's Lot in Seventeenth-Century England*, 1984

On 5 June 1639, the Calvinist Lady Ann Cunningham rode into battle at the head of her troop of horse. She carried pistols and daggers; indeed all her female attendants had to become expert markswomen.[2] That same year, in Sweden, the thirteen-year-old Queen Christina dressed like a man and rode like a woman – that is, expertly.

Queen Anne, who came to the throne of Great Britain and Ireland in 1702, when she was thirty-seven, was enthralled by hunting and by horses, and even more by speed. 'She hunts in a chaise which she drives herself, and drives furiously, like Jehu and is a mighty hunter,' noted Jonathan Swift, in 1711, when Anne was already aged forty-six. The Queen's chaise was a light one-horse chair, with enormous wheels, in which she rode alone. She was known to drive her horse forty or fifty miles in an afternoon.

Anne inaugurated the first race at Ascot. The day before the meeting she went to inspect the course, accompanied by a lady-in-waiting, on horseback, Miss Forester, who, according to Dean Swift and a second, more reliable witness, was dressed like a man. Sensible riding-habits were just coming in.

In 1714, Queen Anne invented racing for money. As usual, she had donated a gold cup to be awarded to the winner of a race at Doncaster. But she also insisted that each horse owner put up a sum of money as well: the winner would take all.

In France, when the 1789 Revolution broke out, women were urged to form 'Amazon battalions'. At Crueil, women from a company of the National Guard used javelins as weapons; at Valence, they used swords. It was war, but it would eventually be sport.

Peacetime, as ever, required women to know their place. The randy, distinguished, seventeenth-century Virginian gentleman, William Byrd, did allow his wife into the billiard room – whenever he felt the urge to 'roger' her or 'give her a sudden flourish'.

There was always an undercurrent of women's sport – much of it unrecorded or lost. There is mention of a woman bullfighter in Spain in 1654. Another story tells of a women's swimming party in Massachusetts in the eighteenth century; and in the South, where the agrarian traditions of Britain were upheld, women rode.

But even Jean-Jacques Rousseau, the 'radical' novelist and philosopher who, in eighteenth-century France, pooh-poohed puritanical strictures, thought woman was there to please man; he didn't think she needed to be athletic to do this. Like his contemporary, the German philosopher Immanuel Kant, Rousseau believed that 'her strength lies in her charms'. At least, though, he advocated that young girls should be allowed to romp and play:

> A little miss ought not, surely, to lead the life of her grandmother. On the contrary, she should be permitted to sing, to dance, to play about as much as she pleases, and to enjoy all the innocent pleasures of her age: the time will come but too soon, when she must be more reserved, and put on a more constrained behaviour.[3]

Thirty years later, in 1792, the fiery polemicist Mary Wollstonecraft, an Englishwoman who had been a governess and a teacher, argued convincingly in *A Vindication of the Rights of Women* that many of the traits which Rousseau and others considered 'naturally' feminine – such as fondness for dolls and dress – were due to upbringing, to nurture. The choice for growing girls was dolls or nothing, she said. Given a chance to play outdoors, to run and skip, every girl would choose to be a tomboy, and it would be good for her (and for men). When the little girl grew up, she would physically be a more beautiful woman: 'While enervated by confinement and false notions of modesty, the [female] body is prevented from attaining that grace and beauty which relaxed half-formed limbs never exhibit.'[4]

That idea might have caught on, but Wollstonecraft added a dangerous notion: a strong mind in a strong female body would lead to marital

101

partnership rather than subservience. It was not a far cry from, shudder, equality. 'The woman who strengthens her body and exercises her mind will . . . become the friend, not the humble dependent of her husband.'

In France, 27-year-old Sophie Armant Blanchard soloed in her gas-powered balloon in 1805. She became famous for her ascents to music from the Tivoli Gardens in Paris. Royalty joined the public to watch her. In 1819, when fireworks ignited her balloon and it began to lose height, Blanchard coolly threw out the ballast, and crash-landed neatly on a roof. It looked as though she had escaped, but suddenly the balloon toppled to the ground and Sophie Blanchard was killed. More than one person pointed out that Madame Blanchard would still be alive had she stayed in her kitchen.

That same year, the eminent English illustrator, George Cruikshank, caricatured two unlikely lady cyclists in ostrich-feathered hats, coasting down a country lane toward stately Lark Hall. The bicycle of the day was an unstable bronco, the pedal-less 'hobby horse'. Cruikshank's satirically intended caption was: 'I do not see why Ladies should not have a lark as well as the Gentlemen.' Women's bicycling, such of it as there was, was entirely a joke, but there must already have been serious rumblings of equality. More than half a century later, women would learn to ride the diamond-frame 'safety bicycle', and it would be more than a lark; it would be an incitement to freedom.[5]

It is hard to overestimate the importance of the two good things that now happened to women: bloomers and the bicycle.

The bloomer was an inadvertent feminist plot. Finding long skirts immobilizing in 1849, the busy New York temperance leader Elizabeth Smith Miller tried shortening her skirt to calf length and wearing Turkish-style pantaloons under it. She was pilloried for her unnatural, mannish apparel. In a show of solidarity, Amelia Bloomer, editor and owner of the *Lily*, a Ladies' Temperance Society newspaper, not only defended her in print, but donned the offending apparel herself. These 'bloomers', as the trousers became known, were debated nationally.

Although highly convenient for women who wanted to move but did not want to offend propriety by baring their legs, bloomers did not truly catch on. What they did do was make trousers for women thinkable.

By the end of the century, when bicyclists and other sportswomen needed apparel that would not become snarled in the chain but would protect modesty, the mind was open to change. Princess Maud, daughter of Queen Victoria, had lead weights sewn into the hem of her skirts to keep them down when she cycled. Like Princess Diana today, where

There is nothing in the book of Genesis to suggest that Adam's apron of fig leaves was bifurcated.

Amelia Bloomer (1818–1894)

Maud led many fashion-conscious women followed. Other women sewed ankle hoops under their skirts. The particularly daring few wore culottes. These 'divided skirts' further paved the way on the road to trousers.

Trousers are still subversive.

Brenda Polan, women's editor, London *Guardian*, 1985

Early bicycles had lacked pedals and chains, not to mention comfort and any ability at all to go uphill. It was only in the 1870s that a rideable steed was invented. The stupidly dangerous 'Ladies Ordinary', aimed at the women's market, was invented in 1874. It was a side-saddle bicycle, which must have been hell on wheels. Many opposed the indecency and unnecessary danger to themselves (and to pedestrians) of women astride two-wheelers. Tricycles were somehow less objectionable morally.

In about 1881, Bertha von Hillern, a young German artist living in America, gave exhibitions of her skill on a two-wheeler. The outspoken social reformer Frances Willard, the nationally-known leader of the American Woman's Christian Temperance Union, and an ardent campaigner for women's suffrage, decided not to go to see her because 'I should certainly have felt compromised' by what people said. A dozen years later Willard herself took to the bike.

When, in 1887, an American designed an open frame bicycle for elderly men 'too clumsy to mount over the rear wheel', he did not aim for the women's market because he thought 'it would be impossible to induce any considerable number [of women] to ride a bicycle'.

But across the Atlantic, that very year, an Englishman bent the crossbar on a bike in an attempt to appeal to women. A second Englishman, James Starley, soon came up with the eminently rideable diamond frame. Within a few years, a third of the bicycles on the by-roads of England were women's models, and half the cyclists were women.

Frances Willard, now even better known as a temperance and

suffrage leader, decided to learn to ride a bicycle at the age of fifty-three. Not a single friend encouraged her. But there was too much propaganda value in 'the conquest of the bicycle' by a woman of great years and reputation for her not to do it, Willard said. It was she who coined the suffragist motto, 'Do Everything.'

For her adventure, Willard donned a loose tweed blouse and skirt, with belt, rolling collar, and loose cravat; a round straw hat; and walking shoes with gaiters. The skirt was three inches from the ground. It was, she felt compelled to say, 'a simple, modest suit, to which no person of common sense could take exception'.

It was also a far cry from the fashionable long, tight-waisted, tight-collared dresses of the day, into which women were crammed with boned corsets, and which were worn with high-heeled shoes, as tight as possible, to minimize the unsightly length of a lady's foot. Willard hated such clothing passionately.

'I "ran wild" until my sixteenth birthday,' she said, 'when the hampering long skirts were brought, with their accompanying corset and high heels; my hair was clubbed up with pins, and I remember . . . the first heartbreak of a young human colt taken from its pleasant pasture.'

Although Willard was already an able tricyclist, learning to ride a bicycle took her three months, with an average of fifteen minutes' practice every day; in all, twenty-two hours of lessons.

> First, three young Englishmen, all strong-armed and accomplished bicyclers, held the machine in place while I climbed timidly into the saddle. Second, two well-disposed young women put in all the power they had, until they grew red in the face . . . Third, one walked beside me, steadying the ark as best she could by holding the centre of the deadly crossbar.
>
> Frances E. Willard, *A Wheel Within a Wheel*, 1895

Clearly women reared to sedentary ways did not find learning to cycle easy, but doctors said bicycling in moderation was not harmful, particularly as it got one into the open air. There were even those who claimed it could cure dyspepsia, torpid liver, incipient consumption, nervous exhaustion, rheumatism, and melancholia – all of which were widespread, particularly among women.

Unlike the then current bugaboo, the pedal sewing-machine, cycling was not thought to have the unpleasant drawback of exciting a woman sexually. With so much to commend it, there were 30,000 female bicyclists in North America before the end of the century.

Now, on both sides of the Atlantic 'the fragile female' accomplished feats of derring-do. Wearing a long-skirted dress and a hat, on a clunky bike, Mrs Ward rode the 120 miles from London to Brighton and back in six and a half hours. Going in the opposite direction, Maggie Foster, who was paced by a motorcycle, cut an hour off the time. No pacemaker accompanied Kate Green of York, who kept pedalling for twenty-four hours and covered 300 miles. Six-day marathon bicycle races had become popular in the United States and Canada. The first for women, held on 6–11 January 1896, was staged in Madison Square Garden. The winner, Frankie Nelson, clocked 418 miles.

Modern sport, with its emphasis on recorded times, measured courses, and strict rules of the game, dates for both sexes from this Victorian age. With the factory and the office replacing the farm, the time-clock was becoming a daily fact of life. Men geared to indoor, sedentary work were less robust than farmers, and there were now fears that men would lose their virility. Magazine articles warned of 'The Feminizing of Culture', or of its 'Effeminization'. There was a perceived need for 'vigorous, manly out-of-door sports'.

In England, public schools took it upon themselves to develop the muscles of the purveyors of Empire; 'muscular Christianity' was an idea whose time had come. Sport built character, manliness. The word 'manly' appeared a dozen times in the address the American President-to-be Theodore Roosevelt delivered in 1893 on 'The Value of an Athletic Training'.

Sport thus excluded women ideologically. It was primarily the women of the leisured classes who slipped in: the wives and daughters of captains of industry; the antecedents of Sloane Rangers, rich girls on both sides of the Atlantic who attended the new women's colleges and were used to having their own way; well-bred countrywomen who lived near stables continued to ride their favourite steeds. Not a far cry from how it had always been anyway; only now there were more of them and there were new sports to master. There was in America an additional impetus for women to participate: one response to the influx of European-born, often Catholic, immigrants was a WASP (white, Anglo-Saxon, Protestant) eugenics movement which believed strong women would bear strong, white, middle-class sons.

Mind you, a woman ought not to be too intensely physical because sport would damage her reproductive apparatus. Too much thinking was dangerous too – intense intellectual effort was still believed by doctors to strain a woman's childbearing equipment. The new colleges for women, it was asserted, might endanger the entire human species. Dr William Withers Moore warned the British Medical Association, in 1886, that educated women became 'more or less sexless' and the result was unborn sons. 'Bacon, for want of a mother, will not be born.'

A dozen years earlier, Henry Maudsley, professor of medical jurisprudence, had raised the alarm when he gave his influential professional opinion that girls underwent the strain of higher education 'at a cost to their strength and health' and could be disabled 'for the adequate performance of the natural functions of their sex'. The year before, in 1873, Harvard Medical School's Dr Edward H. Clarke had blamed college education for uterine disease, hysteria, and other female complaints. Fortunately that bit of male chauvinism eventually backfired.

In response to Dr Clarke, the American women's colleges looked to their curricula, and added 'mild physical activity' to counter overbookishness. As a result, studies in the 1890s showed that college women were healthier than others; magazines spread the word. Women got on their bikes.

In the United States, Vassar College for women had made PE compulsory in 1876, including a choice of riding, swimming, boating, and, in frigid weather, ice skating. There was even a bowling alley.

Young ladies at most colleges could choose between gymnastics – which had been imported from Sweden – and more vigorous sport. Gymnastics, ever the feminine alternative, lost ground as competitive sport became popular, only to rear its graceful head again three-quarters of a century later.

Tennis, which had been tardily introduced into the United States by Miss Mary Ewing Outerbridge in 1887, was available at Wellesley College. In England, back in 1884, the first thirteen ladies, in their long white dresses and corsets, had walked gingerly onto the courts at Wimbledon. In 1892, basketball was invented as a male non-contact sport; the young women at Smith College, in Massachusetts, began to play it. Girls' high schools in Iowa never realized the game was for men, and an inter-school league was started in 1898. At that first all-girls game in Dubuque, Agnes Martin scored all three of the winning team's baskets. Volleyball and hockey followed before the new century.

The Staten Island Ladies Athletics Club, one of several *fin de siècle* private clubs, offered tennis, archery, and darts. The American Association for the Advancement of Physical Education had a women's basketball committee in 1899.

In Britain, Madame Bergman-Osterberg had brought Swedish gymnastics to the elementary schools of London in 1878. Seven years later her Hampstead Gymnasium launched four students on a full-time course in physical education. By the early nineties there were twenty students and the *Women's Herald*, whose correspondent had journeyed ten minutes by rail into the country to get to rural Hampstead, was impressed by Madame's students, whose curriculum allowed them to play tennis, cricket, and to 'plunge, dive, swim'.[6] Bergman-Osterberg brought her message to Roedean, to Cheltenham, to the schools for girls. Parents were not, however, eager for their daughters to step out of tightly whaleboned day clothes – 'a suit of armour that clasped us . . . in all sorts of agonizing places' – and step into short blue serge gym dresses.

Team games, another danger, now began to catch on. *The Lancet* of 1885 prescribed well-padded corsets for female cricketers lest a severe blow to the breast cause cancer or flat-chestedness. The first women's hockey club, the East Molesey, was formed in 1887.

Most women, though, remained glumly on their pedestal. They continued to suffer from a bevy of discommoding female complaints. In 1900, against Pierre de Coubertin's better judgement, eleven well-to-do women competed at the Olympic Games. The short, strong, thrice and former Wimbledon champion, Charlotte Cooper of England, defeated Hélène Prévost of France 6–1, 6–4 to win the first Olympic women's title. It was a timid, decorous, visibly ladylike beginning to what would be a slow revolution in womanhood.

In 1909, Eleonora Sears was sent off the polo ground by her captain for wearing trousers. Sport still had to be ladylike and becoming. One dared not be over-strenuous for health reasons; one dared not be remotely competitive for social ones. Particularly, one dare not play too vigorously or too often either, lest unsightly, unfeminine muscles sprout. It was 'advanced' women who took up sport, just as in the 1920s – after the First World War had shown women they could perform deeds of strength, stamina, and valour – it would be 'fast' women who first wore revealing sports-inspired clothing.

Intellectually, the argument had not advanced a mite. Post-war doctors and governments urged women to flee the playing fields for the bedroom, to save the race and to recover, while it was still possible, their 'natural' femininity.

In Germany, where the declining birth rate and the increasing independence of women were putting doctors on the spot, they did not hesitate to explain that the female was by nature soft, passive, yielding; not really made for sport. A certain Dr Friedel explained in a learned article specifically about women and sport, in 1924, that the female body was, 'a sack, that occasionally needs to be filled and from which things

> One must not overlook that the female body because of its function is open underneath so that with strong physical exercise prolapsus could easily occur.
>
> Dr M. Kloss, *The Body of the German Woman*, 1928

can be removed'.[7] Women everywhere were reminded that God had created them as bags – to hold penises and embryos. And care must be taken lest the stresses of sport put the womb out of kilter.

This notion of the especially vulnerable female had for centuries hampered women's physical development. It was nonsense. But it became a key factor in the corollary notion that sport itself was defeminizing. In 1920, in *Feminism and Sex Extinction*, the British Dr Arabella Kenealy bemoaned the 'craze for making hockey-goals' which had given girls of the middle class builds as 'hard and rough and set as working women'.

Indeed, in 1899, in an article in *Nineteenth Century* she had foreseen the trend and spoken out against women who could walk miles without tiring, who could play tennis or hockey, and bicycle all day – at the cost of a tense 'bicycle face', a 'sterile glint' in the eye, a 'stride' instead of a feminine glide.

In 1973, at the Houston Astrodome, during the King vs. Riggs Battle of the Sexes (see p.000), when Billie Jean King, in rubber-soled tennis shoes, strode onto the court with a spring in her step, the TV commentator said, 'She walks like a man'.

No More Apologies, Please

The Ladies' Professional Golf Association (LPGA) was not even pushing thirty when it looked into the mirror, in the mid-1970s, and saw, metaphorically speaking, crow's feet. No one had ever minded the post-preppy, middle-aged paunch or the shaggy locks of the male pros, but female pro golfers were just too dumpy, too butch, to make Big Bucks. What the LPGA, which runs the American pro tour, did to make its image more acceptably feminine worked so well that it was emulated by rich, but evidently not rich enough, tennis in the late 1980s, and by the fledgling British and European women's golf circuits. Individually, sportswomen had been engaging in apologetics for decades – wearing make-up in the marathon, ear-rings on the track – or the media had done it for them. In a sense, the fastest woman in the world was still reading in print that she was a good cook.

To change the unlovely image of the women's tour, the LPGA hired an advertising man, Ray Volpe, as commissioner. He began to sell golf the way Madison Avenue was selling soap. In selecting promotable heroines, Volpe looked at bustlines rather than drives. In the annual guide to golf tournaments, *Fairway*, the 'ladies' of golf now appeared in pin-up-calendar poses.

The first Beauty of the LPGA circuit was Laura Baugh. She wore tight T-shirts but was playing mediocre golf. Baugh had been a bright amateur, but she turned pro prematurely, lured to the pro circuit by offers of more endorsement money than ever offered before. 'She's never turned out to be the golfer she might have been,' says Nancy Lopez, who has been a top golfer for nearly a decade. 'I suspect she may have been tempted to play upon her looks, rather than her game, and the latter suffered.'

Then the Australian Jan Stephenson, not a stunner like Baugh, but she worked at it, proved willingly promotable, and she could play golf. She had posed for the cover of the American magazine *Sport*. The story goes – impossible to know if it is true – that she had been unaware that the photo *Sport* would use would show a lot of cleavage, and she arrived in Volpe's office in tears at being had. Cheer up, he said, or words to that effect. Madison Avenue uses sex to sell soap and soup and cars, why not use it to sell golf?

Pressure was put on all the women on the golf circuit to slim down. 'A lot of us were naturally heavy,' says Nancy Lopez, who joined the golf tour in 1978. 'We've lost an amazing amount of weight. The LPGA keeps statistics on that, and simply on that basis our image must have improved a lot.' Those extra pounds, though, had put extra weight into some women's golf swing. (Similarly, Olympic discus throwers and pentathletes stay heavy because extra poundage adds power to their throws.)

The poses in *Fairway* began to get decidedly *risqué*. In 1981, Jan Stephenson was seen lying on a bed with a lot of leg visible. That pose sparked a controversy which divided the female pros about fifty-fifty, the most vociferous opponent of the photograph being Jane Blalock: 'Is our organization so unaware of our real glamour and attraction staring it in the face that it must resort to such trash?' she asked.

Evidently it was. The next year, *Fairway* readers got a look at Stephenson impersonating Marilyn Monroe, in a photographic facsimile (not a parody) of the scene in the movie *The Seven Year Itch*, in which a draught rising up from a street grating plays havoc with her skirt. Kathy Reynolds appeared in a night-gown, kneeling on a bed in a pose Rita Hayworth had made famous. Muffin Spencer-Devlin was Betty Grable in a swimsuit. That sort of thing. Stephenson was also on view to the navel in the American men's magazine *Oui*.

It was a shoddy way to sell golf, a reflection of the false distinction women are still cornered into making. 'I may be an athlete, but I'm still a woman,' the line goes. No man ever has to play this apologetic game, and say, 'I am an athlete but I am still a man.' Sport affirms masculine identity; it is still iffy for women, albeit less iffy than in the past. One day they will be secure enough to say that winning at a chosen sport requires no justification, it is what it means to be a woman. One of the things.

Twelve American female golfers had joined together in 1950 to form the LPGA, among them the most famous golfer of her time, the uncompromisingly athletic Texan, 'Babe' Didrikson Zaharias. About as stereotypically feminine as Davy Crockett, Mildred Didrikson, as we have seen, excelled at basketball and baseball and billiards. At the 1932 Olympics, she won medals in three very different athletic events – javelin throwing, hurdles, and the high jump. Later, she married the hefty wrestler George Zaharias, and turned to golf: 'For nearly four months I hit golf balls from early morning until late afternoon – hit balls until tape was piled on top of tape covering the blisters and cracks in my hands. Then I entered my first tournament . . . and won.'

That was in 1935, the Texas Women's Championship in Houston. In 1947, she became the first American to win the British Women's Championship, one of seventeen tournaments she won that year. In 1948, she piled up more tournament wins and $3,400. She was a great all-rounder, and Americans in 1950 voted her the greatest female American sportswoman of the first half of the century, but her muscular image tainted golf.

In 1979, after her highly successful first LPGA pro season, Nancy Lopez, a wife and later a mother, published her autobiography, *The Education of a Woman Golfer.* She felt called upon to begin the chapter on 'Friends and rivals on the tour' with a disclaimer:

The offensively prying will maintain that lesbian relationships exist among any group like ours [which travels together], whether it be in another sport, or the theatre, or the dance, or whatever. Maybe so, but I'm not aware of it, and if I were I'd consider it their concern alone. . . . I'm not so innocent that rumours never reach my ears [but] the tour is not exactly a saturnalia.[1]

> [Chris Evert is] . . . the young lady who would rather be famous for being a girl than for being a tennis player . . .
> Rex Bellamy, *The Times* tennis correspondent, 1972;
> reappeared in *Game, Set and Deadline*, 1986

The LPGA's campaign of pushing the 'pulch' – the pulchritude – of its members worked well. There were also professional PR and financial management firms like Mark McCormack's IMG working on golfers' images individually; all that marketing dove-tailed into dollars. In 1953, the highest paid golfer of the year, Louise Suggs, was earning $20,000, but except for the top two or three, female golfers were earning a pittance. Ten years later, there were twenty-eight tournaments, and Mickey Wright, a woman golfer who won the US Open four times, pulled in $30,000.

Incomes were going up, but they lagged behind tennis. In 1976, five years after Billie Jean King had done it in tennis, the American Judy Rankin became the first woman golfer to win more than $100,000 in a single season. She won $150,734. None of those figures includes endorsement money either, and the money was going up and up.

Only two years later, in 1978, Nancy Lopez's rookie year, the situation had changed completely. Nancy Lopez won almost $200,000 prize money, her official earnings. Lopez says: 'My rookie year produced for me even more in appearances, commercial endorsements, and things like that, than the money I earned by doing well in tournaments.' Three other women topped $100,000 in prize money, and another dozen won more than $50,000 each.

> [Chris Evert is] the Sugar Plum Fairy of the lot.
> Ted Tinling, *Sunday Times* magazine, 1986

Eight years on, Nancy Lopez took seven months off for the birth of her second daughter. Returning to the pro tour in August 1986, she did not win her first tournament, the LPGA Henredon Classic, in North Carolina, but she reached her goal of shooting under-par every day. Betsy King won, pushing her ten-year career winnings past one million dollars. The second placed Joanne Carner pushed hers past two million.

That autumn, a twenty-year-old Swede, Lisolette Neumann, became the first woman to crack the £30,000 barrier on the seven-year-old European professional golf tour. Prize money was finally beginning to go up, even the Americans were coming to play, and in 1987 it hit the one million pound mark for the first time. Only three years earlier, the tour had been almost bankrupt. Then, under the guidance of Colin Snape, the executive director, the women had been urged to exploit their dress sense and sex appeal, as their American sisters had done. Now the sponsors were interested. TV, it was felt, would soon be back.

In Britain, where they had been snide about women golfers since Mary Queen of Scots was derided for playing golf only days after her husband's demise, the foremost proponent of women's golf, Lewine Mair, prescribed an interesting PR antidote in *Golf Monthly*. Reminding players not to 'lose that sense of fun and feminine charm which should be integral to the game on the distaff side,' she suggested that young men should be found to play in the pro-amateur matches. 'There's no denying that a few young admirers getting involved with the tour would do no harm to its image. Rather the reverse.'[2]

Tennis, with plenty of money but two recent front-page lesbian scandals, was feeling the pressure of showing that its women were girly-girly no matter what. A 1986 pin-up calendar appeared in which

[*Times* man Rex Bellamy] always has the capacity to sum up a player perfectly with a single offhand phrase; for example, Chris Evert in the 1972 Wimbledon finals is '. . . the young lady who would rather be famous for being a girl than for being a tennis player . . .' In many ways that still holds true. Yet *Game, Set and Deadline* is not without flaws.

Charles Arthur, *Tennis Magazine*, 1986

Martina Navratilova was done up to the nines in furs, hairspray, and ghastly make-up. It was a ghastly mistake. The makers of it had misunderstood her beauty entirely; she looked like a female impersonator or an expensive prostitute.

At the Munich Olympics, in 1972, the British pentathlete Mary Peters was narrowly saved from going out to collect her gold medal looking just as ludicrous as that. Mary Peters was herded with the other victors to the make-up room, where her Veronica Lake hairstyle – long, straight locks, combed smooth – was not deemed suitable. 'In the makeup room where they doll you up to appear before a television audience,' she says, 'it was intensely serious business. In the hands of the male German hairdresser, I felt like Madame Pompadour getting ready for a night out with the lads. He drew my hair back tightly and used about a hundred pins and clips to weave it into the most elaborate style. I didn't like it.' Neither did her coach, Buster McShane. 'What the hell have they done to your hair?' he said. 'We stood by the side of the track pulling out pin after pin and clip after clip until I was able to shake my hair free and feel myself again.'[3]

Earlier, of course, her own hairstyle had been quite 'nice' enough to keep 50,000 spectators rooted to their seats as darkness fell, to watch her, already victorious and all but alone in the huge stadium, jump higher and higher toward an Olympic record.

[Chris Evert] personifies the Kipling line which is engraved over the door to the Centre Court at Wimbledon, a door through which she has walked so many times: 'If you can meet with triumph and disaster and treat those two impostors just the same . . .'

Carol Thatcher, *Lloyd on Lloyd*, 1985

In the 1986 'Miller Lite Report on Women in Sports', prepared in conjunction with the Women's Sports Foundation, 7,000 American women *to whom sport is important* were interviewed. Nine out of ten said that they personally did not think participation in sport had any real effect on femininity, *but* six out of ten of them thought society often forces a woman to choose between being an athlete and being a woman. The percentage of women who believe that society puts on the pressure would be higher if you asked British or Western European sportswomen the same question. And of course it would be higher still, on both sides of the Atlantic, if the question had been asked of women who did not actively participate in sport – more of whom will have felt and succumbed to the pressure.

Definitions of masculinity and femininity are changing, have changed. Instead of the polarities of masculine and feminine – hard-soft, independent-dependent, agressive-passive, strong-weak – what is deemed healthy today is an androgynous personality, in which there is a melding of these traits. Even the hardly avant-garde *Sunday Mirror* has run a series documenting that androgynous people have better heterosexual sex lives.

> If you can keep your head when all
>   about you
> Are losing theirs and blaming it on
>   you . . .
> If you can meet with Triumph and
>   Disaster
> And treat those two impostors just
>   the same . . .
> Yours is the Earth and everything
>   that's in it,
> And – which is more – you'll be a
>   Man, my son!
>
>   Rudyard Kipling, *If*, 1912

Female sportstars are admired, but they are, even in our so-called post-feminist era, often ridiculed. And because female stars regularly show their aggressiveness, their competitiveness, their ability to master (note the very maleness of the term) highly skilled sports, these world-ranked sportswomen feel the need to parade their femininity.

Even after so long as élite professionals, the women in tennis, the golden racket, still worry that they are perceived as masculine. It is just possible that lately they worry more than ever. They who had led the way to the big-money, high-profile, high-skill revolution in women's sport, have now lost the way.

Mind you, these sports-superstars don't themselves worry about being feminine or even masculine. They have strong, dominant personalities. They like themselves perfectly well as they are. The diamond ear-rings and the vulgar pin-up calendars are for others. For show. Aside from skill, image is nearly everything if you want to make a good living from sport, and images have taken some shakings lately. The sports champions have instinctively developed a set of disclaimers, which they trot out whenever possible.

Thus, after a long interview, many an Olympian or pro will smile and say suddenly, lest you think otherwise, 'But I'm no women's libber. I think a woman's true role is to be a wife and mother – when I retire I will.' Or if it is too late, she says as Billie Jean King did in a TV-documentary recently, 'I like children.'[4] A female athlete's PR rep or her team manager or her own reading of the media soon teaches her to mouth such platitudes.

Sociologists call these disclaimers an *apologetic*. A phoney apologetic, a deference to prejudice. The champions feel they must apologize for their unwomanly activity; or somehow make it all right. What is new is the fact that at the top sportstars are only apologizing for image purposes. No longer feeling ambivalent about their role as sportswomen, they nonetheless feel the need to pretend to be ambivalent.

> 'I quite agree with you,' said the Duchess; 'and the moral of that is – "be what you would seem to be" – or if you'd like it put more simply – "never imagine yourself not to be otherwise than what it might appear to others that what you were or might have been was not otherwise than what you had been would have appeared to them to be otherwise." '
>
> 'I think I should understand that better,' Alice said very politely, 'if I had it written down: but I can't quite follow it as you say it.'
>
> Lewis Carroll, *Alice in Wonderland*, 1911

There is something more complicated than an apologetic going on here. What sportswomen are doing is playing a strange poker game. Many ordinary recreational players still have trouble taking the last piece of cake, winning, particularly against a man. But sportstars have passed beyond that conflict or they wouldn't be winners. No one who has trouble gobbling up her opponents gets to be Olympic or World or Wimbledon champion.

Few truly entertain silly neo-Victorian notions of femininity. But they pay lip-service to them. Billie Jean King, retired now, sums it up nicely: 'When you reinforce somebody's lifestyle, they like you.' And when you don't, they don't.

What is unfortunate is that when élite champions play the PR game they do nothing to change the prejudices. Thus, many women who play at recreational level, and many beginners – unbolstered by living on a pro circuit or an Olympic squad – continue to feel self-doubt. In this way, sportstars are, with only a few exceptions, letting other women down.

Ironically, until women went pro and therefore independent, tennis was considered a perfectly feminine sport. Sports that are deemed dainty or are performed in scanty costumes have always been fairly acceptable, as have sports like horse riding, which have an aura of class privilege. Just as protective labour legislation 'protected' women out of the work they wanted (or needed), so has the cultural stereotype of female fragility limited their participation in sport. It still does, although less and less, thankfully. But, as we have seen, life for sportswomen is far from perfect. Grace is not only under the pressure of winning; she faces the pressure of prejudice.

> You get labelled. People tell me every day how great I am, and they don't even *know* me. I'm no angel . . . I'm a control freak – on and off the court.
>
> Chris Evert, 1986

4

Is Anatomy Destiny?

Is Anatomy Destiny?

A woman's heart is the size of a clenched fist. Her lungs, her bones, her twitch-muscle fibre are given by nature. Nutrition and exercise affect how tall she grows, how strong. And no woman's relationship with her body is entirely a physical matter. Human beings are not simply machines. Even the most physical experience is filtered through expectation and memory. It is affected by the knowledge and prejudices of science, religion, and social class; by advertising and the media; by child-rearing practices; by common-sense notions of male and female.

Physically, boys and girls have the same capacity for sport. At puberty, though, most girls reach a plateau and may even begin to diminish in capacity. How much this is due to the body and how much to the prejudices of the body politic is unknown.

Generations of women were urged to refrain from sport for fear of damaging their child-bearing capacities. But pelvic injuries are rare. Far more frequently, it is testicles that get hurt. On the football field and in non-contact sports, despite jock-straps and 'boxes', those hanging, external, male genitalia are virtually sitting ducks.

> Batsmen in cricket do not wear a metal box covering their genitals for nothing. [Injuries] are more common in activities such as tennis, golf, baseball, and contact sports where protection is not worn; this is why soccer players instinctively protect themselves with their hands when forming part of a wall in front of a free kick.
>
> Norman Harris, et al., The Sports Health Handbook, 1982

The Sports Health Handbook, written by Sunday Times staff in consultation with the sports medicine specialist and former rugby player, Dr

J.G.P. Williams, calmly recommends ice-packs to the scrotum and rigging up some sort of sling for support in cases of 'abrasions and minor tears of the scrotum, bruising, swelling, and bleeding'. Rupture of the testis, and torsion (twisting of the cord above the testis), require fast, specialized, expert treatment. Not only is this injury excruciatingly painful, it can have horrible consequences – and even a bicycle ride can cause it.

Two British doctors writing in the medical journal, *The Lancet*, described cases in which 'a ride on a racing bicycle with a long, narrow saddle' was the culprit. 'It would appear that the testis becomes twisted between thigh and saddle as the legs go up and down. Presumably the dropped handle bars tend to bring the legs closer up to the abdomen and increase the compression of the scrotum and its contents against the saddle.'[1]

> Men are the ones in danger of athletic injuries to reproductive organs because their organs are exposed and relatively unsupported . . . the internal reproductive organs of women are extremely well protected by bony, ligamentous, and muscular structures.
>
> Christine Wells, *Women, Sport, and Performance*, 1986

In some cases the injured contents of the scrotum, namely the testes, become gangrenous – and have to be amputated.

The testes play a role parallel to that of the female ovaries. They produce hundreds of millions of sperm cells daily, plus the male sex hormone, testosterone. Should we not consider banning boys and men of child-spawning age from bicycling? For their own good, of course.

A definitive study of *Women, Sport, and Performance* by the physiologist Christine Wells was published in the United States in 1986. Wells's thorough search of the literature turned up just one case in which a hockey player's uterus had been perforated by an IUD following a blow to the pelvis. There were a few reports of water-skiing mishaps causing 'forceful vaginal douches' leading to internal cuts and bruising. Competitive water-skiers wear reinforced neoprene rubber pants or panty girdles, which provide protection, and there were no records of incidents among them. Pelvic injuries specific to women are not frequent.

It is now a dozen years since the American Committee on the Medical Aspects of Sport reported it very unlikely that girls competing in contact sports would get more injuries than boys doing the same sports. It is even possible that girls and women would get fewer injuries because of their smaller muscle mass in relation to their body size. In other words, females, being smaller-boned and usually less-muscled, generate less momentum and less potentially injurious force when their bodies collide on the football field.[2]

There is a protective aluminium and sponge-rubber bra on the market, but unlike the jock-strap or the metal box, it is not much in demand – although it is probably a good idea for ice hockey, football, and fencing. Bras which offer support, often marketed as sports bras, seem to have answered the problem of breast soreness from running. Elite runners, being thinner than other women, tend not to have bouncing breasts anyway.

Menstruation has long been another female bugaboo. No woman should be prime minister or president, it has been argued, lest she press the nuclear button during PMT (pre-menstrual tension). Similarly, women were (and by many still are) believed to be incapacitated during their pre-menstrual and menstrual period. This doesn't leave much of the month for sport, does it?

At the first international Medical Congress on Women and Sport, held in Rome in 1980, the Dutch researchers F.T.J. Verstappen, *et al.*, of the Department of Physiology at the University of Limburg, in Maastricht, reported that the menstrual cycle seemed not to affect sport performance. Over a period of more than six months, they had monitored their subjects, all women who were active at sport, but not at world-class championship level. Every week these women pedalled an exercise bicycle, called an ergometer, until they were utterly exhausted. The scientists monitored heart rate, oxygen consumption, and other aerobic indicators. 'No effect of the menstrual cycle on work-load could be shown.' They came to the conclusion that there was no physiological reason why women could not exercise and win sports events at all stages of the cycle. Which is exactly what they do.[3]

When the United States Olympic teams were monitored, at the 1964 and 1968 Olympics, it was found that women had won gold medals and set new world records at all stages of their cycles. Some of the women set personal bests while they were having their periods. An unusually thorough analysis, in 1974, of 594 sport data in relation to thirty female athletes – in ice skating, kayak, and swimming – found that competition results were slightly *better* in the eighteenth to twenty-eighth day of the menstrual cycle. Statistically, though, the improvement was not considered significant; what was significant is that it was there at all.

No matter how many studies there are, some doctors and some

coaches, and, therefore, some athletes, continue to feel that all female athletes are affected adversely by their periods, and perhaps partly because they think they are, some athletes do find their powers waning temporarily. Negative self-fulfilling prophecies limit women in all aspects of sport. The golfer Nancy Lopez says she tries to avoid playing when she has hers. Swimmers seem most to falter – perhaps partly because of generations of warnings to stay out of the water during menstruation. One study found that, during their periods, swimming performance was poorer by about six per cent; and when a sample of sixty-six women were asked about their periods at the 1964 Olympics, the minority who thought their performances suffered were mostly swimmers.[4]

Today, many top athletes – runners, body-builders, gymnasts, ballerinas, for example – don't menstruate (amenorrhoea) or have infrequent periods. Some take oral contraceptives to control their cycle. Onset of menstruation is delayed, perhaps for years, in girls who have less than ten per cent body fat, perhaps even less than five per cent; thus gymnasts may not begin to menstruate until they are nineteen or twenty.

Most athletes don't miss their periods at all. Their low body fat, and the physical and psychological stresses of training seem to be what stave off the periods. 'I've been checked by a gynaecologist regularly and have been told not to worry,' said Tina Plakinger, the American body-builder turned soap star. 'I'm actually in favour of not being regular; I'd rather worry about getting my body into tiptop shape than about getting pregnant.'

Although some doctors are worried, the menstrual cycle returns to normal, with no ill effects on the ability to have children, when these athletes retire, or take time off. A favourite reason for a holiday from athletics is to become pregnant.

After a glorious 1985 season on the track, Mary Decker Slaney sat out most of the 1986 season, pregnant. The athletics correspondent of the London *Times*, no fan, asked her pointedly if she had got pregnant because she thought it would improve her running.[5] She allowed it was one reason. Many Eastern Europeans took time out to have babies; and then their sports results got better. Decker Slaney, an American, saw no reason not to take a pointer from the Soviet bloc. Few runners and few Western scientists had noticed the pregnancy boost until recently. But Ernst Jol, a German who taught at the University of Kentucky, had spoken of it in 1957, in the *British Journal of Physical Medicine*.

The tall East German sprinter, Barbel Wockel (Eckert), won the 200 metres title at the 1976 Montreal Olympics, then had a baby, and in

1980, at Moscow, became the first woman to successfully defend that Olympic title. She went on to win gold in the 4 × 100 metres relay. Her total of four Olympic golds equalled the record held by Fanny Blankers-Koen.

Wockel's compatriot, the heptathlete Anke Vater Behmer, was world bronze medallist in 1983. Having sat out the 1985 season to have a baby, she entered the 1986 European Championships and won gold. The Soviet long jumper, Galina Chistyakova, had a baby girl in 1983. Then she added speed and length to her best jump, and won gold at both the 1985 Europa Cup and the 1986 European Championships.

The Dutch runner and hurdler Fanny Blankers-Koen, who won four gold meals at the 1948 Olympics, heads the roster of famous mother-athletes. Blankers-Koen was the most impressive athlete of her time. Ingrid Kristiansen, the slightly-built Norwegian runner, is one of the most impressive of hers. Hollow-cheeked Kristiansen was for years overshadowed by the other great Norwegian marathoner Grete Waitz. Then Kristiansen had a baby, a son called Gaute, and she set new world records over 5,000 and 10,000 metres, and the marathon; no one had ever held all three records at one time. Her rival Joan Benoit Samuelson sat out 1987 pregnant.

Of a lady at Queen Elizabeth's Court: 'As she was playing shuttlecocke, presently retired herself into a chamber and was brought to abed of a child without a midwife.'

Manningham, a courtier, 1602

The Soviets did the first scientific work in the area; and their athletes have shown results. Now Western exercise physiologists have examined the evidence. Many agree with the British sports physiologist Craig Sharp's apt description of pregnancy as 'nature's own aerobic conditioner'.

Physiologists think that pregnancy gradually conditions the heart and lungs as it forces them to become more efficient to cope with the stress of extra body weight. Kristiansen's coach has also noticed that her gait has changed – a pelvis widened by childbirth could have made for a more efficient stride. There is evidence, too, that much of the benefit is psychological: Kristiansen says that she has had a lift from having something important other than running in her life. It is likely, too, that having demonstrated that she is a 'real woman' will reduce any inner conflicts she may have about excelling at sport.

The first mother to win Wimbledon was Dorothea Lambert Chambers, who won seven Wimbledon singles titles between 1903 and 1914, three of them after her first child was born. There haven't been many tennis mothers since. Martina Navratilova has talked of having a child some time. If she gets wind of what the runners know, she may have one sooner.

It is hard to know how many top athletes were pregnant when they competed at high level, or how pregnant they were. At the Helsinki 1952 Olympics, at least one bronze medallist was pregnant.[6] The American sprinter, Evelyn Ashford, had her daughter Raina in May 1985, just forty weeks after breaking the world 100 metres record.

Pregnancy in its first months does not seem to be a real obstacle to performance except possibly at the very highest levels of sport, where milliseconds count, and anything can affect everything. A study of 859 women who ran in the 1977 Portland Oregon Marathon showed that 7.3 per cent were pregnant and running; 3.3 per cent were breast-feeding and running; and 14.2 per cent had run during a pregnancy.[7] Replacing the old worries that sport might imperil the female reproductive system, is the evidence that having a baby may – for physiological and psychological reasons – enhance a woman champion's sport.

There are, though, some sport-engendered physical problems for women. Amenorrhoea doesn't jeopardize future pregnancies, but it may predispose a sports champion to bone fractures – all the evidence isn't in yet. When menstrual periods stop, it is a sign that hormonal levels, particularly of oestrogen, have fallen (there are analogous changes in world-class male athletes). Calcium levels in the bones of these young athletes may fall, just as they do in most women after menopause (when the oestrogen level drops).[8] This may be one reason why athletes take oral contraceptives: synthetic oestrogens are the main components of the pill.

Paradoxically, exercise staves off calcium loss in ordinary women. There is absolutely no doubt that women who exercise throughout their lives tend to have stronger bones than those who are sedentary. They are less prone to fractures in old age. *Sport is good for women.*

But there may be an optimal level of sport for people, a threshold. And most Olympic athletes and most top pros – *both female and male* have gone way beyond that. In China, Lang Ping, Olympic volleyball's first 'iron hammer', entered Peking No. 2 Spare-time Sports School at the age of fourteen. Soon after, she contracted periostitis (inflammation of her shin-bone coverings and stress fractures), caused by overtraining. She had been pushed too hard too soon. Similarly, in her twenties, Billie Jean King required knee surgery; a teenage Mary Decker Slaney underwent three operations on her shins and, in 1987, in her late twenties, has had an operation on her right Achilles tendon, long a sore point. The need for surgery, in all the cases mentioned, arose, as it does in cases of surgery for young male cricketers, footballers, and so forth, from overtraining, called by physiologists an 'over-use syndrome'. Nor is the Olympic gymnast Mary Lou Retton the only one who aches in damp weather.

Even exceedingly misogynist physiologists concede that women are more agile, more flexible, and have better balance than men. They are fatter, too, an advantage in some endurance sports – the eighteen-hour, fifteen-minute record for a two-way crossing of the English Channel, set in 1983, is held by a woman from Holland, Irene van der Laan, who was twenty-two at the time. The official record for a one-way crossing, seven hours, forty minutes, also belongs to a woman – the Californian Penny Dean, who set it in 1978 when she was only thirteen. In 1985 an Australian woman, Shelley Taylor, clocked six hours twelve minutes twenty-nine seconds in the fastest ever swim round Manhattan. Earlier that year, a Broadway actress, Julie Ridge, set the record for the longest swim around Manhattan – six days.

The female of the species' extra fat is a definite advantage in swimming, where women's Olympic records are closest to men's. In long-distance swimming, women can surpass men, partly because that extra margin of fat probably keeps women warm. The greater body fat in women also provides buoyancy and reduces body drag in water. In the gruelling new endurance sport of triathlon, which involves marathon swimming, bicycling, and running, swimming is the event at which women are most competitive with men. Although only seventeen per cent of triathloners are female, spectators at the end of the triathlon swim leg are usually impressed by the high percentage of women among the leaders at that point.[9] In marathon running, the extra fat seems not to give the same advantage because it becomes a burden to carry. Women marathoners at world-class level tend to be rake thin.

> There are wider differences between the trained and untrained bodies of the same sex than between the sexes; and less between the trained man and woman than between the sedentary man and his mate.
> Norman Harris, et al., *The Sports Health Handbook*, 1982

125

Women sweat less than men. Their bodies convert fat to energy faster too. The upshot seems to be that women who are trained as well as men finish a marathon in less discomfort than men do, as they are less dehydrated and less starved of nutrition.

As sport becomes a better regarded pursuit for women, more of them are participating. As the pool of talent increases, so do the standards. Perhaps the women with the greatest potential in a given sport will soon begin to play it. We are nowhere near that now; a lot of women who are athletically gifted still refrain from serious play lest they be considered unfeminine. Taboos on female muscle still exist. Even body-builders are urged to keep their bodies to 'marketable' proportions. The subject of muscle requires a chapter to itself (see the chapter 'If You've Got It, Flex It').

Even women whose stated intention is top-level sport train much less than men. Training fifty to seventy kilometres per week places women among the fastest for their sex; the same amount of training by men results in their finishing well down the field. In other words, top male runners run much more than seventy kilometres a week.[10] 'High level training for girls and women has been practically non-existent,' says the physiologist Christine Wells. 'I suspect that *few* world-class female athletes are trained to the same extent as *most* world-class male athletes.'[11]

Numerous studies bear her out. One from the University of South Carolina compared women and men who had finished a fifteen-mile road race in about one hour, fifty-five minutes. For women this is a good time; for men it is below average. The amount of training the two groups put in turned out to be very similar. Comparing aerobic and other factors showed that when men and women are matched by age and performance, a similar training and racing background is revealed. The physical differences between the sexes seem to balance out and the indications are that good results for women in running events come from average training. If more women trained more – if they trained as much and as hard as top male runners do – the record gap might well be closing at an even greater rate.[12]

History has stunted women's bodies and their sense of physical possibility. And it is ironic that women have particularly been kept out of long-distance events, the very ones in which nature seems to have given them an advantage. In most sports women's records lag about ten per cent behind men's. In some sports, though, women excel. And in nearly all sports, women's records are now improving faster than men's.

The issue of women catching up the men is, though, a red herring, and will continue to be, even when more women do surpass men. The fact that women dominate world equestrian sport is something to crow about, perhaps, but it is not part of a putative sporting sex war with men.

What is important is that women be allowed to engage in the sports they want to engage in – women were barred from the British equestrian Olympic team until 1968, as the sport was believed to be too difficult for the weaker female sex. Equestrianism demands a high level of fitness and strength and courage, as well as timing and balance; the men were at pains to argue that the horse didn't do all the work. The controversy has continued into the 1980s, even after Princess Anne won the 1971 European Championship and Lucinda Prior-Palmer (now Green) had won six Badmintons, two European titles, and the world three-day eventing championship. Nor was Lucinda a one-off – her successor as the world's finest rider (and winner of all three of the above events) is another Briton, Virginia Holgate Leng. Not long after Leng's success, a horsey Virginia country gentleman of sorts (my dear brother, in fact) was heard to say that the horse did do much of the work.

On 3 July 1986, 26-year-old Gail Greenough became the first woman, the first Canadian, and the first non-European to win the open world show-jumping championship. Greenough, a commercial artist from a highly horsey family, had overcome terrible odds at the championship – she was one of only seven female riders in a field of seventy-two. That year, an American team, fifty per cent female, won the fifteen-team Nations Cup. The second- and third-placed British and French teams were entirely male. In 1986, too, Anne-Grethe Jensen, a Dane, won the first Dressage World Cup in Holland. An Englishman was second, and a Swiss woman, Christine Stückelberger, came third.

A large proportion of riders are female. Little girls on ponies have always been considered a graceful, feminine sight. Little inner conflict has added up to many victories, even against men. 'I'm one of the girls who never outgrew the horse-loving stage,' Gail Greenough says.

The issue in sport ought to be comparable physiognomy; weight and height, not gender. On average, women are lighter, smaller, and have less muscle mass than men; all of which are advantages in some circumstances. But few women are jockeys because few are given the opportunity; even though male jockeys, burdened by heavier bones and more muscle mass, must go to dangerous lengths of dieting and dehydrating themselves to make the weight. Women have a lower blood-to-weight ratio, but other factors mean that overall their hearts work about as efficiently as men's.

As Germaine Greer, no physiologist but a highly competent scholar, pointed out in *The Female Eunuch*, in 1971:

> There is much evidence that the female is constitutionally stronger than the male; she lives longer, and in every age group more males than females die, although the number of males conceived may be between ten and thirty per cent more . . . There is no explanation for the more frequent conception of males . . . It is tempting to speculate whether this might not be a natural compensation for the greater vulnerability of males.[13]

Sweat, energy-converting abilities, and a lower centre of balance favour women in some circumstances; favour men in others. As we have seen, humanity is a motley crew: there is as much, or more, physical difference within the sexes than between the sexes.

In boxing and judo, men compete against each other in weight categories. Basketball stars would fail on the football field, and vice versa. No muscle-bound boxer would stand a chance running against diminutive Sebastian Coe.

If women of the same stature and weight were to train at the same level of intensity as men – and if they were to compete against opposition of the same standard – sooner or later we would see a lot of women victorious, even though on average men have more muscle relative to body weight.

It is bound to be later for a number of reasons. First, fewer women than men play sport seriously: we need to get the same number of women in the sport pool so that the female talent that reaches the top will be comparable. Secondly, large numbers of women still have to convince themselves of their right to be better than men. Remember how the tennis player Margaret Court was psyched out as recently as 1973 at the idea of beating a man? Or how even Joan Benoit Samuelson, the winner of the first women's Olympic marathon, had been self-conscious about being seen training. Many potentially fine marathoners, for example, never discover the sport. In addition, studies show that women still train for sport less seriously than men and train less intensely. Thus, they are less fit than they could be.

The prognosis physically for women in sport is good. They have it in them to get better and better for a long time. Sociologically, though, things aren't good enough.

Girls growing up today are still bombarded with conflicting notions of what womanhood is. No longer is it true that most women answer shyly, 'I'm just a housewife.' Today they have double trouble – many being both home-makers and wage-earners. Many are mothers. In the United States twenty-eight million women work. Ninety-three per cent of British women who don't have children work or are looking for work. By 1991, one-third of mothers of children under four will have jobs, as will seventy per cent of those whose youngest child is ten. As their children grow up, even more women will return to work. That figure might be higher if there were more jobs to take.

These statistics suggest that time for leisure often does not apply to women. A much smaller percentage of women than men engages in recreational sport. Indeed, the result of the General Household Study, reported in *Social Trends*, in 1985, showed that men who were employed full-time had, after sleep, personal and domestic duties, and travel to and from work, 42.6 hours a week of free time; fully employed women had 6.3 hours less. Women traditionally are care-givers, facilitators of their children's and their husbands' work and leisure. The lack of leisure for women is worldwide. 'For women age thirty-five and older, taking time for oneself is often felt to be selfish and self-indulgent not only by the family but by the woman herself,' says American psychologist Dr Kay Porter. Add that to the masculinity bugaboo, and the fact that women have less money than men, and it is certainly apparent that social and economic conditions, rather than biology, keep large numbers of women from taking part in sport.

In 1973, the parents of a twelve-year-old American girl, Maria Pepe, went to court when a move was made to oust their daughter from the place she had earned (and initially been allotted) on her local Little League baseball team. Their victory was also a victory for later generations of girls; but I shouldn't think the fuss helped Maria's batting average.

Five years later, in Britain, the Court of Appeal ruled that the Football Association had the right to ban Theresa Bennett from the Muskham United under-12 team for being a girl. Despite the eagerness of Muskham United to have her – she 'ran rings around the boys' – the Football Association said no. So did the Court. Theresa's parents were refused the right of appeal to the House of Lords. She and a generation of British girls were cheated by law of an equal opportunity to play the sport of their choice.[14]

The message was exactly the opposite of what the American judge had said when he ruled in favour of fair play: 'The sooner little boys realize that there are many areas of life in which girls are their equal and that it is no great shame, no great burden to be bested by a girl, then perhaps we come that much closer to the legislative ideal of sexual equality, as well as relieving a source of emotional difficulty for men.'

Young American women are much more involved in organized sport than were those of the previous generation. The law has paved the way. American female sportstars have also played an important part. In 1974, the tennis star Billie Jean King, the Olympic swimmer Donna de Varona, who had become a TV sportscaster and a celebrity, and a few others, created the Women's Sports Foundation. 'The foundation is a support system for women, which we need,' says de Varona, who became its president in 1978. 'We hope to provide more funding and scholarships for women athletes.' In Britain, a Women's Sport Foundation was started a decade later, with little money and no fanfare, mainly by sportswomen involved in sports education; but there were no stars studding the roster. (I was one of the few sports writers among the founder members.)

In the United States, when 7,000 members of the American Women's Sports Foundation were asked about their girlhood sporting histories, in a study published in 1986, it was found that opportunities had improved markedly. Four times as many young women as older women had played organized sport. Those younger than age twenty-five were four times as likely as those older than thirty-eight to have played organized sports during their school and college years.

Two decades ago, when those women over age thirty-eight would have been graduating from high school, they had had little encouragement to play sport. As the tennis star Chris Evert has said: 'A woman athlete wasn't a normal human being, she was a freak, looked down upon.' One factor in changing points of view has been the success of stars like Evert herself.

Another important factor was the 1972 law in America known as Title IX. It was supposed to give girls and women the same access to school and university sport facilities, practice times, teams (except in contact sports), and equipment as their male counterparts. A loophole meant it didn't quite; but there are many more opportunities than before for American women to play sport.

> It's the better female athletes who are frustrated by the lack of coaching, support and recognition. If you have to get on a boys team to get it, so be it.
> Dr Dorothy Harris, sports psychologist, *USA Today*, 1987

The new story is mixed teams, even in contact sports. One reason girls want to play on them is because there isn't a female equivalent. A second reason is that the standard of play is often higher, partly because the boys' game is often taken more seriously not only by the players but by the coaches.

A law suit was necessary to put Linda Garcia, fourteen, and theoretically, therefore, any other girls who play well enough, on her New Jersey high school's football team. In Virginia, in 1986, two girls joined a boys' high school basketball team; in Connecticut there was a female ice hockey goalie (she recorded an impressive shut-out in her first game), and a schoolgirl wrestler (she lost her first two matches).

A *few* women have even integrated professional basketball. In 1985, Lynette Woodward, the finest one-on-one player in the United States and a member of the 1984 Olympic Championship team, was hired by the Harlem Globetrotters. Two years later, Jackie White joined her on the team. And Nancy Lieberman, although well-known for her commitment to women's basketball, played in the United States Basketball League with men. Nor does she think that integrating the male league will create a muscle drain in women's sport. Women will, she says, develop their own skills rather than be lost to women's sport.

'Studies have shown that when girls and boys play together they learn to compete in other life activities better,' said Deborah Anderson, the executive director of the American Women's Sports Foundation. 'I think we belong everywhere.'[15]

Sport is said to build a man's character; to teach the skills of competition and co-operation that lead to success in later life. There is a widely held belief that sports participation, even on a school team, leads to upward social mobility. People believe that sport provides opportunities for fame and fortune and to form connections that will lead to high-paying careers, later, outside sport.

Those who have made it stand up as role models. The school football or cricket star player is presumed to have the self-confidence to do better than most of us in later life. Many studies have shown that even male high school league players earn more money in later life than non-players earn. And what effect does the sport have on the later, non-sporting careers of women?

The heart-breaking but important long-term study, reported in 1985, of thousands of students – male, female, black and white – from six American states found that eleven years after graduation, white male former athletes of similar background had average monthly salaries that were $252 more than the salaries of former non-athletes. Black male former athletes averaged $116 more than black non-athletes. White women earned just $72 more. And the black women's income was *adversely* associated with sport participation in high school.

New jobs in sport – as coaches, trainers, administrators, referees – are being created as more girls and women play sport. Most of those jobs are going to men. So are the jobs in male sports. 'Data at all levels of sport competition suggest that women do not have equal opportunities when it comes to jobs in coaching and administration,' says sociologist Jay J. Coakley. In 1984, athletics directors at fully eighty-six and a half per cent of American co-educational universities and colleges were male; forty per cent of the programmes had no women in administrative jobs. Nor are there many female head coaches. One of the few at the 1984 Olympics was Pat Summit, the head basketball coach of the gold-winning American team. Similarly, the eighty-six-person International Olympic Committee had no women members until 1981.

In the mid-1970s when American law made it necessary to pay attention to college women's sports, 44 new women and 724 men were hired as women's coaches at the 335 colleges and universities studied.[16] Male and female physical education departments were combined.

In the national reshuffle, women lost 294 head coaching jobs while men gained four hundred and thirty-seven. In high schools, the situation was about the same. In Colorado, for example, eighty-nine per cent of the coaches of women's teams were women in 1974; ten years later the percentage had plummeted to thirty-three per cent. Of high school athletes, thirty-eight per cent were women, but only seventeen per cent of officials (referees, etc.), twenty per cent of coaches, and eight per cent of athletic directors were female.[17]

In Canada, where women occupied only a third of sports administrative jobs, few of them at the top, the situation was no better.

In Britain it is even worse. The British sociologists Anita White and Celia Brackenridge have concluded that: 'There is a greater gender dominance by men in the 1980s than in the 1960s and 1970s.' The figures bear them out. In the twenty years between 1960 and 1980 the number of women on the Olympic teams nearly doubled, rising to thirty-two per cent. But the number of female officials rose only two per cent to fourteen per cent. They had jobs as masseuses, hostesses, physiotherapists; not the jobs at the top. They weren't doing well as national coaches either. In 1976 nine per cent of the members of the National Coaches Association were female; in 1984 the number had dropped to seven per cent, though the overall membership mushroomed.

Nor did they have much power in administering individual sports. In the 1980s, at the Royal Yachting Association, three per cent of committee members were women; in the equivalent body for tennis, five per cent; in swimming, twelve per cent; and in cycling there were none. In badminton, where nearly half the adult players were women (forty-four per cent), they had only six per cent of the standing committee posts.

Two-thirds of the adults who ride horses in Britain are women and four-fifths of the members of the Pony Club for riders under twenty-one are girls. At the British Horse Society, women did have nearly two-thirds of the salaried jobs. But Brackenridge and White found that the 'more senior management positions are held by men'. Army officers and aristocrats were well represented on the prestigious council, but only thirty-eight per cent of the members were female. This, however, was the best yet. 'Though Britain may be ruled by a queen and have a woman as head of state, British sport is firmly in the hands of men,' observed White and Brackenridge.[18] Nor is Britain the only place.

When it comes to cashing in on sports-related careers, when it comes to getting social advantages from sport that allow one the opportunity of making money, well, then anatomy definitely is destiny.

When in Rome
Do as the Romans

That cynical old saying took on a new irony in 1987. Blood doping and steroid abuse scandals rocked Italian athletics even as the world's top athletes were in training for the autumn 1987 World Championships in Rome. Doing as the Romans did, the story went, meant engaging in chemical sport.

The Italian scandal was huge in its international implications. No less than the chief coach of the national team was accused of insisting that runners boost their blood and take massive doses of anabolic steroids. L'Expresso printed a photocopy of a written purchase order from the Italian National Athletics Federation for twenty hospital packs of the anabolic steroid Testoviron. Doubt was cast on the means by which the allegedly blood-doped Italian women's team had won the World Cup Marathon in Japan. The president of the Italian Federation, Primo Nebiolo, denied everything.

What was particularly embarrassing was that Nebiolo, who was head of so apparently corrupt a show, was also the president of the International Amateur Athletics Federation (IAAF), which governs the sport internationally. 'The problem exists all over the world,' Nebiolo said.

He was right.

Doing as the Americans did meant chemical sport too. More than one million Americans take anabolic steroids or growth hormones to build muscle.[1] The steroids are man-made versions of the male hormone testosterone. Athletes who take them in massive doses say they can train harder, more often, and in longer sessions. Thus, they quickly build muscle and perhaps strength. Growth hormones, which are more expensive and in much shorter supply, have the same advantages and fewer side-effects. In Britain and Europe (including Eastern Europe) there are perhaps another 100,000 or 200,000, or even 300,000 people, using these substances for the purposes of sport.

How many of the world total could possibly be world-ranked female athletes? Or even ambitious ne'er-do-well female athletes? Not many. Because of society's ambivalence towards female muscle, anabolic steroids are less used by the rank and file of recreational sportswomen than by sportsmen. Steroid and other drug abuse is rife, but it is not particularly a female problem.

It is frequently implied, however, that women in strength and throwing events like weight-lifting, or the shot put, or the javelin, abuse these muscle-building drugs more than men do. Some do abuse them, but not more than men.

The sight of an athlete hurling a javelin can take your breath away. It is a graceful, balletic movement. Yet it requires great strength to make the javelin soar. The difference between the male and female record is the largest of any Olympic sport. Because of the anatomical conformation of a woman's arm, it is all too easy to throw like a girl.

Technical skill is very important, but it isn't everything. Extra muscle and body weight help. Taking anabolic steroids is thought to be one way to build them. The five-foot-six-inch Olympic and Commonwealth champion, Tessa Sanderson, an outspoken Jamaica-born Briton, weighs in at a compact 145 or so pounds. Her fighting weight used to be about fifteen pounds lighter. Tessa Sanderson admits she has been 'tempted to take what many of the other girls did'.

Sanderson even names names.

The powerfully built East German former Olympic marvel, Ruth Fuchs, who used to pop into Tessa Sanderson's room at championships for a talk and the loan of a hairdrier, heads Sanderson's list. 'There were two Ruth Fuchs: the one who broke world records and the other who appeared afterwards, slimmer, her voice several octaves higher, a very feminine lady, an official with the East German athletics teams,' Sanderson has said.

> The first manifestation, twelve stones [168 lb] or so, hard-looking with a deteriorating voice box, was the woman who in Dublin [in 1977] could not register that I, a nine-stone three-pound [129 lb] parcel of skin and bones, had beaten her. She seemed to think I had discovered a secret potion that turned a weakling into a superwoman. 'What medication do you take?' she half-croaked to me. Neither she nor the East German coaches believed my protests that this was just me, unaided by stimulant, booster or pill.[2]

Ruth Fuchs has never failed a drug test. The Greek thrower Anna Verouli has. Five-foot-four-inch Verouli, who went from eleventh place in the World Student Games to gold in the European javelin championship in just one year, tested positive for anabolic steroids at the Los Angeles Olympics. Tessa Sanderson says she had long since noticed in Verouli and some others all the tell-tale signs: 'The neck bulges, sometimes a kind of acne appears, particularly on the back and face, the skin pigmentation changes, and if the drug is inexpertly administered, the patient sometimes blows up grotesquely.'[3] Long-term damage to the heart and liver, uncontrollable aggression, and even cancer are among the long-term side-effects.

Regarding her bitter rival, dark-haired, bubbly, muscular Fatima Whitbread, who in 1986 set a world record, Sanderson says snidely: 'Her aggression ripples through a thirteen-stone frame that has been built up by, I am told, incredibly tough training schedules . . . It is bulk acquired over the last three years that has given her the thrust.'[4]

Whitbread, a vocal opponent of chemical sport, has a tough training schedule, which includes weight training with a male partner. A nutritionist who specializes in sport has always been involved.

Tessa Sanderson denies taking anabolic steroids or anything else: 'I have never taken drugs.'[5] A poison-pen campaign of letters from 'two women', alleging she did, Sanderson says, was a reason the planned *This Is Your Life* television programme about her was cancelled. She hints that Fatima Whitbread and the coach who adopted her, Margaret Whitbread, may have been involved. 'I have heard [Margaret] talk openly of throwers who, she alleged, were taking anabolic steroids.'[6] Although this is surely the pot calling the kettle black, it is not an unfounded allegation.

Indeed, there is no love lost on either side of the rivalry. Fatima Whitbread speaks of tell-tale anabolic steroid signs too. One she sometimes mentions is a thick, muscular neck. This is one of the notable aspects of Tessa Sanderson's physique. Sanderson's mother, who is no athlete, has that thick neck too.

The point of this is not to imply that, like Anna Verouli, Tessa Sanderson, or Fatima Whitbread, or even Ruth Fuchs, get their muscle from an illegal male hormone. The point is that it is a terrible slur to imply such a thing – not just because it is illegal, not just because, technically, it is cheating. Those libels would apply to male athletes, and very few people bother to slander them.

But because anabolic steroids are male hormones, for women who are accused of using them, that double trouble of going against sex type is there. It is the steroid testosterone which differentiates the seven-week-old male embryo from the female; it is this hormone which also affects such secondary sex characteristics as moustaches and breasts. So the slander becomes edged. If you want to slur a woman's reputation in a strength event, you say she has too many muscles, looks mannish, uses anabolic steroids – the implication being that she has turned herself into a freak. It is analogous to a man calling a woman he isn't having any luck with whore or dyke. Whether she is or isn't, whether she uses anabolic steroids or not, the barb is something that is anti-woman.

In her autobiography, Sanderson recalls that at the end of a Woman of the Year dinner, where 300 female luminaries, including the Duchess of Kent and the first woman in space, had assembled, she 'was longing to see and chat with a man. They are funnier.' No doubt some are. But her statement, which is apropos of nothing in the text, is part of a paragraph stuck in just to stress, 'I'm normal.'

'I am no ardent feminist,' she says. Yet she is all for equal pay.

As a javelin thrower she has felt the pressure of asserting her femininity in this way; of dissociating herself from the frontier of womanhood, even while she is blazing a trail up to and across the Great Divide. It is dismayingly characteristic of women in stereotypically unfeminine sports. What it amounts to is spitting over your shoulder lest someone else spit in your face.

There is blatant bigotry towards women throwers. Often steroid abuse is presented as the basis of their sport. In *World Sporting Records*, published in 1986, the British writers David Emery and Stan Greenberg in their account of field events, speak approvingly of 'increasingly mighty men' but disparagingly of 'elephantine females'. There is no mention of male use of anabolic steroids, surely relevant to the male throwers, who are described in heroic terms. The discussion of the women *focusses* on drug abuse.

Because of society's ambivalence about women's muscle, using muscle-building drugs is less frequent among the rank and file of female athletes than among men. It is a problem at the top. But in sport, where women get far less mention than they are due, they get rather more mention than is fair when the subject is anabolic steroids. Interestingly, the anabolic steroid that is traded on the American black market for about $100 million a year is called Dianabol.

There is no shame any more for men in taking anabolic steroids. They admit it right and left. Out of the ear of the authorities if they are still competing; in print if they are not. The American power-lifting champion, Ron Hale, said in 1987 that after twenty years on anabolic steroids, he had no medical problems: 'Used properly they are no more of a threat to an adult than liquor is.'

Steroid abuses by male athletes are rife. And have been for years. Olympic records show that shot-putters got fourteen per cent heavier in the sixteen years between 1956 and 1972. At those Munich Olympics, sixty-one per cent of male discus throwers admitted using anabolic steroids in their six-month build-up to the Games; and two-thirds said they had taken them at some time. The IAAF did not ban steroids until 1970. The US AAA did not ban them until 1971. And the Olympic committee didn't get around to it until 1975. By this time, though, they were widely used, by women too.

In 1976, at the Montreal Olympics, seven male weight-lifters and one woman failed the steroid test. But because of the competition timetable, the woman, Danuta Rosani, a discus thrower from Poland, became the first athlete disqualified at the Olympics for using anabolic steroids. Rosani had qualified for the discus final, but before she had a chance to compete, the steroid test proved positive. This highlighted the abuse by women although men were seven times as guilty.

The next year, at the European finals in Helsinki, the six-foot-tall East German shot-putter Ilona Slupianek was one of the five athletes caught. In fact, this caused much dismay among the athletes.

The East Germans were supposed to know more about sport science than anybody else, and if one of theirs got caught, well, it was worrying. Hefty Geoff Capes, the top British shot-putter, says:

> We were told it was because her doctor did not use a long enough needle. He had injected the drug into the body fat instead of the muscle and it had been retained in her body for longer than it should have been. So the usual clearance period of two to four weeks was not enough, and she was caught. And that is the only way the testers catch anybody – when the athletes make a mistake.[7]

Now, a new scenario began to appear in top-level sport: she got caught, she got banned, and then she won an Olympic gold medal. Or, he got caught, he got banned, and then he won an Olympic medal. Sixteen days after she completed her year's ban – during which no one tested her for anabolic steroids and she probably trained on them – Slupianek won the European championship. Then came the 1980 Olympic gold medal, two new world records in the shot, and bronze in the first ever athletics world championships, in 1983. A hand injury had cost Mrs Slupianek-Briesenick the gold.

In 1978, another East German, the runner Renate Neufield, who had defected to the West, said that she had been forced by her coaches to take drugs and that when she refused, threats were made against her family. The samples of the drugs she had brought with her to the West were identified by the West Germans as anabolic steroids. It was in Eastern Europe, according to Western sports officials, that the real drug abuse went on. In the East, of course, doping was spoken of as a Western problem. On visits to the West, some Soviet coaches have tried to buy steroids, suggesting to more than one expert that the drugs may be scarce back home, except for top athletes.[8]

But the problem of drug abuse is, as the Italian athletics chief Primo Nebiolo had said, worldwide. The countries with the worst records – the most track and field athletes caught – are: the Soviet Union (ten athletes); the United States (nine); Bulgaria, Cuba, and Greece (five each).[9] These countries may not be the worse abusers, they may simply have the worst techniques of disguising drug abuse. Over the past dozen years, more than seventy athletes of both sexes have been suspended from competition for refusing or failing a drug test.

Most athletes who have been caught have been banned for no more than a year or eighteen months. During that period they can continue to take the drugs and continue to train – with no worry of having to show up for competitions where they might be tested for drugs. Not a discouraging story to prospective users of anabolic steroids, is it?

But it does deeply discourage 'clean' competitors. The shot-putter Judy Oakes, who has been British number one for nearly a decade, but is well out of the world number one position, says, 'I was very sick about Gael Martin out-throwing me' at the 1984 Olympics. The Australian was caught, banned for eighteen months, and came back stronger than ever. With no Eastern Europeans to contend with in Los Angeles, at the age of twenty-eight, she won Olympic bronze. And Westerners, like Eastern Europeans, know how long it takes to get the drug out of their systems so it will not show up in tests. Gael Martin ended the 1986 season in nineteenth place on the world ranking list – the highest non-Eastern European in the sport. Is something wrong with the system?

'This eighteen months' ban is just a farce,' says Oakes, who is two years younger than Martin, but who in frustration has retired from shot-putting competition. She was ten places behind Martin on the ranking list. 'I feel that anyone in any sport caught taking steroids should be banned for life: no second chances. This happens in weight-lifting now and is the only way to eventually eliminate drug abuse.' Oakes has now turned to weight-lifting, although it is not yet an Olympic sport for women.

The scientists have supplied ever more sophisticated means of testing. But the administrators have tended to cover up where possible. Where it is not, they name individuals – usually athletes, rarely the coaches, team doctors, and sports officials who prescribed the drugs and dosages. Then the athletes are banned just long enough to get in some undisturbed training.

Random drug testing during the training season is far better in some countries than in others. Many let the athletes, who know they are subject to testing at events, just get on with it during training. This means athletes can take anabolic steroids all winter, use the advantage they give in allowing one to train harder, and come off them long enough before competition so that chemicals do not show up in tests, which are now routine at major competitions.

Whether or not anabolic steroids build strength is still debated in the laboratory, although athletes are convinced, and there is no doubt that the drugs do make muscles bigger. When athletes bulk out, they feel more powerful. Some who have been told they were being given anabolic steroids, but who got dummy injections called placebos, have performed better than those who knew they were getting the placebos, and even as well as athletes who thought they were getting placebos but were actually given steroids. But scientific experiments are done only on 'safe' dosages – which are miniscule compared to the amounts athletes actually take. Measurable changes in strength may only happen at massive doses. William N. Taylor, the author of *Hormonal Manipulation: A New Era of Monstrous Athletes*, presents a welter of evidence that they do. So do the record books.

Amphetamines, or 'uppers', were the first widely talked about abused drugs. In the early days of drug testing, a lot of athletes seemed suddenly to have colds. The Canadian middle-distance runner, Joan Wenzel, was disqualified from third place at the Pan American Games in 1975 when amphetamine was found. She was banned for life. On appeal Wenzel claimed that she hadn't known there were traces of amphetamine, a stimulant, in the medication she had taken for a cold. The IAAF evidently believed her, as she was reinstated after only a year. She did, however, lose her bronze medal.

At the 1976 Winter Olympics, in Innsbruck, the cross-country skier Galina Koulakova had to give back her bronze medal when ephedrine – an upper – was detected. Koulakova, who had won three gold medals at the previous Olympics, attributed the banned substance to a nasal spray she had taken to relieve her bad cold. She was allowed to compete in the remaining events.

Steroid abuse was soon to be an even bigger problem.

Blood-doping – which is also known as blood-boosting or blood-packing – was next. It is 'natural', in that an athlete usually uses her own blood, which she 'donates' sometime between three weeks and three months before a major competition.

How does blood-doping work? The first stage is exactly what happens to anyone who donates blood and takes about twenty minutes. Two pints of blood are given, frozen, and stored. The athlete's red blood cell level soon returns to normal like anyone else's would. Shortly before competition – a couple of days or the night before – her blood is reinjected. This extra boost of red cells increases the oxygen-carrying ability of her blood; in short, more oxygen becomes readily available to the muscles; she runs up to five per cent faster, perhaps rather less at the very highest levels. In the marathon, five per cent would cut the world record time by about seven minutes; in the 5,000 metres it would be close to a minute. As world records are judged in milliseconds, the potential effects on sport – if you get the dosage and time right – are enormous.

The method was pioneered in Stockholm, at the Institute of Physiology and Performance, in the late 1960s and early 1970s. It was all done in the interest of science. The first rumours of abuse by athletes were not until 1976, when the great Olympic runner Lasse Viren, the 'Flying Finn', was asked if he boosted his blood. Viren said his only secret was sipping reindeer milk. The Finns were, at the time, almighty good runners.

In 1981, a reliable double-blind study in *Medical Science and Sports Exercise* showed that *average* runners could improve by fifty seconds on a five-mile run. World-class athletes would do much less well; but even a hair's length counts at the top. Blood-doping caught on worldwide. It was regarded as seedy but it was not yet illegal.

In 1985, there was dismay when it became known that the red-blooded American boys and girls on the Olympic cycling teams, which won nine medals at the Los Angeles Olympics, had met the night before competition in a hotel room to pack their blood. Rebecca Twigg, the women's road race silver medallist, refused to comment when she was named in the *New York Times*.

The Americans had not packed their own blood; they had used that of near relatives. The cyclists appeared to be doping their blood too often to rely solely on their own resources.

This scandal preceded the Italian brouhaha. In 1986, the International Olympic Committee got around to banning blood-doping. Two months later, the United States Olympic Committee followed suit. In Italy, the Minister of Health stepped in to do likewise. Meanwhile, the drug Pentoxyfilin had come into use to expand blood vessels, and Japanese and American researchers were developing an artificial red blood cell which should be virtually undetectable.

And there was now another widespread offender: technicians looking for anabolic steroids in the urine samples taken at the 1983 world athletics championships in Helsinki had found traces of growth hormone, somatotrophin, known as STH. Some thought it even more effective than anabolic steroids, and it had fewer side-effects. It was expensive though, and scarce, because it could only be extracted from the pituitary gland of *human* corpses. There was not enough somatotrophin in the world for treating children who had growth problems, but athletes who could pay for it had no trouble getting what they called the 'dead man's drug' on the black market.

Diuretics and thyroid-type drugs were also in use, and fad drugs. Five years ago it had been bee pollen; the latest was inosine, a clever chemical said to boost the metabolism, if taken in doses of 3,000 milligrams, enabling athletes and body-builders to train with less fatigue. The American weight-lifting doctor who first picked it up at the Moscow Institute of Sport, in 1983 (so he said), was but one advocate. As the headline introducing it in *Flex Magazine* said: 'At last a safe, legal, super replacement for steroids – But does it work?'

The notion that women can only be good with chemical help of some sort is one part of the stereotype of the weaker sex. It is fostered by the fact that women with muscles look different from the average woman, who historically has worked hard to *avoid* muscles.

There is also the belief that little girls, being made of sugar and spice, ought not to take part in nasty, unnatural practices. Better leave nastiness to the boys, who will be less corrupted, being made anyway of puppy dogs' tails and snails. In the old days, sport itself was regarded as unnatural for women; now the prohibition is against arduous sport and, in particular, chemical sport, which means, of course, top-level sport, as success is now only attainable for both sexes in many events by chemical means. One could argue that this is a step forward for women; I won't.

I do insist, though, that women in sport are no better than they should be; no better than the men. Like men they take drugs to delay puberty, stay awake, build muscle, increase strength, weight and speed, slow their pulse, steady their nerves, disguise their pain, increase their courage. Nor will drugs be stamped out until the win-at-all-costs philosophy itself is changed. And when, dear reader, do you think that will happen?

Is She,
or Isn't He?

Because men are presumed to have an advantage in most sports, there is a suspicion in all sports that women who do well may be men in disguise. At the Olympics and other sacred sporting events, it is routine for women – but not men – to undergo sex tests. In 1966, when the sex tests were introduced, they were controversial. They still are. Twenty years on, in 1986, the *Journal of the American Medical Association* questioned their validity and called for an end to the unnecessary indignity of the tests.

In the first year of sex testing, 1966, at every major championship, female athletes lined up, sometimes dressed only in a towel, in the medical officer's waiting room. In turn, each woman walked, passport in hand, into the examining room, dropped the towel, and the examiners had a good look. The British pentathlete Mary Peters remembers dropping the towel at the European Championships in Budapest. But even though, in that first year of sex testing, Mary Peters had already had her genitals gawked at – inside and out – at the Commonwealth Games in Jamaica, she was so fraught at Budapest that she cannot remember how many doctors there were – she thinks about ten – or even whether they were male or female.[1] She was relieved when she again passed the test.

> 4.2 . . . Competitors who have been registered as females must report to the femininity control head office. Those competitors who fail to report cannot take part in the Games.
>
> From Rule 29, Item Four: Femininity Control,
> *Olympic Charter*, 1983

By 1967, the mass strip-teases were over. Now the test was done by a

143

less embarrassing saliva test. Chromosomes looked at under the microscope would reveal any man trying to pass as female. It was in Mexico, in 1968, that the tests were to get their Olympic début.

Before they started, a nervous Mary Peters, who was captain of the British Olympic team, demanded to know what the British officials would do if any of the team failed the new chromosome test. The tests were being conducted in the name of fair play. But they could be terribly unfair in their social effects. 'Supposing a girl just failed the test and was eliminated from the games in a blaze of publicity?' Peters asked the officials. 'She may well have been leading a perfectly balanced life until that moment with boyfriends and marriage prospects, only to be exposed to millions of people as a freak,' Peters said. 'A life could be ruined in the very brief time it would take for the news to leak out.'

That was precisely what had happened to Eva Klobukowska. The Polish sprinter, who had been a member of the winning 4 × 100 metres team at the previous Olympics, looked like a woman when you removed the towel but she didn't under the microscope. She passed in Budapest. But in Kiev, at the 1967 European Cup, the six doctors reporting said that Eva Klobukowska had 'one chromosome too many to be declared a woman for the purposes of athletic competition'. It was a sad case; a distraught Klobukowska was stripped of her Olympic and other athletics medals. It was conceded that she was one of the six women in a thousand who seem female in every way, but whose chromosomes are anomalous. Most men have XY chromosomes; most women XX. Hers was the rare XXY genotype. Critics said the test was examining the wrong factor, and it was cruel.

Now Peters proposed a fail-safe plan to protect women on her team.[2] Any athlete who failed the sex test would be rushed to the isolation ward of a hospital, and the press would be told that she had developed a highly contagious disease. Hence, she could not participate in the Games; nor could she be interviewed. 'We would then just pray that our word would be accepted.' A migraine headache or some other sudden, but boringly ordinary, illness would have been a more believable option. In any event, the melodramatic British plan did not have to be put into play.

Mary Peters was not the only one who had been wary of the chromosome sex test. From the start, there were outcries against it. On many counts. There still are. The test is expensive in money and time, and in the psychological stress it puts on female athletes. The American sports psychologist Thomas Tutko was one of the first to point out the underlying message of the sex test: 'It's a way of saying, "If you're this good at sport, you can't be a real woman." '

The Wimbledon singles champions: smiling Lottie Dod and pouting Ernest Renshaw probably after their tennis Battle of the Sexes at Exmouth, 1888

The American weekly *Sports Illustrated* named Chris Evert its 1977 Athlete of the Year – but played it as a joke. Some feminists were outraged

The first female sports superstar, La Grande Suzanne Lenglen, playing the Wimbledon she left in disgrace, 1926

Still an outsider in 1951, Althea Gibson, who broke the colour bar in tennis, at her second Wimbledon

Young Steffi Graf (*above*) has made an indelible impression but Martina Navratilova (*below*) remains the sportswoman men feel most threatened by

Gaunt Ingrid Kristiansen, the only athlete in history to hold the 5,000, 10,000 half-marathon, and marathon world records simultaneously

Settling a bitter Olympic score, Mary Decker Slaney beats Zola Budd at the grudge-match Peugeot Talbot Games, Crystal Palace, London, in 1985

'Fastest woman in the world is good cook' was the headline when Fanny Blankers-Koen (nearest camera) won her unprecedented four gold medals at the London Olympics in 1948

Eighty-eight years late women were allowed to run the marathon at the Olympics. Joan Benoit, victorious in Los Angeles, 1984

Too much muscle? Australian body-builder and power lifting champion Bev Francis

Shotputter Judy Oakes could top the British list but not the world because, she says, she will not take anabolic steroids

Going for it: East Ender Fatima Whitbread (*left*) and Russian Tamara Press (*below*), setting new records. Whitbread's in the javelin, Stuttgart, 1986; Press's in the shot-put, Tokyo, 1964

Bantam weight world judo champion, Karen Briggs, throws her team-mate, the European champion Diane Bell, in practice at their home ground, Crystal Palace

4.5 . . . women competitors [must] present themselves with their identity cards at the examination room on the day and time appointed, accompanied by an interpreter (if necessary).

From Rule 29, Item Four: Femininity Control,
Olympic Charter, 1983

In California, the swimmer Debbie Meyer, at the age of sixteen, felt more panic at the prospect of the first Olympic chromatin sex test, scheduled for Mexico 1968, than she did at the coming Olympic competition. 'I hadn't had my period yet, and I started worrying that maybe there was something wrong with me.' Frightened lest she had trained herself out of being female, Debbie Meyer went to her doctor, who performed a chromosome test so that she would know the worst or, in her case, as in most others, the best. Sport hadn't made a man of her. Relieved, the world 200 metres freestyle record holder set a new Olympic record in Mexico. But if she had not been able to afford to take the test privately, she might have given up sport.

That the test is an unnecessary indignity has even been recognized by some Olympic officials. As early as 1975, the American representative on the IOC's medical committee, Dr Daniel Hanley, derided sex testing as 'an expensive over-reaction to a remote possibility'.

The controversy continues. In 1986, a detailed article in the *Journal of the American Medical Association* by a geneticist, Dr Albert de la Chappelle, of the Department of Medical Genetics at the University of Helsinki, questioned the fairness and even the validity of the tests. 'Neither sex chromatin nor gynaecological examination is suitable for screening purposes,' he said. 'The present screening method is both inaccurate and discriminatory in that it excludes women who should be allowed to participate.' These are the six women in a thousand who look like women, think they are women, and whose body composition, strength and muscle seem entirely female – but who fail the test because they have Y chromosomes.

The sex test is done with a swab or with a hank of hair. Either a scraping is taken of the mucous membrane inside each woman's mouth, or the root of a hair is examined, and these are scrutinized under a microscope. What they are looking for is Barr bodies, which are the genetic difference that results from men having XY chromosomes and women having XX. Men have no Barr bodies; women have them in twenty to fifty per cent of their cell nuclei. A few women, like Eva Klobukowska, have the XX Barr bodies but they also have a Y chromo-

145

some. Dr de la Chappelle concluded that they were being unfairly 'denied a career in sports'. The *JAMA* editorial called for an end to the tests. 'Eliminating screening would probably have little or no effect' on who won the championships, said the *JAMA*, 'and it might restore a few personal dignities.'

Indeed, if there were competitors who should be barred because they had an unfair advantage, the test was failing to spot them. A hormonal imbalance called adrenal hyperlasia does give one woman in 5,000 the shape and muscular strength of a man; such women have female genitalia and they would pass the chromatin test.

4.6 . . . Female competitors who have a valid certificate of femininity, which has been issued by the IOC Medical Commission, will be exempted from another examination upon presenting that certificate to the femininity head office.

From Rule 29, Item Four: Femininity Control,
Olympic Charter, 1983

Ever since they talked their way into the Olympics, women have been medically examined far more frequently than men. In 1925, the Olympic Medical Sub-Commission decided that women's 'special functions' and 'special organization' required 'carefully chosen' events, and these had to be 'reduced considerably' in comparison with events for men. There were also clothing regulations 'to prevent regrettable exhibitions'. It is the psychological message – the demeaning subtext – of these and the present sex tests which have caused so much dismay.

The sex test is the pass card of organized sport. It is not, like the pass card of South Africa, intended as an instrument of evil, but it does keep women in their place.

In South Africa, the pass card not only allowed the government to keep tabs on the underclass, it also communicated the message to blacks that they were an underclass, that they were under the control of the 'bas' and that there was something so suspicious about them that they required watching.

As women don't need a special card in other walks of life, the sex test obliquely tells women that they are second-class citizens in Sportsworld, and that there is something worrying, something suspicious, perhaps even unnatural, about women doing well at sport.

Those who pass are issued with a certificate of femininity so that they need not take the test again and again. Female athletes bring their certificates with them whenever they go to a major competition to compete.

Many athletes have admitted that the prospect of the test has frightened them. Most are still in adolescence, like Debbie Meyer, at an age when personal insecurity is frequent. More than one coach has wondered if it is the psychological barrier of the sex test rather than any lack of speed and muscle that keeps women from running the four-minute mile – when times in the 1,500 metres show clearly that they have the ability.

4.7 . . . The identification of the competitor appearing for the control will be made by the identity card and will include the competitor's photograph, weight, size, and accreditation number. In some cases, the individual's passport could also be requested.

From Rule 29, Item Four: Femininity Control,
Olympic Charter, 1983

Women do excel at those sports which are not considered to be particularly masculine or masculizing. They now outride men at the top levels of equestrian sport, for instance. Yet what is innately female about riding a horse? Nothing surely. It takes enormous athleticism: strength in the thighs, and the courage to jump fences and speed forward in a sport that is known for spills and injury. Equestrian sport has always been expensive (horses eat a lot; so do trainers), hence it has attracted riders of high social status, rich enough to afford the sport. Princess Anne was no exception in this respect. And as cute little girls love ponies, women who ride well are not made to put their womanhood in question. Hence they can win the world championship and the competition at Badminton, as they have, even though they compete against men.

Are women scared to run faster than men lest their femininity come under suspicion? Ten years ago, a top female athlete muttered that it was unfeminine for a woman to run the 100 metres faster than 11 seconds. Now women have done it; but not that one. And perhaps some woman who could run even faster dares not. Would the roughly ten per cent difference between the male and female record be diminished even more, be overcome, if women didn't have that psychological worry too? Is it this which keeps them from throwing further, and from swimming faster and further than men, as often as they could?

147

Which is not to say there have been no anomalies or masquerades. A few unscrupulous men, probably in cahoots with unscrupulous governments, have pretended to be female athletes. But more often it has been a question of sad cases – a hermaphrodite ruled against, or individuals who were genetically male but had reason to believe they were female, and others who simply very much wished they were.

In 1938, the German high-jumper Dora Ratjen, who set a world record of five feet seven inches, was found to have both male and female sexual organs. She was banned, and although she had lived as a woman previously, she changed her name to Hermann.

> 4.8 . . . the determination of X and Y chromatins will be conducted on a smear of buccal mucous membrane.
>
> From Rule 29, Item 4: Femininity Control,
> *Olympic Charter*, 1983

Two Frenchwomen in the 1946 European silver-medal-winning relay team later were found to be living as Frenchmen. Claire had become Pierre; Lea was Léon. Whether they had pretended to be women or whether they were later pretending to be men was not absolutely clear.

The downhill skier Erika Schineggar was caught with her chromosomes down in the first year of the tests. It was said that her male sex organs had been hidden inside her body since birth. With sublime self-possession, Erika later changed her name to Eric, married, and became a father. For the Polish sprinter Eva Klobukowska, however, the discovery had been only tragic.

In 1980, elderly Mrs Stella Olsen, the former Stella Walsh, was shot dead during a robbery in Cleveland, Ohio, an innocent bystander. The autopsy revealed that the 1983 Olympic 100 metre sprint champion, who had won forty-two American national titles, had male sex organs.

The most notorious case involved two Russian sisters, Tamara and Irina Press, who dropped out of world competition just before the sex tests were to be introduced. Because of the timing of their retirement, it was *presumed* in the West that they had something to hide. The rumour was that the muscular sisters were really the Press brothers.

Tamara Press had had an impressive career: she held the world shot-put record from 1959 to 1965, and the world discus record from 1960 to 1965. At the 1960 Olympics, she won gold at the shot put and was the silver medallist in the discus; in 1964 she won gold in both events. Irina, two years younger, was the finest hurdler in the world. In

> 4.9 . . . If the test is inconclusive, the competitor must undergo
> further tests. . .
>
> From Rule 29, Item Four: Femininity Control,
> *Olympic Charter*, 1983

1960, she became the Olympic 80 metres hurdles champion; in 1964, she scored gold at pentathlon with a world record of 5,246 points. The sisters had racked up a total of five gold medals in two Olympics.

There is no proof that the Presses' retirement at the ages of twenty-nine and twenty-seven was in any way connected with the introduction of the sex tests. There are dozens of reasons why the sisters might have retired: after so many years at the top in sports that required arduous training, they may have had enough or simply have gone stale. The sisters were close; if one withdrew, it was understandable that the other did too. And there might have been family reasons, or injury problems (common in throwing events), or even the advent of a new fair-haired shot putter in Russia.

Indeed, Tamara's world shot-put record was broken by a Russian, Nadyezhda Chizhova, who went on to become Olympic champion. Neither she nor the greatest discus thrower of the modern era, Faina Melnyk, another post-sex-test Russian, who held the world record for nearly five years, lasted as long at the top as had Tamara Press.

Yet maybe the Press sisters really were the Press brothers. The point is that we do not know. To this day, they claim to be sisters. Tamara Press, who turned fifty in May of 1987, lives by herself in the Lenin Hills in a three-room apartment. She has a Ph.D. in education, holds a high-level administrative job in recreation, and has found time to write two memoirs. It is said that Tamara Press swims regularly at a local pool.

> 4.12 . . . The Medical Commission will issue a femininity
> certificate to those competitors whose tests are conclusive.
>
> From Rule 29, Item Four: Femininity Control,
> *Olympic Charter*, 1983

The younger of the two, Irina Press, also has a Ph.D. in sports education. A Muscovite now, she lives in two rooms, likes to attend first nights at the theatre, and works on the grounds of Moscow's oldest stadium, as chief of sports education at the Dynamo Sports Society. Irina takes some of the credit for the success of Dynamo's athletes. Olga Vladykina, the 400 metre runner, won at the inaugural Goodwill Games in 1986, and the same year, Rimas Ubartas became the European discus champion. The younger Press still does strenuous exercises and runs twice a week. The two sisters, I am told, are great friends although they live their own lives. Twice a month they run three or four kilometres together in a city park.[3] This is one Westerner who would like to go and have a talk – and look through the family photograph album.

Consider the other much-discussed case: Maria Itkina, another Russian and a talented 400 metres runner. Her event has had two great post-sex-test champions, the much-admired Pole, Irena Szewinska, who held the world record *intermittently* from 1974 to 1978, and the East German, whom many regard as the greatest athlete of her era, Marita Koch, who has dominated the event since 1978, holding the world record for most, but not all, of the period. But Maria Itkina, who departed pre-sex-test, held the record for five *consecutive* years. Yes, she may have been a man masquerading as a woman; or, after so long a reign, she may just have been a woman who was worn out.

Far more commonplace in world history is the fact of women disguising themselves as men: Joan of Arc; seventeenth-century foot soldiers; ordinary refugees trying to avoid rape; not to mention Shakespeare's Rosalind in *As You Like It*, and Vita Sackville-West on her very bohemian Paris sojourn. Women have usually disguised themselves as men to gain autonomy – safety on the street, the right to earn a living, perhaps also the right to participate in sport.

In fact, the very first sex test in Olympic sport, way back in ancient Greece, was instituted to keep women from disguising themselves as men. Athletes and trainers had to pass naked as they arrived at the ancient Olympics lest any women sneak in. It is surely unlikely that women have suddenly stopped masquerading as men. In some endurance sports – long-distance swimming certainly, the marathon and equestrian sport (which has both single-sex and mixed-sex competition) possibly, and others – women even have a yet-to-be-properly-tapped physical advantage. There are no sex tests for men. When there are more women for coaches to choose from, will they sneak a few on to the men's team?

It would be an extreme and unlovely use of women for national pride; it would call for a huge sacrifice: the woman would have to become a man. It is unlikely that many could live a false life from childhood ever after – for unless one covered one's tracks thoroughly, someone would find out. It is equally unlikely the Press sisters could have sprung grown from the head of some sports scientist. Surely, Tamara and Irina grew up somewhere. Someone remembers their childhood.

It is, however unlikely, perfectly possible that in the future women could be rejigged and sneaked on to men's teams. Indeed, in the early years of the century, many of the top male athletes were no more fit and no more muscular than strong countrywomen. Even now one finds some hefty rural Amazons about. It is entirely possible that some of the great purportedly male Olympians of the twentieth century were – and are? – women.

5

The Shape
of the Future

The Girls Who Don't Want to Grow Up

The answer to sexual alchemy was supposed to be gymnastics. A feminine sport. Gymnasts are girls, not tomboys.

In many sports, being little is a liability. In gymnastics it is an asset. In many sports, bulging muscles are called for. In gymnastics being muscle-bound would impede flexibility and agility, which are everything. This is the one sport in which girls can be girls.

The problem is they dare not become women.

Gymnasts appear to have the highest rate of anorexia nervosa in sport.[1] This starvation disease has been linked by doctors not only to fear of being fat, but also to a fear of growing up.

At fourteen, that dark-haired, *petite* embodiment of gymnastic perfection, Nadia Comanenci, scored seven perfect tens at the 1976 Montreal Olympics. Comanenci of Romania was the first gymnast ever to attain a perfect score at the Olympics. They called her 'Little Miss Perfect'. Her technique was flawless, and at the Olympics she had a perfect strength to weight ratio for the sport. At sixteen, though, her budding breasts and increased height began to upset her perfect balance. Like many girls who did not want to grow up, Nadia Comanenci stopped eating. She became thinner, and thinner, and thinner. Anorexia is known among gymnastics coaches as the 'Nadia Syndrome'. It is not, technically, a contagious disease. But the two British champions, Suzanne Dando and Mandy Gornall, came down with anorexia. Seventy-four per cent of the college-age American gymnasts tested in Michigan in 1986 had some pathological eating behaviours aimed at keeping them slim.[2]

Gymnasts in California, in another key 1986 study, averaged 300 calories a day less than they needed. More than forty per cent of them were eating *less than two-thirds* of the RDA (recommended daily allowance) of calcium, vitamin B6, iron, folate, and zinc. 'These nutrients are essential for normal growth, development, and tissue repair,' noted the researchers in *The Physician and Sports Medicine*.[3]

155

Female gymnasts have good reason for their fear of food – it would take them on the road to puberty and mature them out of their sport. Unlike male gymnasts, females in the sport now have a very short career span indeed, peaking at sixteen or seventeen; the 1986 male world champion was twenty-four.

The legacy of the two prima gymnasts, Olga Korbut, the Russian who brought the sport to the attention of the world in 1972, and Nadia Comanenci, who took gymnastics to its apogee, is tainted. Most people think that gymnastics is ideal for girls: it is a sport which seemingly does not put their femininity on the line.

But the sport as it is now practised causes gymnasts enormous anxiety about fitting its stereotype of lithe Lolita. Before Korbut, the feats that gymnasts performed were accessible to a mature body; after Korbut, only short hyper-flexible waifs could become champions.

Gymnastics now is also more dangerous to life and limb than it ought to be. The Korbut somersault and the Korbut loop, once considered daring, still considered dangerous, are virtually mandatory for victory. And the risk stakes continue to rise. Comanenci added a full turn to her dismount routine specifically 'to gain a risk value'. 'The world has me to thank or blame for the Comanenci somersault and the Comanenci dismount,' she says. On the blind forward somersault done on the high bar, 'the gymnast doesn't get to see the bar while trying to catch it until the last possible moment'.[4] Cruel and unusual peril is now enshrined in the customary rules of the game. Olympic champion Mary Lou Retton calls it Killer Gymnastics.

Few people on the outside realize how hard it is for gymnasts to live up to their sport's feminine stereotype. Insiders know.

If enough people at the top cared enough, gymnastics could clean up its act.

The young gymnasts still talk about Olga Korbut. It is fifteen years since satellite television brought the pre-pubescent seventeen-year-old Russian to the attention of the world. A world audience saw her wink and flirt and contort her body splendidly in her 1972 Olympic début at the Munich Sportshalle.

Fifteen years is a millennium in sport. But posters of Olga are still to be seen on the bedroom walls of young up-and-comers. The willowy seventeen-year-old British champion, Lisa Elliott, who has long since had her blonde Olga pony-tail clipped short, is not the only one who will tell you, 'I started because of Olga Korbut.' Lisa Elliott was just two years old and living in Surrey when Olga played Munich. But for years afterwards Olga came to London to perform, part of her tour of the

Western World. Little girls in the audience, and their Mums and Dads – there are always a lot of Dads at gymnastics – came to see her perform. Or they watched her on television and read books about her, and about Nadia. Today they spend their evenings practising the Korbut somersault and the loop, which are listed on the international classification of gymnastics elements. Girls, by the millions, took up gymnastics after Olga Korbut's Olympic début. Olga Korbut set off a revolution in the West. Or was it a counter-revolution?

But let us not get ahead of our story. What actually happened in the Munich Sportshalle in the last days of August in 1972? And why?

When the spectre of masculizing sport began to loom in the West, when Billie Jean King was first talking big, when the about-to-be enacted American law, Title IX, was making American colleges think they would have to field female footballers, when women's liberation was getting too much muscle, along came Olga.

She was an unlikely seventeen-year-old. She stood four-foot-eleven, weighed in at 84 pounds, and looked no more than twelve. Her blonde hair was pulled back in a childlike pony-tail, and although she was Russian she had a face like a Barbie doll. No breasts, no sign of puberty, but Olga Korbut knew how to flirt with an audience, knew when to wink, when to toss that pert blonde head. And she was a daring gymnast. She did a backward somersault on the four-inch-wide beam. No one had ever before performed a somersault on the beam. And she did a half-back somersault on the uneven parallel bars, which had never been done before.

But in her thirty seconds on those asymmetrical bars during the competition for the overall championship, she made two bad mistakes. She fluffed her take-off, and then, spinning through her exciting routine, her hand slipped off the bar. She finished her performance as gracefully as possible, but there was no chance of a prestigious over-all medal.

And then what did she do? Dear, sweet, delicate girl, she cried. Four hundred million people saw. Satellite TV's contribution to the then almost unknown sport of gymnastics.

At the next day's individual-event competitions it all came right. Olga Korbut, who had come to the Olympics as a reserve, remembered to put enough chalk on her calloused little hands, she didn't lose concentration, and she didn't fall. The crowd applauded her every move. When she was awarded only 9.80 on the asymmetrical bars, the crowd jeered and whistled for fully five minutes. In the next event, the beam, the judges awarded Olga 9.90 and thus, to the dismay of some of the *aficionados*, the gold medal. The same thing happened in the floor exercise, where she just bested the darling of the purists.

There are fistfuls of gold medals in the gymnastics pot. Even with those two dubious golds and her share of the Soviet team gold medal, Olga Korbut came fifth overall. The most coveted Olympic title in the sport, the individual overall championship, had gone to another Soviet gymnast, the better gymnast Ludmila Tourischeva – but who remembers her name? Tourischeva didn't cry.

It was Olga Korbut who was the star. Hers are perhaps the most momentous tears in sport. Olga Korbut's vulnerability coupled with her flirtatiousness – translation, feminine dependence – charmed. A generation of little Western girls immediately pulled their hair back, donned leotards, and walked a four-inch plank called the beam.

Their Mums (in Britain), and their Moms (in the States) chauffeured them to gymnastics class. Their eager Dads accompanied them to gymnastic displays. Sometimes Uncle Jack went along. Quite a number of unaccompanied men turn up in every gymnastics audience.

Within six months of Olga's appearance in Munich, the participants in the sport quadrupled in Great Britain alone. The *Sunday Times* sponsored gymnastics, and in less than a decade three million British girls earned badges. Fifteen years later, at least twelve million American, British, and European girls are active in the sport. Probably more.

The Soviets say that no drugs are necessary to stave off puberty. Keeping a young gymnast's body fat below seven per cent of body weight will do the trick. Some estimates say even seventeen per cent will work. The seventeen-year-old joint world overall champion, Oksana Omeliantchik from Kiev, who is a dark-haired version of Olga Korbut, looks about eleven. But neither Omeliantchik, nor her coach, nor the head of the Soviet team could be drawn on the subject of the champion's puberty. They spoke only of long hours of training, begun at an early age. Lisa Elliott's body fat is five point three per cent. This is comparable to the Russian stars. Most competitive gymnasts fall in the eight to nine per cent range. The body weight of most teenage girls is about twenty per cent fat. Tony Murdoch, who has helped forge links between British and Soviet gymnastics, is but one of many Westerners who insist there are no anti-puberty drugs in the sport: 'Diet and intensive training do it,' he says.

The Russian gymnasts start at the age of six and attend specialist boarding school so that they train full-time from an early age. This body shape has been necessary – it hasn't always been – at least since the advent of Korbutian gymnastics. Ludmila Tourischeva was, in fact, the last of the grown-up-looking gymnasts. Now a short, extremely flexible

body is necessary for such elements as that Korbut somersault an
which are now standard moves in international competition.

Some members of the Fédération Internationale de Gymna
(F.I.G.) had wanted the difficult new elements kept out of the interna-
tional classification tables – in other words, discouraged if not banned.
They lost the battle. Gymnastics has become a high-risk sport.

Throughout Olga Korbut's performances, an intent, dour, dark-
haired man who hated noise – even when it was applause, and there
was plenty – stood nearby, his arms folded on his chest. Renald Knysh,
a taciturn man, and Korbut's coach, had devised those daring – and
dangerous – new elements. 'There's no point in mastering the ordinary
exercises that everybody knows because they won't impress the
judges,' he told the gymnasts at his school in Grodno, where there were
500 girls, but only one Olga Korbut. Precision, finesse, artistry, were all
necessary ingredients of any new trick; but forget not, Renald Knysh
would say, 'perceptibility'. If the judges couldn't see the daring of it,
what was the point? For years he had believed that the backward
somersault was possible. It had taken Olga Korbut, whose short body it
was designed for, fully two years to learn.

Comanenci, no coward, has even remarked on the danger now
inherent in the sport. 'The Code of Points was created with a view to
keeping the escalation of risk elements in the various exercises in check,
but it does not yet seem to have succeeded in its aim. The quest for
those precious ROV bonus points has continued to oblige competitors
to take more risks.'[5]

One who fell and became paralysed was Elena Mukhina. Tony
Murdoch and Nik Stuart have called her 'the most daring of performers'. And she was. In 1978, at eighteen, Elena Mukhina became the
world overall champion. She had taken Korbut's loop from the high bar
and added a full twist, catching the high bar once again and continuing
with her routine. This routine had taken her two years to learn.

Mukhina, who had a shelf full of world and European championship
gold, was expected to shine at the Moscow 1980 Olympics. Three days
before the Games, during a routine somersault in the seemingly least
dangerous part of the sport, the floor exercise, disaster struck. The final
somersault in Elena Mukhina's tumbling sequence required her to land
on her neck and shoulders and then roll to a standing position, in a
common enough gymnastics movement called a 1½ or 1¾ Arabian front
somersault. Mukhina had practised this routine thousands of times, but
she landed on her neck too heavily; it broke. She was rushed to hospital
and underwent surgery. Her life was saved, but Mukhina was severely
paralysed. For six months she could not even talk.

It was not a freak accident. As Comanenci explained, even the floor exercise has to be dangerous if you want to be champion: 'As one of the world's top gymnasts, she could be expected to include many elements of high risk, in order to give her a chance of acquiring the necessary bonus points. . . . She was,' said Comanenci, 'a fine exponent of our sport.'[6]

Most gymnastics injuries are less dramatic, but they may be just as serious, and accidents are frequent. Many Olympic-style gymnasts get injured each year.[7] It appears that there is an average of more than one injury per gymnast each year. One two-year study conducted in Yorkshire showed that eighty per cent of the injured gymnasts did take some time off from training. But few take off as long as they should.[8]

Ankles get taped; so do wrists, thighs, and calves. At the 1979 Texas world championships Comanenci was inveigled into making a short appearance to save the team's chances, although she was really too ill to perform.

The Olympic champion, Mary Lou Retton, who became the first American to hold the title at Los Angeles in 1984, was trained in part by Comanenci's demanding former coach, Bela Karolyi, who defected to the United States in 1981. Four-foot nine-inch Retton has had to bite her lip and go on plenty of times in training. The British champion, Lisa Elliott, almost put out her eye one year; the next year she injured her ankle; she took what time off she could. But in the weeks before the national championships she trained and competed although she was in constant pain. This is quite usual.

Severe back problems often need six to nine months off – unthinkable in a female gymnast's short career.

Accidents occur because gymnasts are undernourished and because gymnasts put themselves at risk so often. Moreover, these two factors are linked in an inter-acting downward spiral. Gymnasts starve themselves to stay thin and pre-pubescent. The resulting malnourishment makes them prone to accident and weakens their bones so that any accident is apt to be more serious than it would be if they ate properly. There are also 'over-use' injuries – the results of performing a repetitive motion 20,000 times, thereby over-stressing growing bones and muscles.

Female gymnasts and distance runners have the lowest body fat percentage of all female athletes, and are under great pressure to maintain a low body weight. The runners' training runs the weight off; the gymnasts, however, perform in bursts; pathological eating behaviours tend to be the only way. In fact, these young athletes go to great lengths to stay slim. The sports medicine specialists in the

Michigan study cited at the beginning of this chapter found that seventy-four per cent of the gymnasts vomited more than twice a week, used laxatives, diet pills, diuretics, or starved themselves.[9]

Vanity was *not* a factor: 'What emerged is not a pattern of eating disorders designed to enhance physical beauty, but rather a naive, desperate, and high-risk attempt by female athletes to lower their body weight to achieve the highest possible level of performance.'

> When it's cold and damp outside I just ache all over. *And I* hadn't had a big fall or anything, but I guess with all the stress over such a long period that bone finally cracked. So they put the wrist in a cast and told me that it would be eight to twelve weeks. But when you have big competitions coming up, you're not going to stay out that long. I got the cast off in four weeks.
> Olympic champion Mary Lou Retton, 1986 (aged eighteen)

The girls in their study were aged eleven to seventeen and practised at least nine hours a week. Many practised for twice that long. On average they ate 300 calories less than the 2,100 a day recommended for sixty-inch-tall thirteen-year olds.[10]

Quite a few studies have shown that 'chronic calorie restriction' can lead to 'growth failure and impaired maturation'.[11] There are added dangers for gymnasts who do not eat properly. Fatigue is a result of poor nutrition. It is when gymnasts feel tired that they have accidents. There is another sort of triple trouble. Too little calcium affects bones. Gymnasts have a high rate of stress fractures. When they fall, too, they are likely to cause more damage than they would if they were healthy. Too little zinc interferes with wound healing and is a cause of short stature. Too little folate also seems to play havoc with the healing process.

In Texas, Comanenci, who was visibly anorexic, fluffed a simple move. Then she was taken to hospital with an inflamed wound on her wrist which had not healed. Poor resistance to infection is a symptom of anorexia.

Many more children and adolescents than used to now engage very intensely in sport. There are many more injuries, too. In fact, intensive gymnastics programmes have become standard. Young gymnasts now *expect* to lose a few months to injury. What they don't realize is that they may be affecting their whole lives.

Injuries to the growing parts of bones can have serious long-term effects. Gymnastics particularly puts girls at risk.

Before maturity, the ends and the shafts of bones are separated by cartilage. These plates of cartilage are responsible for growth in the length of bones. By maturity – that is, when bones have achieved their adult length – the cartilage plates harden into bone. This ossification occurs between the ages of fourteen to twenty; it may happen at a different rate in different bones of the body. If the cartilage plates are damaged, however, there can be serious growth abnormalities.[12]

Overloading is what causes damage. This can be sudden excessive strain; or it can be continued strain, damaging little by little. In gymnastics training, the bones and joints of a child's body are frequently subjected to squashing, stretching, and sheer force. Every time a gymnast does a backbend or 'walkover' great stress is put on bending the bones and muscles. Twisting vaults – so commonplace in the sport – cause enormous torsion.

Girls doing gymnastics stress their bodies as much as men carrying heavy loads. What is more, they may do it over and over again. It took Olga Korbut two years to learn the Korbut somersault, so she must have done it at least 20,000 times. Thereafter, she did it another 5,000 or even 10,000 times. Such movements cause repeated impact, stretching, or tissue elongation, acceleration and then deceleration of the limbs, and then there is the loading or weight put upon parts of the body.

It is not just the shape and size of the bones that may be affected. Repeated impact and muscle contractions can change the internal architecture of the bones. Jumping over and over again, landing over and over, can cause mineral changes that make the bones fragile.[13] Using the limbs is good for them; using them too much causes the stress. Training at the intensity necessary for national and international competition causes problems in the young adults who practise most sports; the problems are compounded in children – that is, most competitive gymnasts.

While it is clear that such training can lead to all sorts of problems, it is not at all clear that sustained training really does increase a child's strength greatly. Growing children get five to ten per cent stronger a year anyway. This is a normal consequence of maturation of the nervous system and increased muscularity. Adolescents seem to respond rather like adults to training; but the evidence about children is conflicting. About twelve weeks of training may be all that is needed (or desirable) to attain the child's maximum strength,[14] but more training may be needed to perfect technique. This additional training can be harmful.

Coaches and gymnasts themselves *should* expect decreased results per unit of training work in post-adolescent girls. This is a natural result of maturation. But often this decrease in the rate of improvement leads to frantic overtraining.

Inadequate rest between training sessions – very common in intensive gymnastics training – accumulates, leading to stress fractures, tendinitis, and bursitis, all being 'over-use syndrome' injuries. Over-use injuries happen when a muscle or bone is repeatedly subjected to stress; practising a vault or a somersault over and over again can eventually lead to a stress fracture, or a painfully inflamed tendon (tendinitis). The cartilage growth plates, in particular, can be damaged, leading to short or crooked bones. In other words, deformity can result.

It is hard to say how many children have been damaged in this way. Studies show that at least five per cent, and perhaps up to eighteen per cent, of children's sports injuries are to the growth plates. And many injuries just are not reported. Only recently have such large numbers of children become involved in gymnastics and other sports; many of the long-term effects of their intense training are still not known.

During the adolescent growth spurt, the discrepancy between the strength of bones and muscles can be very large, and the risk of injury becomes very great. These may, though, be the prime years of a gymnast's competitive life.

The safeguards – proper medical care and screening, good coaching and physical conditioning, and safe facilities – are, unfortunately, in short supply. Elite athletes do have access to sports medicine specialist care – but injuries can happen on the way up to national ranking. Moreover, there are many occasions on which an injured gymnast has been called upon to 'save' the team.

There is, too, a conflict of interest felt by many coaches, who are often physical education teachers as well. 'There are disparate or incongruous philosophies between these two professions,' admits Keith Russell of the University of Saskatchewan, a PE teacher and coach.

As a physical educator I believe in the values derived from children receiving a 'balanced diet' of regular physical activity and that instruction and facilities should be made available, not only for the 'select' few, but for the masses. But, as a former national coach and present mentor of many young elite gymnasts, I teach that to reach international prominence in many sports requires that athletes must start young and train intensely in specially designed facilities.[15]

An ambitious coach is perhaps a *sine qua non* of championship attainment. Olga Korbut's coach Renald Knysh kept a card-file of young married couples in his town of Grodno who might produce gymnastic fodder.

In Onesti, Romania, in the school-yard during break, six-year-old Nadia Comanenci caught the eye of the distinguished gymnastics coach Bela Karolyi, who was scouting for talent. As he walked over to talk to her, the bell rang. Karolyi went from classroom to classroom to find her. No luck. He searched a second time. A third time, he went into the classrooms. He asked if any of the girls liked gymnastics. Nadia Comanenci was one of the ones who shouted, 'I do!' Karolyi used to scour Romania in search of six-year-olds, because he aimed to have his gymnasts mastering the international repertoire by the age of twelve. At seven Comanenci was entered in the Romanian junior championships; she finished thirteenth. At eight, she won. At thirteen, now a student at the special gymnastics high school in Gheorgehiu Dej, she won the women's European championship. After her 1975 début in the West, at the 'Champions All' tournament at Wembley, on the outskirts of London, gymnastics fans knew her name. After the Montreal Olympics the world knew it. At fourteen years 313 days she became the youngest ever Olympic gold medallist in the sport. What Korbut's coach had started, Comanenci's sealed.

Both gymnasts, though, got the best of everything their countries could provide. Elite gymnasts usually do get proper conditioning and coaching. In the West, though, particularly at the early stages, it can be hit and miss. One big danger is poor equipment and facilities: landing areas are often insufficiently padded; the run up to the vault is usually too hard and thin. Even the British national champion, Lisa Elliott, has to travel 200 miles a week to find gyms which are properly equipped in all aspects. And the one in Surrey, which is considered prime, was muscle-pulling cold when I was there.

Gymnasts arch their back when doing walkovers and handsprings. Twisting and hyperextension movements cause many competitors to complain of lower back pain. Hyperextension when presenting yourself to the judges – a Comanenci innovation – has led to many a young gymnast's backache. Gymnasts have five times as many arthritic lower back problems as other women.[16] The situation may be even worse than the figures suggest, as many such problems only begin to show up more clearly as the gymnasts age.

Eleven per cent of gymnasts had spondylolysis (a defect of the lumbar neural arch); only two point three per cent of non-athletic white females of the same ages had the problem. By the mid-1970s specialists in medical journals were referring to the 'current epidemic' of back injuries among female gymnasts.

Because the arms carry so much weight – on the asymmetric bars, for example, or when vaulting – there is also a high rate of arm and wrist injuries.

There is even some evidence that risk of injury can be predicted. One indicator, alas, is previous injury record. Girls with relatively poor musculature and short stature are particularly prone to injury, especially if they are relatively heavy. That short stature is necessary, though, to perform the contortions now required by the sport. So champion gymnasts must arm themselves with supermuscle, perhaps causing growth problems, as we have seen; and they must be superlight, perhaps leading to anorexia or other pathological eating behaviours. And so the spiral of debilitation goes down and down.[17]

If the rules were changed so that the sport did not rely so heavily on the hyperextensions and other movements best done by a short-waisted immature body – in other words, if a gymnast had the career expectancy of a marathon runner or even a tennis player – gymnasts and their coaches would have to train at last. Permanent injury would not be risked so regularly for short-term gain.

If there were no kudos, no 'bonus points', for risks surely the situation would be much improved? It is indeed ironic that gymnasts are credited with grace, agility, soft, traditionally feminine, skills when they are really as courageous – and foolhardy? – as the 'daring young man on the flying trapeze'.

If officials wanted to, say the many concerned coaches, they could clean up the sport. The gymnasts blame the judges and the judges blame the gymnasts. As Hazel Wearmouth, who heads gymnastics at Carnegie Department, Leeds Polytechnic, explains, 'You don't have to hyperextend when you present yourself to the judges; but it is expected. Hyperextension on presentation is not a rule. It is just a habit, introduced by Nadia, which other gymnasts feel they must copy.' What is expected should be changed.

The code of points is itself at fault. 'It encourages high-risk elements and routines, and extreme hypermobility. The need for suppleness and an appropriate strength-weight ratio favours pre-pubertal girls,' says Wearmouth. 'The older age group finds it increasingly difficult to maintain strength/weight ratios, percentage body fat, and routines showing high levels of difficulty.'

There is an impasse because gymnasts blame the judges who do not award bonus points unless they do the advanced series. Judges meanwhile blame the gymnasts for raising the stakes by showing extremes of flexibility. The judges feel they must award the prize to the most flexible, the most daring, and so on.

What makes it really dangerous is this. Gymnasts must show a series of moves, they must exhibit extreme flexibility, *but* they cannot do the hard elements all at the beginning – they must sprinkle them through the programme and finish on one to earn the bonus points. And doing them at the end when they are tired puts them more at risk of injury. 'The underlying problems in female elite Olympic gymnastics require international co-operation (with all the political complexities involved) to evaluate critically the very structure of the competitive sport and the morally unacceptable demands it makes on young people under our care,' says Wearmouth.

Perhaps the heroine of this sport will once again be Olga Korbut, long since retired. In 1986, she suggested that gymnastics be divided into age categories. Then the girls in their early teens would compete against their peers and those who had become women could stay in competition. Anorexia would be physically unnecessary. The young group might still be the élite – because certain contortions can only be performed by short, undeveloped bodies. The older group, though, might just catch on – their interpretation could go back to the intense levels of old. Acrobatics might again give way to something akin to ballet.

If You've Got It, Flex It

At Caesar's Palace in Las Vegas, during the World Women's Body-building Championships, one woman sitting in the audience leaned close to the woman next to her and whispered, 'You wouldn't want to look like that, would you?'

Betty Weider, whose husband Joe is the Hugh Heffner of body-building – that is, he has built a financial empire purveying muscle – was the woman asked. No, she didn't want to look like that.[1]

Body-building is a brand new sport; some people don't even accept it as sport. Like weight-lifting (an Olympic sport for men but not women) and power-lifting, body-building *embodies* precisely what worries people about women in sport. All that rippling muscle on a woman, that 'unnatural' bulge in the wrong places, puts long-held ideas of feminine grace under pressure.

To many, female body-builders look like freaks. So, in fact, do male body-builders – although more people find them more nearly acceptable. Betty Weider had less problem with the men: she liked Joe Weider's muscles. She says she eventually came to appreciate the shape of women body-builders, but admits it is a developed taste. 'When I began to attend women's physique contests, it took me a while to get used to what I saw,' Betty Weider says. 'It takes time to appreciate the aesthetics involved,' she wrote in one of Joe Weider's magazines, *Muscle and Fitness*. 'I had always associated muscles with masculinity, so a lot of the women seemed masculine to me. I was not used to women with such low body fat, so this lean, muscular look seemed strange to me.'[2]

Once she understood the nuances, Betty Weider did see the beauty in some – but not all – women body-builders' physiques. 'When I look at the women in a contest these days, I can see detail I would not have appreciated before and have a much better feel for the real beauty that a woman body-builder can develop.' But some body-builders, she feels,

167

go too far. How far is too far? How much muscle is beautiful and how much ugly? How lean, how tight, how 'ripped', should a woman be?

And how heavy, how mighty, should a discus thrower get to build the strength that will lengthen the distance of her throw? Does that dark-haired Briton with the dark mosquito eyes, the javelin world record holder Fatima Whitbread, feel uneasy about the muscularity of her biceps and thighs? And does her rival, the Olympic javelin champion, Tessa Sanderson? Is Chris Evert's strong right arm, are her bulging calves, any less lovely, any less acceptable, than the slimmer ones of the champions of the past? Sports champions look different from sedentary women. Do they look better – or worse? Are they Wonder Women? Or are they Mock Men? The answer, the shifting boundary of acceptability – that point where the line is drawn, the new beauty – is the frontier of femininity.

In the movie *Pumping Iron II*, the most muscled body-builder, the one who had the best etched muscles – the most cut, the most ripped – that utterly uncompromising Australian, Bev Francis, did not win the competition at Caesar's Palace because she had too much muscle. The film shows the argument that raged. A certain amount of muscle – far more than the average suburbanite would find normal or 'nice' – was considered desirable by the majority of the judges; beyond that, the women were not feminine enough. Bev Francis, they whispered, and then when the argument got bitter, fairly shouted, looked like a man. But, asked a dissenting judge, if the contest is for body-building, shouldn't the contestant who has built the most muscle on her body, and who parades it in the classic body-building manner, win?

The answer was no. And this sport's early star, the much mascara'ed Rachel McLish had bigger biceps, deltoids, and the rest than the average life-guard of Elizabeth Taylor's, or even Meryl Streep's, youth. But she was not the most muscled; she was, though, in the old sense of the phrase, the most 'built'. Technically, this is *not* what is meant by body-building. There is already a double standard in the sport.

But Corinna Everson, thrice Ms Olympia, is no dolly-girl. Her massive back and thighs ripple with mounds of muscle, each so defined, so cut, that it has a very definite shape. She is a former pentathlete, and works out with weights six hours a day. After her first Ms Olympia victory, in 1984, Robert Kennedy, the editor of *Muscle Mag*, spoke of her as 'on the borderline of being too masculine'. Such a ruckus resulted that the following year he felt called upon to explain, rather confusingly: 'Obviously I meant how the average lay person would perceive her in a body-building show, not her personality or her body outside the body-building arena.' He found her defined 'glutes', the long, large muscles of her buttocks, ravishing, he said expansively. 'On top of all this, she just happens to be a timid and nice person.' Timid still a feminine virtue? Ah, perhaps that was an answer to the charges that the women were all 'on the juice' and subject to steroid rages. The result of this commentary was that in her poses on the 1986 Ms Olympia stage, at New York's Madison Square Garden, another victory, a mollified Corinna Everson gave the audience plenty of back views.

There were two Dutchwomen that year on the otherwise entirely American victory roster – and they looked different from the Americans. But not in the muscle development. Corinna Everson harked to the sex-pot image of Raquel Welch; there was more of Jeanne Moreau in the dark-haired, carefully-sultry Juliette Bergmann. But she has been European and world amateur light-weight champion, a Ms Universe. Kennedy sounds like an art historian when he talks of her: 'Monumental potential blazes from her frame.' 'Full, long, beautifully-shaped muscles. Awesome size. Wide shoulders with an extravagant "V" shape.' A small, neat bone structure sets off the enormous muscles. 'When she poses . . . ah! each position . . . divinely shaped muscle mass.' That kind of voyeurism is intrinsic to the sport. In body-building, the women, tanned and oiled, pose to music and are judged on symmetry, proportion, and muscle. The latter is judged with a connoisseur's eye. Everson herself speaks of 'muscle quality' – 'a very delicate combination of definition, size, hardness, shape, and vascularity'.

Everson's husband, Jeff, who was the weight-training co-ordinator at the University of Wisconsin when they met, says she has always had a 'natural muscularity' and 'a real capacity for hard work. Everything she tried she excelled at. I saw her throw a football spiral fifty yards. Amazing really. She deadlifted 325 pounds on about her fifth training session.' He was the collegiate weight-lifting champion; she was a Big 10 pentathlete. They tried couples body-building and won the national title.

Like the rest of the women in the Olympia parade a month before Christmas 1986, Corinna Everson had passed a drug test for anabolic steroids. This was not proof that she had done it without drugs. It was only proof that there was no trace of the drugs in her body at the time of testing. Nor is there any reason to suspect her or Bev Francis, who had come tenth, more than their opponents. Anabolic steroids are illegal, but they are known to be rampant in the gym. They have been the dirty little secret of male body-building since they became available and widely used in the 1950s. The women have long since caught on to them, and to human growth hormones, known in the gym as STH, and said to work best when combined with anabolic steroids. The only well-known body-builder who is reputed to have done it entirely without steroids was Gladys Portuguese.

The trouble with the Australian Bev Francis wasn't that anyone thought she took more steroids than anybody else. The trouble was that in refashioning her body, 'she had gone too far'. As Brian Moss, the owner of Better Bodies Gym in New York put it, if the sport was to grow, if they wanted to attract commercial sponsors, it had to have female body-builders 'acceptable to someone in Illinois or Ohio'. It had to have 'marketable physiques'.

What is marketable changes with the century, sometimes with the decade. The ideal woman of Rome was broader and heavier than her Greek predecessor. Portia was broader and heavier than Helen. Those vase drawings of Atalanta show us she was quite svelte. The Roman matron style was supplanted in the gothic period, and women became wide-eyed anorexic Twiggies.

Renaissance woman was chubby. The expression 'Rubensesque' refers to soft, fleshy women like the ones Rubens painted in the 1600s. The bosomy hour-glass figure of the 1890s gave way in the 1920s to the somewhat flat-chested, hipless, boyish flapper. But not that boyish. Nor that athletic. But the beginning of a new look. In 1932, *The Young Rower*, Lancelot Glasson's idealized painting of a female rower, bare-breasted, narrow and unmuscled in the shoulder, was named the Royal Academy's 'Picture of the Year' (see Plates).

In the 1950s came that fantasy figure for husbands with femininely mystiqued, home-body wives, Marilyn Monroe. In the 1980s, when the British singer and dancer, Stephanie Lawrence, had to play Marilyn in a musical in London's West End, it was necessary for her to gain twenty pounds. Stephanie Lawrence's hips were whirly-twirly, and her figure was hardly straight up and down; but to play Marilyn she had to get *fat*. To plug another show she was in, Lawrence, the dancer, had run a marathon without particularly training for it. She finished in a dreadful time, but could Marilyn Monroe have done it, with all that flesh on her? Never.

Times had changed. Or had they? Nina Blanchard, the American model agent, says, 'Models' measurements haven't changed since 1961.'

The Marilyn Monroe-inspired, big-busted sex-pot sells beer and cars, and do-it-yourself equipment, and girlie mags; the cool, expensive, elegant vamp sells sophisticated cocktails, chocolates (which, of course, she would in real life utterly shun), and cars (a different make), and luxuries. The middle-middle housewife sells soap powder and such. In features, too, actresses tend to be cast according to these stereotypes. The 'unlovely' women on the screen are objects of comedy or compassion – unless they turn out to be the villains of the piece.

Women are aware of the acceptable stereotypes, and grow up trying to fit them. Even the body-building magazines have tips on 'grooming', and earnest articles on the advances of breast implantation surgery. (Body-builders have big pectorals but small breasts as they have so little fat on their bodies.)

Ads often focus on women bit by bit, encouraging men to look at women bit by bit instead of as whole people – hence statements like, 'I'm a leg man.' Or, as the sex researcher William Masters, of Masters and Johnson fame, complained in the *Observer* recently: 'You can't, on TV, advertise a new car unless you have a well-filled sweater holding on to the fender somewhere.'

Women, too, are encouraged to focus on, and worry about, bits of their anatomy. An enormous percentage of women, even in these post-feminist times, feel that some part of their anatomy is substandard – their breasts are too small, their buttocks too big, their thighs too flabby. At seventy, they are still dieting. And it is not vanity; it is insecurity. Men are not reared with this degree of self-dissatisfaction.

Now comes the interesting part. Muscles.

Muscles are new and not everyone likes them.

But everyone likes what they do to flab. Muscled – toned, trained, fit – bodies annihilate flab. Burn it off. Weight-training for women – in *moderation* (ah, what a complicated word) – is gaining widespread acceptability. From 1974 to 1976 the number of women weight-lifters in the USA increased from a few hundred to 10,000. Then women invaded the body-builders' gyms. In March 1980, that glossy American, Time Inc. weekly, *Sports Illustrated* decided female weight-lifters were sufficiently prevalent to be featured.

The faintly muscular look had been appearing in women's magazines since the late 1970s. It was part of the fitness movement which swept the States, Canada, and Australia a decade before it was to reach Britain and Europe. British *Cosmopolitan* featured it with zest. And as the tennis player Zina Garrison puts it, 'Tone is in.'

Models on the covers of American women's magazines may not have changed their bust, waist, and hip measurements, but some now had tiny biceps and there were signs of muscle inside the European women's mags too. They will make the cover by the year 2000 surely. *Muscle and Fitness* had long since put hard-muscled, bulging female body-builders on its cover. Kodak had responded by advertising its product with a beefy female in mid-frame.

A lot of women are dabbling a little in hard muscle. About 35 million Americans exercise with machines; forty-eight per cent of them are women. But more than half of the new-comers flocking to the gym to train with weight machines are female.

Weight-lifting was serious business, a sport in itself. Weight training – exercising with graduated weights and often with Nautilus-type machines – was widely used to build strength in all sports. Chris Evert did it, Fatima Whitbread did it, as did Annabel Croft, and every Olympic swimmer, sprinter, and rower. And it had many, many dabblers. Recreational weight training – a little at the health club or public sport centre, or at the Y, or in the privacy of one's own bedroom – began to be very popular. Nautilus machines were kept busy. Jane Fonda wasn't the only 45-year-old whose body looked terrific. Ordinary young women trained hard too. Sarah Coope of Britain would have been unlikely to become the 1987 European Triathlon Champion without weight training.

Many a girl-next-door had her own bench press. The discount stores sold them. Wrist and ankle weights, even bar bells, came in pastels. You could buy them at any Joe Weider shop. Or at most department stores.

Women who exercised with weights no longer had to worry about floppy upper arms or orange-peel thighs. All they needed to worry about was – ready? – muscle. Too much muscle.

But how can you have too much of a good thing? Yet another double-bind for women. A new problem, a contentious issue, even though it has been known for years that a lot of the soft roundness of women's bodies was caused by their sedentary lives, which, historically, have been far more sedentary than the sedentary lives of their husbands. In other words, in the nineteenth century men strode, women sewed, and women, unfit to an appalling degree, were depressed, neurotic, crazy. There were more incarcerated in insane asylums, and more suicides among women. Which is not to say that three twenty-minute sessions in the gym per week would have put everything right for females trapped into the Victorian leisured class. The poor physical condition of women was, of course, not the only reason they were depressed, neurotic and – free at last – insane. Arguably, though, had they become fitter sooner they would have found a way forward sooner.

One consequence of regular sport is fitness; and a consequence of that is a feeling of well-being. Your sense of your physical self – your body image – improves. This is true of men quite as much as of women. The judo champion, Neil Adams, saunters out of the gym feeling cocky, feeling good. So does the judo champion Karen Briggs. But perhaps we need another term for her. Somehow, feeling 'cunty' does not have the right ring to it. But this issue is not a matter of words; it is a matter of muscle. Or ought to be. All too often it is also a matter of ideology: you know, those notions of sport unwomaning woman.

> If being independent and having a good self-image with high self esteem is masculine, then exercise does masculinize women.
> Dr Elizabeth Ferris, former Olympic diver, 1982

The front line of this issue, which affects all contemporary women, is being pushed forward today by the female champions. Navratilova's veiny forearms come under fire, as does Bev Francis's articulated muscle; the physique of the British javeliner, Fatima Whitbread, is stared at nervously in Essex, but admiringly in Los Angeles. The *Sunday Times* sends a man to a village in Czechoslovakia to report that the mightily muscled Olympic runner, Jarmila Kratochvilova, trains as hard as any man, indeed harder than most, and so she may, despite appearances, be all woman.

One reason for the suspicion of body-builders and other muscled women is the widespread belief that real women do not have it in them to build muscle naturally. They don't have the right hormones. Health clubs – unless they specialize in heavy muscle – make sure they mention this to prospective female members. The classic study, done a dozen years ago, showed that men and women who took part in an intense ten-week weight training experiment both became stronger, but only the men developed bulging muscles. Both sexes gained lean body weight, and lost body fat, but women only gained a quarter of an inch on upper body measurements, whereas men gained five to seven times as much bulk. Another key study showed that after six months of maximum resistance training women got much stronger, but their arms bulked just two per cent and their thighs just four per cent.[3]

Yet these days it is not at all hard to find ordinary women, in their twenties to fifties, who work out moderately hard twice or three times a week for an hour or so a time at a health club. Many such women, softies, dilettantes – including me – have been surprised to develop a few muscles. Nothing like the physiques of body-builders, but well over four per cent. If this seems poor science, it is salutary to remember that athletes were getting big on steroids for years while laboratory tests

173

were showing it was impossible, or unlikely, anyway. It is possible that training methods, using Nautilus-style equipment, and knowing better how many sets to do, have made muscle more possible for women today.

Not only that, some women are born with a bit more 'fast-twitch muscle fibre' than others. Women come in different shapes and sizes, don't they? They also come with a varying potential to build big muscles; it is the fast-twitch muscle fibre that responds to resistance training. Says Corinna Everson: 'Genetics play a part in body-building, but they are not everything. Besides it's impossible to tell what genetics you have until you get into training for a significant time. Some people will develop muscle faster than others.'

> It takes a great deal of courage and independence to decide to design your own image instead of the one that society rewards, but it gets easier as you go along.
> Germaine Greer, *The Female Eunuch*, 1971

Isn't it likely that women who see their body take shape will stay with it in the gym, just as tall, agile ones turn to basketball; or light-boned Decker Slaneys or Budds keep running? Thus, those with 'the best genetics' for the sport will move toward the top.

What is new is the number of women who train at the enormous intensity required for world competition. Nor did they study already very muscular women who, it is quite possible, have undergone changes in body chemistry – some of which, of course, may have come from a bottle or a hypodermic. One top body-builder, Gladys Portuguese, is often cited as having done it all on her own genetics.

It now appears, though, that very highly trained sportswomen (not only body-builders) may have changed hormone levels (as may men). Just as there is some evidence that very intense exercise may keep the metabolism whirring for a few hours after it finishes, so it may be that intense exercise affects oestrogen levels. If this is true, it is a bit like getting matching funds from government for any business investment you raise privately: if you train hard to build muscle, nature co-operates, and gives your body a boost.

And many top body-builders, weight-lifters, and throwers (discus, shot put, javelin) use drugs. Anabolic steroids are synthetic testosterone, a male hormone which is used to increase the amount of work a muscle can do, so that women and men who take them can train more intensely – and build more muscle faster. The chapter on drug abuse, 'When in Rome, Do As the Romans', gives a fuller account of muscle-building drugs. A woman taking them may be able to do two, or maybe three, training sessions in a day without feeling worn out. Whereas, without the steroids she would flag much sooner. For male athletes, steroids do exactly the same thing: they reduce the amount of time the body takes to recover from exercise. But because women have less natural testosterone they may be helped up to ten times as much. The primary way the drugs make athletes stronger is by enabling them to increase their work load.

Body-builders believe that anabolic steroids work not only when you are taking them, but ever after. 'If a woman has taken her arms to sixteen inches with the help of steroids,' says Joe Weider, 'she's going to be able to reach fifteen without using chemicals. But if she had never used the juice in the first place then she might be eternally stuck with a measurement of fourteen inches.' This he calls the 'muscle memory factor'.

Female body-building champions often have husbands or boyfriends who are themselves body-builders. So the little woman maintains her own sense of being more fragile than the male. This notion of comparative muscle – farmers' wives being physically tougher than accountants' wives – goes back a long way. Women in macho, militaristic ancient Sparta felt free to be more athletic than those in effete Athens.

Interestingly, the narcissism of male body-builders seems to many a feminine trait; the muscles of female body-builders seem to many masculine.

Unlike body-building, weight-lifting is not about being beautiful; it is about being strong. What is so startling in these early days of female weight-lifting is how ordinary the light and middleweights look. No Sumo wrestler air to any of them. No hint of Frank Bruno or Muhammad Ali.

No particularly defined muscles. Weight-lifting throws the old dichotomies out: these women may be stronger than the body-builders, but they don't look very different from week-end walkers, and they can lift more than their own body weight. In their sport they act upon the weights. The body-builders have huge muscles, traditionally associated with masculinity, but they are the supreme objects of contemplation; acted upon by the observer's eye.

It is weight-lifting, though, which seems to have been designed with women in mind. Contrary to popular prejudices, weight-lifting is a sport, *more suitable for women than for men*. This is not my idea. I wish it were. The physical education teacher turned weight-lifter, Sally Jones, the British champion at her light-middle weight, put the case to me: 'It's an incredibly feminine sport this,' she says. 'The woman's body is far more suited to weight-lifting than a man's because we've got a lower centre of gravity and better balance. We're naturally more supple than men so we can do the movements a lot easier. In relation to our upper body, our lower body is much stronger than men's and all lifting is in your legs, not in your upper body. So, women are far more suited to weight-lifting than men are.'

Beryl Crockford agrees. 'It's more technique than strength anyway. You only need strength for the first part of the movement.'

Most observers don't realize the womanly nature of the sport. Weight-lifters are still bombarded with 'what about your femininity' questions from the press.

But women could conceivably compete against men in the future without even changing the structure of this sport, in which small weight-lifters are not expected to lift the same poundage as giants.

Like boxing and judo, weight-lifting has its featherweights, its middleweights, its heavyweights. David competes against David. Goliath against Goliath. The same is true of Davida and Goldy.

In 1908, weight-lifting became a men's Olympic sport. In the tests for anabolic steroids at the 1976 Montreal Olympics, seven were caught with their anatomy on crooked. There is no immediate prospect of women getting into the Olympics. But although female weight-lifters have yet to attain the big O of sport, their sport is thriving without it – *vide* the first women's world championships, in Florida, in November 1987.

In Britain, weight-lifting is attracting strong women who are champions in other unsung sports – Beryl Crockford, the Olympic rower now well past thirty, and Judy Oakes, the shot-putter, competed when Britain's first official weight-lifting championship was held in 1986, in a dark, wee corner of the Crystal Palace national sport centre, on the outskirts of London. The audience was paltry for sport – about the size you'd get in a fringe, or off-off Broadway, theatre for a hit play. The warm-up area was too crowded and ill-lit. There was a muscle-pulling chill in the air. There was no uniformity even as to what to wear when lifting the weights, and there were runs in the elasticized leotards of some of the lifters. It was very much a loving-hands-at-home sort of spectacle. But it won't be for long.

In competition, lifters get three attempts at each of the recognized two-handed lifts: the snatch, and the clean and jerk. The clean and jerk is the one in which the heaviest weights are lifted. The barbell is raised to the shoulders in a clean movement and then, to complete the lift, it is jerked above the head. Beryl Crockford says she turned to this young sport of weight-lifting because she wanted to stay active in sport, and she had trained with weights throughout her career as a rower. Competing at weight-lifting gave her goals.

Like any good lifter, Beryl Crockford, a middleweight, pulled the barbell close to her body. She knew that the closer the pull was, the easier it would be for her to fix it in the finishing position. Her arms, her shoulders, and the hint of muscle at her neck, were a far cry from the Royal Academy's 1932 painting. They were an even further cry from the bulging muscles of Ms Olympia, Corinna Everson.

Now Crockford bent her knees and reached down to get a grip on the barbell. Then in a clean continuous movement, she lifted the barbell from the floor to her shoulders without any violent contact with her body, heaving it above her thighs, and moving one leg forward, the other backward, in a kind of split, to get balance. Then, suddenly, she jerked into an erect position, and stood stock still with her feet in a line parallel to the bar.

The top British shot-putter, Judy Oakes, was there to break a British heavyweight record. Despairing of getting any better in the world shot-putting lists without taking anabolic steroids, to which she is vehemently opposed, she went for the easier option of weight-lifting and its cousin, power-lifting. The latter is a good choice for a shot-putter, as the three lifts in this end of the sport rely more on arm strength. Immense weights are possible, and as long ago as 1977, Jan Todd bench-pressed 176 and a quarter pounds, dead-lifted 441 pounds, and lifted 424 and a quarter pounds from a squat position, to become the first woman ever to lift more than 1,000 pounds in the three power lifts.

The events in which women grapple also make men – and some women – particularly nervous: they have, in the past, been viewed as semi-pornographic events. Women's judo was, early on, tarred by the unsavoury reputation of women's mud wrestling. The first national judo championships in Britain were held in Liverpool twenty years ago behind closed doors. That hefty, talkative Brooklynite with the gargantuan thighs, Rusty Kanekogi, who has for years been manager of the American team, had to threaten to sue in the courts to get women's judo into the Olympics. Millions of women worldwide compete in the sport; there are European, American and world championships; men's judo is an Olympic sport. So is the little-practised, ladylike sport of synchronized swimming. But the admission of women's judo has been grudging: a début in 1988, as a demonstration sport, and, *probably*, in 1992, full competition, eight years after synchronized swimming.

The one unforgivable question is the one female judokas are always asked. As the British team, which boasts three world champions at their weights, departed for the world championships, someone quipped, 'What are seven, nice girls like you doing in a [violent, aggressive, muscular] sport like this?' Of course, no one would ask the *raison d'être* of a men's team off to the world championships.

Judo requires enormous stamina. But at the end of a long day of bouts at any championship event, who gets gold and who gets silver is decided by four minutes on the tatami mat. There is nothing ladylike about it: a sliding collar stranglehold; an armlock; a swift shoulder throw which makes your opponent tap the mat to indicate her submission. Women's judo used to rely on its exponents of technical agility and grace; now it has mostly powerhouses.

Occasionally, it has a phenomenon. The bantamweight 1980 world champion, Jane Bridge, a four-foot-ten-inch, 105-pound whirlwind, who had plenty of red hair and tiny freckles on her tiny nose, was such a phenomenon. On the tatami mat, Jane Bridge was as balletic as she was brawny. You could go to a match ignorant of judo and pick her out. She was the little one who threw her opponent in twenty seconds. Or, if the match went longer and became a feisty game of cat and mouse, she was the fleet feline. Quick, skilful, innately talented, Jane Bridge was to judo what Pele in his prime was to soccer.

In New York, at the first ever world championships in 1980, Jane Bridge's genius prevailed although she was ill. She became champion at her weight and was recognized for the astounding champion she was. A month later, Jane Bridge walked out of her sport, and on to the north of England dole queue, a disappointed twenty-year-old, with no future lined up and not a spare two pence piece in her pocket.

It was the indifference when she returned from New York with the world title that drove Jane Bridge out of the sport. 'When I came back, nothing,' she said. 'In England if you are not a footballer or a runner, you get nothing really. Being a world champion didn't help me at all, I was just in the same position as if I had lost. I do think you should get recognition for what you achieve.'

In 1981, a year after Bridge became Britain's and the world's first women's world judo champion so quietly, she could not help noticing the thunderous acclaim which greeted the world title of that other Briton, Neil Adams, erroneously reported by most of the media as Britain's first world judo champion. He wasn't a footballer and he wasn't a runner. He was a man.

After that Jane Bridge told *The Times*: 'I'm not a feminist. I think women should stay in the kitchen and do the washing up.' The intrepid *Times* man knew bitterness when he heard it, and reported that her words were surely tongue-in-cheek.[4]

In *My Fair Lady*, when Rex Harrison asked, 'Why can't a woman be more like a man?' he wasn't thinking of the Australian body-builder Bev Francis. Nor did he have the muscle-laden Czech runner, Jarmila Kratochvilova, in mind. The Press sisters of Russia were not in his ken, and it is unlikely that he would have welcomed the small, hard muscles of Jane Bridge's heiress to the bantam world title, that five-foot tall, peroxide blonde judoka, Karen Briggs. Yet such thoroughly muscled women – including many of the East German and American sprinters and swimmers, and all the women in the world's top twenty in the javelin, the shot put, and the discus – are engaged in something very interesting, whether or not one believes they have bodies beautiful, whether or not one believes they are going too far – making women too muscular – which is to say, too strong.

They are stirring the gender cauldron. And despite all the ribaldry, the pointed remarks, and their own fears and self-doubts, there is no stopping them.

Notes

1: Golden Racket pp.1-53

La Prototype

1 Some sources say that at this match Lenglen did not swig brandy, but instead sucked a cube of brandy-laced sugar which Papa Lenglen tossed her between sets. In either case, to the Lenglens it was cognac.
2 William T. Tilden, *The Art of Lawn Tennis*, Methuen, London, 1921, p.159.
3 Laurie Pignon, 'Kitty Godfree: A Lifetime's Love Affair', *Tennis Great Britain*, Lawn Tennis Association, London, 1986, p. 7.
4 Norah Gordon Cleather, *Wimbledon Story*, Sporting Handbooks, London, 1947, p. 46.
5 Ted Tinling, *Sixty Years in Tennis*, Sidgwick & Jackson, London, 1983. pp. 40–1.
6 Norah Gordon Cleather, op. cit., p.57.
7 Virginia Wade with Jean Rafferty, *Ladies of the Court*, Pavilion, London, 1984, p. 48.
8 Norah Gordon Cleather, op cit., p. 59.

English Roses

1 Christopher Brasher, 'The Changes That Made a Champion', *The Sporting Year*, ed. by John Rodda and Clifford Makins, Collins, London, 1977, pp. 173–8.

Strangers

1 Althea Gibson, 'I Always Wanted to Be Somebody', in *Out of the Bleachers*, ed. by Stephanie L. Twin, Feminist Press, Old Westbury, N.Y., 1979, p. 137.
2 Ibid., pp. 138–9.
3 Doris Corbett, *Black Women in Sport*, ed. by Tina Sloan Green *et al.*, Reston, Va., American Alliance for Health, Physical Education, Recreation and Dance, 1981, p. 21.
4 'Maestro: Reminiscences of a Master Sportswoman', BBC Television, 1986. Transmitted 1987.

Hype and Circumstance

1 Bobby Riggs, *Court Hustler*, New American Library, New York, 1974, p. 16.
2 Ibid., p. 14.
3 Ibid., p. 149.
4 Billie Jean King with Frank Deford, *The Autobiography*, Granada, London, 1982, p. 14.

5   Jane Kaplan, *Women and Sports*, Viking, New York, 1979, p. 52.
6   Billie Jean King, op. cit., pp. 196–7.
7   Auberon Waugh, 'Another Voice', *The Spectator*, 12 July 1986, p. 8.

Czechmate
1   Bill Glenton, 'Inside Czechoslovakia', *Tennis*, no. 58, London, June 1986, pp. 12–14 and 16.

2   Passion and Defiance   pp. 55–86

The Long Run
1   Like Atalanta and the Amazons, Melopene may be a figment of some feminist's imagination; similarly, she figures large in marathon history. Cited in David Emery and Stan Greenberg, *World Sporting Records*, Bodley Head, London, 1986. p. 54; Norman Giller, *The Marathon*, Secaucers, N. J., Chartwell, p. 88.
2   The New York course was later found to be slightly short. All of the men's and Grete Waitz's records were invalidated. Her victories and her position in the race, of course, remained unchanged, and she nonetheless broke the two and a half hour barrier.
3   Emery and Greenberg, op. cit., p. 54.
4   After much mathematical scurrying, Kenneth Dyer even predicted marathon parity by 1988 and more: 'The dates predicted for reaching equality, based on the top ten performers in each event, are: 100 metres – 2071; 200 metres – 2088; 400 metres – 2029; 800 metres – 2039; 1500 metres – 1995; 3000 metres – 1996; Marathon – 1988.' In *Catching Up the Men*, Junction, London, 1982, p. 142.
5   These points are still debated by some die-hards, but even Emery and Greenberg, who are by no means feminists, concede that women have a physiological advantage facing 'the wall'. Op. cit., p. 55.

The Mistake of the Century?
1   Fatima Whitbread's world javelin record set at the 1986 European Championships, and the other under-reported achievements by women at Stuttgart that August occasioned his thoughtful analysis of the issue.
2   'Attack on Single-Sex Races', *Running Magazine*, London, January 1987, p. 19.
3   Pierre de Coubertin, 'L'éducation des jeunes enfants et des jeunes filles', *Revue Olympique*, Octobre: 61, 1902.
4   Nina Kuscik, 'The History of Women's Participation in the Marathon', *Road Runners Club*, New York, 1976, p. 28.
5   Harold Abrahams, *The Olympic Games Book*, James Barries, London, 1956, p. 29.
6   Lord Noel-Baker, in *The Olympic Games*, ed. by Lord Killanin and John Rodda, Macdonald & Jane's, London, 1979.
7   K. Dyer, op. cit., p. 126.

Our Medals vs. Their Medals
1   Budd's first 5,000-metre record had not been officially ratified as South Africa had been expelled from the IAAF.
2   Neil Macfarlane, *Sport and Politics*, Willow, London, 1986, p. 156.
3   Harry Edwards, in *The Book of Predictions*, ed. by David Wallechinsky, *et al.*, Corgi, London, 1982, p. 262.

4   Iain Macleod, 'The Legend that is Koch and Gohr', *Athletics Weekly*, London, 18 October, 1 November and 8 November 1986, *passim*.

5   *Sport in the GDR: Past and Present*, Panorama, DDR, 1984, p. 39.

6   Cited in Mary A. Boutillier and Lucinda SanGiovanni, *The Sporting Woman*, Champaign, Illinois, 1983, p. 233.

7   Sebastian Coe with Nick Mason, *The Olympians*, Pavilion, London, 1984, p. 74.

3   The Worm in the Apple   pp. 87–116

The Celebration of Heroines

1   Mary R. Lefkowitz, letter to the author, 22 November 1986. For a thorough, cautious study of the tempestuous area of classical scholarship, see Mary R. Lefkowitz, *Women in Greek Myth*, Duckworth, London, 1986.

2   Charles Seltman, *Women in Antiquity*, Pan, London, 1956, p. 122.

3   Mary R. Lefkowitz, op. cit.

4   Pausanias, *Description of Greece*, V 6.7 (2nd century AD), quoted in Judith Swaddling, *The Ancient Olympic Games*, British Museum, London, 1984, pp. 41–2.

5   *Greek Anthology*, XIII 16, after Drees, in Swaddling, op. cit., p. 42. See L. Drees, *Olympia*, Pall Mall, London, 1968.

Courage Above Her Sex

1   C. Hare, *The Most Illustrious Ladies of the Renaissance*, Harper & Bros, London & New York, 1904, pp. 119–24, as cited by E. B. English, in J. M. Borms, M. Hebbelinck and A. Venerando, eds., *Women and Sport*, S. Karger, Basel, 1981.

2   Antonia Fraser, *The Weaker Vessel: Woman's Lot in Seventeenth-Century England* Weidenfeld & Nicolson, London, 1984, p. 224.

3   Jean-Jacques Rousseau, *Emile*, 1762, quoted in *Woman in Western Thought*, ed. by Martha Lee Osborne, Random House, New York, 1979, p. 115.

4   Martha Lee Osborne, op. cit., p. 133.

5   Philip Boys, 'Riding Away to Independence', *Science for People*, London, summer 1981.

6   Sheila Fletcher, *Women First: The Female Tradition in English Physical Education, 1890–1990*, Athlone Press, London, 1984, p. 30.

7   J. Borms, *et al.*, op. cit.

No More Apologies, Please

1   Nancy Lopez, *The Education of a Woman Golfer*, Simon and Schuster, New York, 1979, p. 94.

2   Lewine Mair, 'Ladies Tour: A Boom but Not without Problems', *Golf Monthly*, Glasgow, March 1986, p. 88.

3   Mary Peters, p. 95.

4   'Maestro', BBC TV, op. cit.

4   Is Anatomy Destiny?   pp. 117–151

Is Anatomy Destiny?

1   Letter, *The Lancet*, 1978, cited in *The Sports Health Handbook*, ed. by Norman Harris *et al.*, World's Work, Surrey, 1982, p. 156.

2   Christine Wells. *Women, Sport, and Performance: A Physiological Perspective*, Champaign Illinois, Human Kinetics, 1986, p. 266.

3   Vertappen, F. T. J., *et al.*, in J. Borms, op. cit.

4   Ibid.

5   Alison Turnbull, 'Does Pregnancy Improve Athletic Performance?' *Running Magazine*, London, October 1986, p. 73; also Michele Kort, 'Can Maternity Make You a Better Athlete?' *Women's Sports and Fitness*, Palo Alto, Calif., May 1986, pp. 38–40 and 58. Pat Butcher was the *Times*man.

6   L. Speroff and D. B. Redwine, 'Exercise and Menstrual Function', *The Physician and Sports Medicine*, no. 8, 1980, pp. 41–52.

7   Questions were set and responses were analysed by trained researchers. Questionnaire appeared in the *Oregonian* newspaper.

8   This is one reason why some of the athletes take oral contraceptives: synthetic oestrogens are the main components of the pill.

9   Robert Douglass, 'Gender vs. Performance', *Tri-Athlete*, Allentown, Pa., June 1986, p. 36.

10 Ron Maugham, 'Men vs. Women', *Running Magazine*, London, January 1987, p. 79. Cites Russell Pate, *et al.*, *Research Quarterly for Exercise and Sport*, no. 56, 1985, p. 245.

11 Christine Wells, op. cit., p. 45.

12 Ron Maugham, op. cit., p. 79; Christine Wells, op. cit., pp. 45–6.

13 Germaine Greer, *The Female Eunuch*, Paladin, London, 1971, p. 25.

14 The court held that there was no discrimination when the physical strength, stamina or physique of a woman would put her at a disadvantage. In 1987, when two eight-year-old girls, Kate Wilson and Joby Williams, were banned, the Equal Opportunities Commission noted that recent medical evidence shows that until puberty there are no such physical inequalities and the mothers of the girls and the prospective Labour MP voiced protest, reported in the *Guardian*, 6 April 1987.

15 Deborah Anderson, *USA Today*, 6 January 1987, p. 14.

16 Jay J. Coakley, *Sport in Society: Issues and Controversies*, Times Mirror/ Mosby College, St Louis, 1986, pp. 123 and 126.

17 Ibid., p. 292.

18 Anita White and Celia Brackenridge, 'Who Rules Sport?', paper presented at the *Olympic Scientific Congress*, University of Oregon, 1984.

When in Rome Do as the Romans

1   'Steroid Abuse', *USA Today*, 6 January 1987, p. 6.

2   Tessa Sanderson, *Tessa: My Life in Athletics*, Willow, London, 1986, p. 160.

3   Ibid., p. 160.

4   Ibid., p. 150.

5. Ibid., p. 159.

6   Ibid., p. 156.

7   Geoff Capes, *Big Shot: An Autobiography*, Stanley Paul, London, 1981. Cited in *Foul Play* by Tom Donohoe and Neil Johnson, Blackwell, London, 1986, p. 62.

8   Tom Donohoe and Neil Johnson, op cit., *passim*.

9   Figures as at end of 1986, cited by Mel Watman, in 'Trackwise', *Athletics Weekly*, 15 November 1986, p. 58.

Is She, or Isn't He?

1   Mary Peters *op. cit.*, with Ian Wooldridge, *Mary P.*, Arrow, London, 1974, p. 56.

2 Ibid., p. 57.
3 Alex Srebnitsky, APN article filed for *Soviet Weekly*, 29 September 1986, pp. 1–4.

5 The Shape of the Future   pp. 153–179

The Girls Who Don't Want to Grow Up

1 Lionel W. Rosen, *et al.*, 'Pathogenic Weight-Control Behaviour in Female Athletes', *The Physician and Sports Medicine*, no. 14 (January 1986), pp. 79–86.
2 Ibid. p. 83.
3 Alvin R. Loosli *et al.* 'Nutrition Habits and Knowledge in Competitive Adolescent Female Gymnasts', *The Physician and Sports Medicine*, no. 14, August 1986, pp. 118–30.
4 Nadia Comanenci and Graham Buxton Smither, *Nadia, My Own Story*, Proteus, London, 1981, p. 99.
5 Ibid., p. 123.
6 Ibid., p. 57.
7 V. A. Steele and J. A. White, 'Injury Amongst Female Gymnasts', *Proceedings of the Society of Sports Sciences*, no. 2, 1983.
8 V. A. Steele and J. A. White, 'Injury Prediction in Female Gymnasts', *British Journal of Sports Medicine*, no. 20, March 1986, pp. 31–3.
9 Lionel W. Rosen, *et al.*, op. cit. pp. 83 and 84.
10 Alvin R. Loosli, *et al.*, op. cit., p. 118.
11 Ibid., p. 129.
12 James Watkins, 'An Overview of Sports-related Lower-limb Epiphyseal Injuries', Scottish School of Physical Education, unpublished, 1986, pp. 1–8.
13 Keith Russell, 'Stress or Distress', paper presented to British Association of National Coaches, 1985, p. 9.
14 Op. Cit., p. 5.
15 Ibid., p. 2.
16 A. M. Kochan, 'Spondylolysis and Spondylolisthesis in Young Athletes', *Coaching Review*, no. 8 (November 1985), p. 64. Also D. W. Jackson, *et al.*, *International Gymnast* (December 1976). Also B. Goldberg, 'Paediatric Sport Medicine', *Principles of Sports Medicine*, Williams & Wilkins, Baltimore, 1984.
17 V. A. Steele, and J. A. White, 1986, op. cit., p. 33.

If You've Got It, Flex It

1 Bette Weider, 'Love Thyself', *Bodybuilding and Conditioning for Women*, Contemporary, Chicago, 1983, p. 5.
2 Betty Weider, op. cit., p. 5.
3 Christine Wells, op. cit.
4 *The Times*, 16 October 1981.

Database:

Women's Sporting Records

Women Who Surpass Men

Surprisingly, since fewer women participate in fewer sports and have been doing so for a shorter period than men, the record books show that women often have more range and endurance than men in sport. This is not an exhaustive list.

*   The youngest person ever to break a non-mechanical world record was New Yorker Gertrude Ederle who set a new women's 880 yard freestyle swimming record of 13 minutes 19.0 seconds at Indianapolis, USA, on 17 August 1919, when she was 12 years 298 days old. As if that were not milestone enough, seven years later Ederle tackled the world's then most gruelling long distance swim, becoming on 6 August 1926 the first woman to swim the English Channel. Her time of 14 hours 39 minutes from Cap Gris-Nez, France, to Dover was two hours faster than the existing record.

*   The youngest Olympic individual gold medallist, American Marjorie Gestring, won the 1936 springboard diving title when she was 13 years 268 days old.

*   The youngest ever international, eight-year-old table tennis player Joy Foster, represented Jamaica in the West Indies Championships in 1958.

*   The youngest ever British international, diver Beverley Williams competed at Crystal Palace against the United States in 1967, when she was 10 years 268 days old.

*   The longest reigning British champion, archer Alice Blanche Legh (1855–1948), won 23 national titles (1881–1948) in a career which spanned 41 years. Her mother was champion from 1882–5.

*   The oldest ever British international, Hilda Lorna Johnstone, placed twelfth in dressage at the 1972 Olympic Games at the age of 70 years 5 days.

*   The most versatile athlete ever, in the impartial view of *The Guinness Book of Records*, was Charlotte 'Lottie' Dod (1871–1960) of Cheshire, England. She won the first of her five Wimbledon ladies singles championships in 1887 when she was three months shy of sixteen (and is still the youngest winner). She became the British Ladies Golf Champion in 1904, Olympic archery silver medallist in 1908, England hockey international in 1899, and a skater and tobogganer to reckon with. In 1888, Dod bested the Wimbledon men's champion in the first exhibition tennis battle of the sexes.

*   The runner-up Texan Mildred 'Babe' Didrikson (later Zaharias) won gold medals at the 80 metre hurdles and the javelin and silver in the high jump at the 1932 Games. The first female 'shamateur' also set a baseball world record and was an all-American basketball player. Her sporting life culminated in fame and fortune as a professional golfer.

*   The largest cache of individual Olympic medals is that of Soviet gymnast Larissa Semyonovna Latynina who won eighteen.

*   The first person to win four Olympic gold medals at one year's winter games was Soviet skater Lydia Skoblikova in Innsbruck in 1964.

Archery: the most world titles ever were won by Janina Spychajowa-Kurkowska of Poland whose seventh women's title came in 1947.

Athletics: Norwegian Ingrid Kristiansen, the only athlete ever to hold the 5,000, 10,000 and marathon world records, topped up her tally with the half-marathon record. American Wyomia Tyus became the first runner ever to win the Olympic 100 metres sprint twice in a row, in 1964 and 1968.

Bowls: the most world titles belong to Australian Merle Richardson whose third women's title came in 1985.

Cricket: Christina Willes probably invented the round-arm bowling style, in 1807.

Cycling: the most British titles were won by Beryl Burton, who competed against men. She has twenty-five British all-round time trial champion (1959–83), seventy-one individual road TT titles, fourteen track pursuit titles and eleven road race to 1986. In 1967, her twelve-hour race distance beat the men's top distance. Says *The Guinness Book of Records*: 'Mrs Burton's career overshadows all male achievements.'

Equestrianism: the first rider to cross the American continent solo, Nan Jane Aspinwall, covered the 4,500 miles in 301 days, 108 of them travelling, arriving in New York City from San Francisco on 8 July 1911. Lucinda Green (née Prior-Palmer) has a record six victories at the Badminton Three-Day Event. (See also 'Equestrian Records'.)

Fencing: the only Briton ever to win Olympic gold was Gillian Mary Sheen in the foil in 1956.

Field hockey: a record 65,165 people turned up at Wembley to see the women's teams, England vs. US, on 11 March 1978.

Flying: in the first successful helicopter flight, German pilot Hanna Reutsch flew the Focke FW-61 in free, fully controlled flight on 4 July 1937. In the first ever long-distance solar-powered flight, Californian Janice Brown flew the *Solar Challenger* six miles in twenty-two minutes on 3 December 1980. The first balloon flight over the North Pole was made jointly by Eleanor Conn and her husband Sidney in the *Joy of Sound* on 11 April 1980.

Gymnastics: the fourteen-year-old Romanian Nadia Comaneci received the first Olympic perfect gymnastics score, in Montreal in 1976. Soviet Larissa Semyonovna Latynina, who retired in 1966, had the most ever world titles (thirty-one) of which eighteen are Olympic titles.

Horse racing: Queen Anne, who reigned 1702–14, not only originated racing for money in 1714 at Doncaster, but in the same year she became the first owner to win any.

Hunting: Jean Bethel McKeever, the longest reigning Master of Hounds in Britain (and probably the world), began her tenure as Master of the Blean Beagles in Kent in 1909, aged eight.

Ice skating: at the 1972 Tokyo Olympics American speed skater Anne Henning won the 500 metre gold medal twice in one day. Henning, clearly the winner, but given the second run because her opponent has infringed the rules, used it to set a world record.

Motor racing: in the two-day 1898 Marseilles to Nice race, a woman named Laumaille, the first female motor racer, finished fourth; her husband finished sixth.

Powerboat racing: Betty Cook, who took up the sport at fifty, in 1977 became the first person to prove the suitability of catamarans (tunnel hull boats) for offshore powerboat racing, changing the nature of the sport.

Rodeo: the youngest winner of a world title, eleven-year-old Metha Brorsen of Oklahoma, became the International Rodeo Association's champion cowgirl barrel racer of 1975 and earned over $15,000 (£10,000).

Rowing: the first woman in the Oxford–Cambridge Boat Race, Susan Brown, coxed the winners Oxford in 1981 and 1982.

Shooting: Canadian Susan Nattrass, with six, has won the most world clay pigeon shooting titles.

Ski-ing: the German alpine skier of the 1930s, Christel Cranz, has won the most world championships – seven individual (four slalom, three downhill) and five combined; a Russian woman, Galina Koulakova, won a record nine world titles in nordic ski-ing.

Squash: the shortest championship match ever was Deanna Murray's 9½-minute, 1979 victory over Christine Rees for a Ladies Welsh title.

Swimming: Dane Ragnhild Hveger, known as the 'Golden Torpedo', set her first world record in 1936, and up to now has set the most in the sport (forty-two). The first swimmer ever to win three individual gold medals in one Olympiad was the American Deborah Meyer in 1968; at the next Olympiad, Australian Shane Gould won three golds, each in world record time. East German Kornelia Ender has won the sport's most world medals to date, ten. The official record for crossing the English Channel, 7 hours 40 minutes, was set on 29 July 1978 by Californian Penny Dean, from Dover to Cap Gris-Nez, France. The fastest round-Manhattan swim, by Australian Shelley Taylor, was 6 hours 12 minutes 29 seconds on 15 October 1985; and the longest round-Manhattan swim over six days in 1985 was by New Yorker Julie Ridge. (See also 'youngest person' p. 187.)

Table tennis: the youngest international in any sport, Joy Foster, was eight when she represented Jamaica in the 1958 West Indies Championships.

Tennis: Margaret Court's twenty-four singles championships in grand slam events is double the men's record. Helen Wills Moody's eight Wimbledon singles titles has yet to be surpassed; the youngest player ever to win a match at Wimbledon, 14-year-92-day-old American Kathy Rinaldi, beat South African Sue Rollinson in 1981 in the first round; Lottie Dod (see 'most versatile' p. 188) was the youngest singles champion.

NINE MARTINA NARATILOVA.

Water ski-ing: in 1901, Anne Taylor, a middle-aged school teacher, became the first person to ride a barrel over Niagara Falls. In 1969, Elizabeth Allan-Shetter became the only person ever to win all four world titles (jumping, slalom, tricks and overall) in one year.

Olympic Champions

No sport was deemed suitable for women at the first modern Olympic Games of 1896. Tennis provided the first female Olympic gold medallist, Charlotte Cooper of Britain, whose singles victory over a Frenchwoman was not popular at the 1900 Paris Olympics. By the 1984 Olympics, in Los Angeles, seventy-five events were exclusively for women, including thirteen new ones, and 45 per cent of the competitors at the games were female. The records here date from the first year of competition for each sport, unless otherwise indicated. There were no Games during the war years of 1940 and 1944.

Athletics

100 METRES

1928	Elizabeth Robinson (US)	0:12.2
1932	Stella Walsh (POL)	0:11.9
1936	Helen Stephens (US)	0:11.5
1948	Fanny Blankers-Koen (NDR)	0:11.9
1952	Marjorie Jackson (AUS)	0:11.5
1956	Betty Cuthbert (AUS)	0:11.5
1960	Wilma Rudolph (US)	0:11
1964	Wyomia Tyus (US)	0:11.4
1968	Wyomia Tyus (US)	0:11
1972	Renate Stecher (GDR)	0:11.07
1976	Annegret Richter (GFR)	0:11.08
1980	Lyudmila Kondratyeva (USSR)	0:11.06
1984	Evelyn Ashford (US)	0:10.97

200 METRES

1948	Fanny Blankers-Koen (NDR)	0:24.4
1952	Marjorie Jackson (AUS)	0:23.7
1956	Betty Cuthbert (AUS)	0:23.4
1960	Wilma Rudolph (US)	0:24
1964	Edith McGuire (US)	0:23
1968	Irene Szewinksa (POL)	0:22.5
1972	Renate Stecher (GDR)	0:22.4
1976	Baerbel Eckert (GDR)	0:22.37
1980	Barbara Wockel (GDR)	0:22.03
1984	Valerie Brisco-Hooks (US)	0:21.81

400 METRES

1964	Betty Cuthbert (AUS)	0:52
1968	Colette Besson (FRA)	0:52
1972	Monika Zehrt (GDR)	0:51.08
1976	Irena Szewinska (POL)	0:49.29
1980	Marita Koch (GDR)	0:48.88
1984	Valerie Brisco-Hooks (US)	0:48.83

800 METRES

After 1928, banned until 1960.

1928	Lina Radke (GER)	2:16.8
1960	Ljudmila Shevcova (USSR)	2:4.3
1964	Ann Packer (GB)	2:1.1
1968	Madeline Manning (US)	2:0.9
1972	Hildegard Falck (GFR)	1:58.6
1976	Tatiana Kazankina (USSR)	1:54.94
1980	Nadezhda Olizarenko (USSR)	1:53.5
1984	Doina Melinte (ROM)	1:57.60

1,500 METRES

1972	Ludmila Bragina (USSR)	4:1.4	
1976	Tatiana Kazankina (USSR)	4:5.48	
1980	Tatiana Kazankina (USSR)	3:56.6	
1984	Gabriella Dorio (ITA)	4:3.26	

3,000 METRES

1984	Maricica Puica (ROM)	8:35.96

80 METRE HURDLES

1932	Mildred Didrikson (US)	0:11.7
1936	Trebisonda Valla (ITA)	0:11.7
1948	Fanny Blankers-Koen (NDR)	0:11.2
1952	Shirley S. de la Hunty (AUS)	0:10.9
1956	Shirley S. de la Hunty (AUS)	0:10.7
1960	Irina Press (USSR)	0:10.8
1964	Karin Balzer (GER)	0:10.5[1]
1968	Maureen Caird (AUS)	0:10.3

[1] Wind assisted

100 METRE HURDLES

1972	Annelie Ehrhardt (GDR)	0:12.59
1976	Johanna Schaller (GDR)	0:12.77
1980	Vera Komisova (USSR)	0:12.56
1984	Benita Fitzgerald-Brown (US)	0:12.84

400 METRE HURDLES

1984	Nawai El Moutawakel (MOR)	0:54.61

400 METRE RELAY

1928	Canada	0:48.4
1932	United States	0:47
1936	United States	0:46.9
1948	Netherlands	0:47.5
1952	United States	0:45.9
1956	Australia	0:44.5
1960	United States	0:44.5
1964	Poland	0:43.6
1968	United States	0:42.8
1972	West Germany	0:42.81
1976	East Germany	0:42.55
1980	East Germany	0:41.6
1984	United States	0:41.65

1,600 METRE RELAY

1972	East Germany	3:23
1976	East Germany	3:19.23
1980	USSR	3:20.2
1984	United States	3:18.29

MARATHON

1984	Joan Benoit (US)	2:24.52

HIGH JUMP

1928	Ethel Catherwood (CAN)	5ft 3in	(1·60m)
1932	Jean Shiley (US)	5ft 5¼in	(1·65m)
1936	Ibolya Csak (HUN)	5ft 3in	(1·60m)
1948	Alice Coachman (US)	5ft 6⅛in	(1·67m)
1952	Ester Brand (SA)	5ft 5¾in	(1·66m)
1956	Mildred McDaniel (US)	5ft 9¼in	(1·75m)
1960	Iolanda Balas (ROM)	6ft ¾in	(1·84m)
1968	Iolanda Balas (USSR)	6ft 2¾in	(1·89m)
1968	Miloslava Rezkova (CZL)	5ft 11¾in	(1·81m)
1972	Ulrike Meyfarth (GFR)	6ft 3⅝in	(1·90m)
1976	Rosemarie Ackerman (GDR)	6ft 4in	1.93m
1980	Sara Simeoni (ITA)	6ft 5½in	(1·96m)
1984	Ulrike Meyfarth (GFR)	6ft 7½in	(2·01m)

LONG JUMP

1948	Olga Gyarmati (HUN)	18ft 8¼in	(5·70m
1952	Yvette Williams (NZ)	20ft 5¾in	(6·25m)
1956	Elzbieta Krzesinkska (POL)	20ft 9¾in	(6·33m)
1960	Vera Krepkina (USSR)	20ft 10¾in	(6·36m)
1964	Mary Rand (GB)	22ft 2in	(6·75m)
1968	Victoria Ciscopoleanu (ROM)	22ft 4½in	(6·83in)
1972	Heidemarie Rosendahl (GFR)	22ft 3in	(6·80m)
1976	Angela Voigt (GDR)	22ft ½in	(6·72m)
1980	Tatiana Kolpakova (USSR)	23ft 2in	(7·05m)
1984	Arisoara Stanciu (ROM)	22ft 10in	(6·95m)

SHOT-PUT

1948	Micheline Ostermeyer (FRA)	45ft 1½in	(13.75m)
1952	Galina Zybina (USSR)	50ft 1½in	(15·28m)
1956	Tamara Tishkyevich (USSR)	54ft 5in	(16·60m)
1960	Tamara Press (USSR)	56ft 9⅞in	(17·32m)
1964	Tamara Press (USSR)	59ft 6in	(18·13m)
1968	Margitta Gummel (GDR)	64ft 4in	(19·60m)
1972	Nadezhda Chizhova (USSR)	69ft	(21·03)
1976	Ivanka Christova (BUL)	69ft 5in	(21·16m)
1980	Ilona Sluplanek (GDR)	73ft 6in	(22·40m)
1984	Claudia Losch (GFR)	67ft 2¼in	(20·47m)

DISCUS THROW

1928	Helena Konopacka (POL)	129ft 11⅞in	(39·62m)
1932	Lillian Copeland (US)	133ft 2in	(40·60m)
1936	Gisela Mauermayer (GER)	156ft 3³⁄₁₆in	(47·62m)
1948	Micheline Ostermeyer (FRA)	137ft 6½in	(41·92)
1952	Nina Romaschkova (USSR)	168ft 8⁷⁄₁₆in	(51·72m)
1956	Olga Fikotova (CZL)	176ft 1½in	(53·70m)
1960	Nina Ponomareva (USSR)	180ft 8¼in	(55·08m)
1964	Tamara Press (USSR)	187ft 10¾in	(57·87m)
1968	Lia Manoliu (ROM)	191ft 2½in	(58·30m)
1972	Faina Melnik (USSR)	218ft 7in	(66·62m)
1976	Evelin Schlaak (GDR)	226ft 4in	(69·0m)
1980	Evelin Jahl (GDR)	229ft 6½in	(69·96m)
1984	Ria Stalman (NDR)	214ft 5in	(65·35m)

JAVELIN THROW

1932	Mildred Didrikson (US)	143ft 4in	(43.70m)
1936	Tilly Fleischer (GER)	148ft 2¾in	(45·17m)
1948	Herma Bauma Austria	149ft 6in	(45·57m)
1952	Dana Zatopek (CZL)	165ft 7in	(50·47m)
1956	Inessa Janzeme (USSR)	176ft 8in	(53·85m)
1960	Elvira Ozolina (USSR)	183ft 8in	(55·97m)
1964	Mihaela Penes (ROM)	198ft 7½in	(60·55m)
1968	Angela Nemeth (HGY)	198ft 0in	(60·36m)
1972	Ruth Fuchs (GDR)	209ft 7in	(63.87m)
1976	Ruth Fuchs (GDR)	216ft 4in	(65·94m)
1980	Maria Colon (CUBA)	224ft 5in	(68·40m)
1984	Tessa Sanderson (GB)	228ft 2in	(69·55m)

PENTATHLON

1964	Irina Press (USSR)	5,246 pts
1968	Ingrid Becker (GFR)	5,098 pts
1972	Mary Peters (GB)	4,801 pts
1976	Siegrun Siegl (GDR)	4,745 pts
1980	Nadyezhda Tkachenko (USSR)	5,083 pts

Replaced by heptathlon

HEPTATHLON

1984	Glynnis Nun (AUS)	6,390 pts

Swimming

100-METRE BUTTERFLY

1956	Shelley Mann (US)	1:11
1960	Carolyn Schuler (US)	1:9.5
1964	Sharon Stouder (US)	1:4.7
1968	Lynn McClements (AUS)	1:5.5
1972	Mayumi Aoki (JAP)	1:3.34
1976	Kornelia Ender (GDR)	1:00.13
1980	Caren Metschuck (GDR)	1:00.42
1984	Mary Meagher (US)	59.26

200-METRE BUTTERFLY

1968	Ada Kok (NDR)	2:24.7
1972	Karen Moe (US)	2:15.57
1976	Andrea Pollack (GDR)	2:11.41
1980	Ines Geissler (GDR)	2:10.44
1984	Mary Meagher (US)	2:06.90

200-METRE INDIVIDUAL MEDLEY

1968	Claudia Kolb (US)	2:24.7
1972	Shane Gould (AUS)	2:23.07
1984	Tracy Caulkins (US)	1:12.64

400-METRE INDIVIDUAL MEDLEY

1964	Donna de Varona (US)	5:18.7
1968	Claudia Kolb (US)	5:8.5
1972	Gail Neall (AUS)	5:2.97
1976	Urike Tauber (GDR)	4:42.77
1980	Petra Schneider (GDR)	4:36.29
1984	Tracy Caulkins (US)	4:39.21

400-METRE FREESTYLE RELAY

1912	Great Britain	5:52.8
1920	United States	5:11.6
1924	United States	4:58.8
1928	United States	4:47.6
1932	United States	4:38
1936	Netherlands	4:36
1948	United States	4:29.2
1952	Hungary	4:24.4
1956	Australia	4:17.1
1960	United States	4:8.9
1964	United States	4:3.8
1968	United States	4:2.5
1972	United States	3:55.19
1976	United States	3:44.82
1980	East Germany	3:42.71
1984	United States	3:44.43

400-METRE MEDLEY RELAY

1960	United States	4:41.1
1964	United States	4:33.9
1968	United States	4:28.3
1972	United States	4:20.75
1976	East Germany	4:07.95
1980	East Germany	4:06.67
1984	United States	4:08.34

SPRINGBOARD DIVE

		Points
1920	Aileen Riggin (US)	539.90
1924	Elizabeth Becker (US)	474.5
1928	Helen Meany (US)	78.62
1932	Georgia Coleman (US)	87.52
1936	Marjorie Gestring (US)	89.27
1948	Victoria M. Draves (US)	108.74
1952	Patricia McCormick (US)	147.30
1956	Patricia McCormick (US)	142.36
1960	Ingrid Kramer (GER)	155.81
1964	Ingrid Kramer Engel (GER)	145.00
1968	Sue Gossick (US)	150.77
1972	Micki King (US)	450.03
1976	Jennifer Chandler (US)	506.19
1980	Irina Kalinina (USSR)	725.91
1984	Sylvie Bernier (CAN)	530.70

PLATFORM DIVE

		Points
1912	Greta Johansson (SWE)	39.9
1920	Stefani Fryland (DEN)	34.60
1924	Caroline Smith (US)	166
1928	Elizabeth B. Pinkton (US)	31.60
1932	Dorothy Poynton (US)	40.26
1936	Dorothy Poynton Hill (US)	33.92
1948	Victoria M. Draves (US)	68.87
1952	Patricia McCormick (US)	79.37
1956	Patricia McCormick (US)	84.85
1960	Ingrid Kramer (GER)	91.28
1964	Lesley Bush (US)	99.80
1968	Milena Duchkova (CZL)	109.59
1972	Ulrika Knape (SWE)	390.00
1976	Elena Vaytsekhovskaia (USSR)	406.59
1980	Martina Jaschke (GDR)	596.25
1984	Zhou Jihong (CH)	435.51

100-METRE FREESTYLE

1912	Fanny Durack (AUS)	1:22.2
1920	Ethelda Bleibtry (US)	1:13.6
1924	Ethel Lackie (US)	1:12.4
1928	Albina Osipowich (US)	1:11
1932	Helene Madison (US)	1:6.8
1936	Hendrika Mastenbroek (NDR)	1:5.9
1948	Greta Andersen (DEN)	1:6.3
1952	Katalin Szoke (HUN)	1:6.8
1956	Dawn Fraser (AUS)	1:2
1960	Dawn Fraser (AUS)	1:1.2
1964	Dawn Fraser (AUS)	0:59.5
1968	Marge Jan Henne (US)	1:0
1972	Sandra Neilson (US)	0:58.59
1976	Kornelia Ender (GDR)	0:55.65
1980	Barbara Krause (GDR)	0:54.79
1984	Carrie Steinseifer & Nancy Hogshead (tie) (US)	0:55.92

195

200-METRE FREESTYLE

1968	Debbie Meyer (USA)	2:10.5
1972	Shane Gould (AUS)	2:3.56
1976	Kornelia Ender (GDR)	1:59.26
1980	Barbara Krause (GDR)	1:58.33
1984	Mary Wayle (US)	1:59.23

400-METRE FREESTYLE

1920	Ethelda Bleibtrey (US)	4:34[1]
1924	Martha Norelius (US)	6:2.2
1928	Martha Norelius (US)	5:42.8
1932	Helene Madison (US)	5:28.5
1936	Hendrika Mastenbroek (NDR)	5:26.4
1948	Ann Curtis (US)	5:17.8
1952	Valerie Gyenge (HUN)	5:12.1
1956	Lorraine Crapp (AUS)	4:54.6
1960	Chris von Saltza (US)	4:50.6
1964	Ginny Duenkel (US)	4:43.3
1968	Debbie Meyer (US)	4:31.8
1972	Shane Gould (AUS)	4:19.04
1976	Petra Thumer (GDR)	4:09.89
1980	Ines Diers (GDR)	4:08.76
1984	Tiffany Cohen (US)	4:07.10

[1] 300 metres

800-METRE FREESTYLE

1968	Debbie Meyer (US)	9:24
1972	Keena Rothhammer (US)	8:53.68
1976	Petra Thumer (GDR)	8:37.14
1980	Michelle Ford (AUS)	8:28.90
1984	Tiffany Cohen (US)	8:24.95

100-METRE BACKSTROKE

1924	Sybil Bauer (US)	1:23.2
1928	Marie Braun (NDR)	1:22
1932	Eleanor Holm (US)	1:19.4
1936	Dina Senff (NDR)	1:18.9
1948	Karen Harup (DEN)	1:14.4
1952	Joan Harrison (SA)	1:14.3
1956	Judy Grinham (GB)	1:12.9
1960	Lynn Burke (US)	1:9.3
1964	Cathy Ferguson (US)	1:7.7
1968	Kaye Hall (US)	1:6.2
1972	Melissa Belote (US)	1:5.78
1976	Ulrike Richter (GDR)	1:01.83
1980	Rica Reinisch (GDR)	1:00.86
1984	Theresa Andrews (US)	1:02.55

200-METRE BACKSTROKE

1968	Pokey Watson (US)	2:24.8
1972	Melissa Belote (US)	2:19.19
1976	Ulrike Richter (GDR)	2:13.43
1980	Rica Reinisch (GDR)	2:11.77
1984	Jolanda DeRover (NDR)	2:12.38

100-METRE BREASTSTROKE

1968	Djurdjica Bjedov (YUG)	1:15.8
1972	Catherine Carr (US)	1:13.58
1976	Hannelore Anke (GDR)	1:11.16
1980	Ute Geweniger (GDR)	1:10.22
1984	Petra Van Staveren (NDR)	1:09.88

200-METRE BREASTSTROKE

1924	Lucy Morton (GB)	3:33.2
1928	Hilde Schrader (GER)	3:12.6
1932	Clare Dennis (AUS)	3:6.3
1936	Hideko Maehata (JAP)	3:3.6
1948	Nel van Vliet (NDR)	2:57.2
1952	Eva Szekely (HUN)	2:51.7
1956	Ursala Happe (GER)	2:53.1
1960	Anita Lonsbrough (GB)	2:49.5
1964	Galina Prozumenschikova (USSR)	2:46.4
1968	Sharon Wichman (US)	2:44.4
1972	Beverly Whifield (AUS)	2:41.71
1976	Marina Koshevaia (USSR)	2:33.35
1980	Lina Kachushite (USSR)	2:29.54
1984	Anne Ottenbrite (CAN)	2:30.38

SYNCHRONIZED SWIMMING

One of the two Olympic sports with no male equivalent. The other is rhythmic gymnastics.

1984	Solo	Tracie Ruiz (US)
	Duet	Candy Costie and Tracie Ruiz (US)

Gymnastics

ALL-ROUND

1952	Maria Gorokhovskaya (USSR)
1956	Larissa Latynina (USSR)
1960	Larissa Latynina (USSR)
1964	Vera Čáslavská (CZL)
1968	Vera Čáslavská (CZL)
1972	Ludmila Tourischeva (USSR)
1976	Nadia Comaneci (ROM)
1980	Elena Davidova (USSR)
1984	Mary Lou Retton (US)

RHYTHMIC GYMNASTICS

Like synchronized swimming, this event has no male equivalent at the Games.
1984   Lori Fung   (CAN)

Other Summer 1984 Games

ARCHERY
Hyang-Soun Seo   (SK)

BASKETBALL
United States

CANOEING
1500m one-woman kayak – Agneta
   Andersson   (SW)
500m two-woman kayak – Sweden
500m four-woman kayak – Romania

CYCLING (individual road race) – Connie
Carpenter   (US)

FENCING
Foil – Luan Jujie   (CH)
Team foil – West Germany

FIELD HOCKEY
Netherlands

GYMNASTICS (see also earlier Overall listing)
Floor exercise – Ecaterina Szabo   (ROM)
Balance beam – Simona Pauca and Ecaterina
Szabo, both Romania
Vault – Ecaterina Szabo   (ROM)
Uneven Parallel Bars – Ma Yanhonjg   (CH)
and Julianne McNamara   (US)
Team – Romania

HANDBALL
Yugoslavia

ROWING
Single skulls – Valarie Racia   (ROM)
Double skulls – Romania
Coxless pairs – Romania
Coxed pairs – Romania
Eights – United States

SHOOTING
Air rifle – Pat Spurgin   (US)
Small Bore rifle, 3 positions – Vu
   Xiaoxuan   (CH)
Sport pistol – Linda Thom   (CAN)

VOLLEYBALL
China

Winter 1984 Games

ALPINE SKI-ING
Downhill – Michela Figini   (SWI)   1:13.36
Slaloms – Paoletta Magoni   (I)   1:36.47
Giant slalom – Debbie Armstrong
   (US)   2:20.98

CROSS-COUNTRY SKI-ING
5km, 10km & 20km – Marja-Liisa
Haemaelainen   (F)
20km relay – Norway

FIGURE SKATING
Singles – Katarina Witt   (GDR)
Pairs – Elena Valova and Oleg
Vasiliev   (USSR)
Dance – Jayne Torvill and Christopher
   Dean   (GB)

Luge – Steffi Martin   (GFR)   2:46.570

SPEED SKATING
500 metres – Christa Rothenburger
   (GDR)   0:41.02
1,000 metres – Karin Enke   (GDR)   1:21.61
1,500 metres – Karin Enke   (GDR)   2:03.42
3,000 metres – Andrea Schoene   (GDR) 4:24.79

WORLD RECORDS (TO APRIL 1987)

Women's records are improving faster than men's as more women participate more seriously in more sports. But few women have yet overcome the taboo of being better than men, even in the sports in which they have a phsiological advantage. Men's running records, for example, are on average nearly 10 per cent faster than women's.

Athletics

Event	Record	Holder	Venue	Date
RUNNING				
100 m	0:10.76	Evelyn Ashford (US)	Zurich	22 Aug 1984
200 m	0:21.71	Heike Drechsler (GDR)	Stuttgart	28 Aug 1986
400 m	0:47.60	Jarmila Kratochvilova (CZL)	Helsinki	10 Aug 1983
800 m	1:53.28	Jarmila Kratochvilova (CZL)	Munich	26 July 1983
1,500 m	3:52.47	Tatyana Kazankina (USSR)	Zurich	13 Aug 1980
1 mile	4:16.71	Mary Decker Slaney (US)	Zurich	21 Aug 1985
3,000 m	8:22.62	Tatyana Kazankina (USSR)	Moscow	26 Aug 1984
5,000 m	14:37.33	Ingrid Kristiansen (NOR)	Stockholm	5 Aug 1986
10,000 m	30:13.74	Ingrid Kristiansen (NOR)	Oslo	5 July 1986
Marathon	2:21:06.0	Ingrid Kristiansen (NOR)	London	21 April 1985
HURDLES				
100m	0:12.36	Yordanka Donkova (BUL)	Sofia	13 Aug 1986
400 m	0:53.33	Maria Stepanova (USSR)	Stuttgart	28 Aug 1986
RELAY RACES				
400 m (4×100)	0:41.53	East Germany	Berlin	31 July 1983
800 m (4×200)	1:28.15	East Germany	Jena, E. Ger.	9 Aug 1980
1,600 m (4×400)	3:15.92	East Germany	Erfurt, E. Ger.	13 June 1984
3,200 m (4×800)	7:52.3	USSR	Podolsk, USSR	16 Aug 1976
FIELD EVENTS				
High jump	6ft 9¾in (2.07m)	Stefka Kostadinova (BUL)	Sofia	25 May 1986
Long jump	24ft 5½in (7.45m)	Heike Drechsler (GDR)	Dresden	3 July 1986
Triple jump	44ft 6¾in (13.58m)	Wendy Brown (US)	Austin, Tex.	30 May 1985
Shot put	73ft 11in (22.53m)	Natalya Lisovskaya (USSR)	Sochi, USSR	27 May 1984
Javelin throw	254ft 1in (77.44m)	Fatima Whitbread (GB)	Stuttgart	28 Aug 1986
Discus throw	244ft 7in (74.55m)	Zdena Silveha (CZL)	Prague	26 Aug 1984
Heptathlon	7,161 pts	Jackie Joyner (US)	Houston, Tex.	1–2 Aug 1986

Database

Swimming

Event	Record	Holder	Venue	Date
FREESTYLE				
50 m	0:25.28	Tamara Costache (R)	Madrid	Aug 1986
100 m	0:54.73	Kristin Oto (GDR)	Madrid	Aug 1986
200 m	1:57.75	Kristin Otto (GDR)	Magedeburg, E.Ger.	23 May 1984
400 m	4:06.28	Tracey Wickham (AUS)	W. Berlin	24 Aug 1978
800 m	8:24.62	Tracey Wickham (AUS)	Edmonton, Canada	5 Aug 1978
1,500 m	16:04.49	Kim Linehan (US)	Ft Lauderdale, Fla.	19 Aug 1979
BREASTSTROKE				
100 m	1:08.11	Sylvia Gerasch (GDR)	Madrid	21 Aug 1986
200 m	2:27.40	Silke Hoerner (GDR)	Madrid	Aug 1986
BUTTERFLY				
100 m	0:57.93	Mary T. Meagher (US)	Brown Deer, Wis.	16 Aug 1981
200 m	2:05.96	Mary T. Meagher (US)	Brown Deer, Wis.	13 Aug 1981
BACKSTROKE				
100 m	0:59.89	Betsy Mitchell (US)	Los Angeles	26 April 1987
200 m	2:08.60	Betsy Mitchell (US)	Orlando Fla.	27 June 1986
INDIVIDUAL MEDLEY				
200 m	2:10.60	Petra Schneider (GDR)	Gainesville, Fla.	1 Aug 1982
400 m	4:36.10	Petra Schneider (GDR)	Ecuador	1 Aug 1982
FREESTYLE RELAYS				
400 m (4×100)	3:42.41	East Germany	Madrid	Aug 1986
800 m (4×200)	7:59.33	East Germany	Madrid	Aug 1986
MEDLEY RELAYS				
400 m (4×100)	4:03.69	East Germany	Moscow	24 Aug 1984

1986 Equestrian Champions

Event	Winner
World Endurance Riding	British four-woman team
World Show Jumping	Gail Greenough, Canada
World Three-Day Eventing	Virginia Leng (née Holgate), Great Britain
World Dressage	Anne-Grethe Jensen, Denmark
Burghley Horse Trials	Virginia Leng (née Holgate), Great Britain

In the same year Princess Anne rode her first winner on the flat; one of the Queen Mother's horses won the Grand Military Gold Cup at Sandown for the third time; and Caroline Beasley became the first woman to ride a winner over the Grand National fences at Aintree.

TENNIS

At Wimbledon women still receive less money than men, but there is equal pay at the US Open. The largest crowd ever at a tennis match, some 30,472 people, came to the Houston Texas Astrodome on 20 September 1973 to see Billie Jean King play Bobbie Riggs in the battle of the sexes. She won.

Wimbledon Singles Champions

(Unless otherwise stated, 1884–1926 Champions are from Great Britain and 1927–1986 Champions are from the United States.)

Year	Champion
1884	Maud Watson
1885	Maud Watson
1886	Blanche Bingley
1887	Lottie Dod
1888	Lottie Dod
1889	Blanche Bingley Hillyard
1890	Helena Rice
1891	Lottie Dod
1892	Lottie Dod
1893	Lottie Dod
1894	Blanche Bingley Hillyard
1895	Charlotte Cooper Sterry
1896	Charlotte Cooper Sterry
1897	Blanche Bingley Hillyard
1898	Charlotte Cooper Sterry
1899	Blanche Bingley Hillyard
1900	Blanche Bingley Hillyard
1901	Charlotte Cooper Sterry
1902	Muriel Robb
1903	Dorothea Douglass
1904	Dorothea Douglass
1905	May Sutton, United States
1906	Dorothea Douglass
1907	May Sutton, United States
1908	Charlotte Cooper Sterry
1909	Dora Boothby
1910	Dorothea Douglass Chambers
1911	Dorothea Douglass Chambers
1912	Ethel Thomson Larcombe
1913	Dorothea Douglass Chambers
1914	Dorothea Douglass Chambers
1915–18	*Not played*
1919	Suzanne Lenglen, France
1920	Suzanne Lenglen, France
1921	Suzanne Lenglen, France
1922	Suzanne Lenglen, France
1923	Suzanne Lenglen, France
1924	Kathleen McKane
1925	Suzanne Lenglen, France
1926	Kathleen McKane Godfree
1927	Helen Wills
1928	Helen Wills
1929	Helen Wills
1930	Helen Wills Moody
1931	Cilly Aussem, West Germany
1932	Helen Wills Moody
1933	Helen Wills Moody
1934	Dorothy Round, Great Britain
1935	Helen Wils Moody
1936	Helen Jacobs, Great Britain
1937	Dorothy Round, Great Britain
1938	Helen Wills Moody
1939	Alice Marble
1940–45	*Not played*
1946	Pauline Betz
1947	Margaret Osborne
1948	Louise Brough
1949	Louise Brough
1951	Doris Hart
1952	Maureen Connolly
1953	Maureen Connolly
1954	Maureen Connolly
1955	Louise Brough
1956	Shirley Fry
1957	Althea Gibson
1958	Althea Gibson
1959	Maria Bueno, Brazil
1960	Maria Mueno, Brazil
1961	Angela Mortimer, Great Britain
1962	Karen Hantze Susman
1963	Margaret Smith, Australia
1964	Maria Bueno, Brazil
1965	Margaret Smith, Australia
1966	Billie Jean King
1967	Billie Jean King
1968	Billie Jean King
1969	Ann Haydon Jones, Great Britain
1970	Margaret Smith Court, Australia
1971	Evonne Goolagong, Australia
1972	Billie Jean King
1973	Billie Jean King
1974	Chris Evert
1975	Billie Jean King
1976	Chris Evert
1977	Virginia Wade, Great Britain
1978	Martina Navratilova
1979	Martina Navratilova
1980	Evonne Goolagong Cawley, Australia
1981	Chris Evert Lloyd
1982	Martina Navratilova
1983	Martina Navratilova
1984	Martina Navratilova
1985	Martina Navratilova
1986	Martina Navratilova
1987	Martina Navratilova

US Singles Champions

(Unless otherwise stated, the Champions are from the United States.)

Year	Champion
1887	Ellen Hansell
1888	Bertha Townsend
1889	Bertha Townsend
1890	Ellen Roosevelt
1891	Mabel Cahill
1892	Mabel Cahill
1893	Aline Terry
1894	Helen Hellwig
1895	Juliette Atkinson
1896	Bessie Moore
1897	Juliette Atkinson
1898	Juliette Atkinson
1899	Marion Jones
1900	Myrtle McAteer
1901	Bessie Moore
1902	Marion Jones
1903	Bessie Moore
1904	May Sutton
1905	Bessie Moore
1906	Helen Homans
1907	Evelyn Sears
1908	Maud Barger Wallach
1909	Hazel Hotchkiss
1910	Hazel Hotchkiss
1911	Hazel Hotchkiss
1912	Mary Browne
1913	Mary Browne
1914	Mary Browne
1915	Molla Bjurstedt
1916	Molla Bjurstedt
1917	*Not played*
1918	Molla Bjurstedt
1919	Hazel H. Wightman
1920	Molla Bjurstedt Mallory
1921	Molla Bjurstedt Mallory
1922	Molla Bjurstedt Mallory
1923	Helen Wills
1924	Helen Wills
1925	Helen Wills
1926	Molla Bjurstedt Mallory
1927	Helen Wills
1928	Helen Wills
1929	Helen Wills
1930	Betty Nuthall, Great Britain
1931	Helen Wills Moody
1932	Helen Jacobs
1933	Helen Jacobs
1934	Helen Jacobs
1935	Helen Jacobs
1936	Alice Marble
1937	Anita Lizana, Chile
1938	Alice Marble
1939	Alice Marble
1940	Alice Marble
1941	Sarah Palfrey Cooke
1942	Pauline Betz
1943	Pauline Betz
1944	Pauline Betz
1945	Sarah Palfrey Cooke
1946	Pauline Betz
1947	Louise Brough
1948	Margaret Osborne du Pont
1949	Margaret Osborne du Pont
1950	Margaret Osborne du Pont
1951	Maureen Connolly
1952	Maureen Connolly
1953	Maureen Connolly
1954	Doris Hart
1955	Doris Hart
1956	Shirley Fry
1957	Althea Gibson
1958	Althea Gibson
1959	Maria Bueno, Brazil
1960	Darlene Hard
1961	Darlene Hard
1962	Margaret Smith, Australia
1963	Maria Bueno, Brazil
1964	Maria Bueno, Brazil
1965	Margaret Smith, Australia
1966	Maria Bueno, Brazil
1967	Billie Jean King
1968	Virginia Wade, Great Britain
1969	Margaret Smith Court, Australia
1970	Margaret Smith Court, Australia
1971	Billie Jean King
1972	Billie Jean King
1973	Margaret Smith Court, Australia
1974	Billie Jean King
1975	Chris Evert
1976	Chris Evert
1977	Chris Evert
1978	Chris Evert
1979	Tracy Austin
1980	Chris Evert Lloyd
1981	Tracy Austin
1982	Chris Evert Lloyd
1983	Martina Navratilova
1984	Martina Navratilova
1985	Hana Mandlikova, Czechoslovakia
1986	Martina Navratilova

Sources and References

Abrahams, Harold. *The Olympic Games Book*, James Barries, London, 1956.
Anderson, Dave. *Sports of Our Times*, Random House, New York, 1979.
Athletics Weekly, 15 November 1986.
'Attack on Single-Sex Races', *Running Magazine*, London, January, 1987.
Boehm, David, *et al.* eds. *Guinness Sports Record Book, 1986–1987*. Sterling, New York, 1986.
Borms, J., M. Hebbelinck and A. Venerando, eds. *Women and Sport*, S. Karger, Basel, 1981.
Boutilier, Mary A. and Lucinda SanGiovanni. *The Sporting Woman*, Champaign, Illinois., 1983.
Boys, Philip. 'Riding Away to Independence', *Science for People*, London, Summer 1981.
Brake, Mike, ed. *Human Sexual Relations: A Reader*, Penguin, London, 1982.
Brasher, Christopher. 'The Changes That Made A Champion', *The Sporting Year*, ed. by John Rodda and Clifford Makins, Collins, London, 1977.
Cambridge Women's Studies Group. *Women in Society*, Virago, London, 1981.
Capes, Geoff. *Big Shot: An Autobiography*, Stanley Paul, London, 1981.
Central Statistical Office. *Social Trends*, Her Majesty's Stationery Office, London, 1986.
Cetron, Marvin and Thomas O'Toole. *Encounters with the Future*, McGraw-Hill, New York, 1982.
Clark, Patrick. *Sport Firsts*, Facts on File, New York, 1981.
Cleather, Norah Gordon. *Wimbledon Story*, Sporting Handbooks, London, 1947.
Coakley, Jay J. *Sport in Society: Issues and Controversies*, Times Mirror/Mosby College, St Louis, 1986.
Coe, Sebastian with Nicholas Mason. *The Olympians*, Pavilion, London, 1984.
Comaneci, Nadia and Graham Buxton Smither. *Nadia, My Own Story*, Proteus, London, 1981.
Coubertin, Pierre de. 'L'education des jeunes enfants et des jeunes filles', *Revue Olympique*, Octobre: 61, 1902.
Coward, Rosalind. *Female Desire*, Paladin, London, 1984.
Donohoe, Tom and Johnson, Neil. *Foul Play: Drug Abuse in Sports*, Blackwell, London, 1986.
Douglass, Robert. 'Gender vs. Performance,' *Tri-Athlete*, Allentown, Pa., June 1986.
Dyer, K.F. *Catching Up the Men: Women in Sport*, Junction, London, 1982.
Dyer, Richard. *Stars*, British Film Institute, London, 1979.
Edwards, Harry. 'The 21st-Century Gladiators', in *The Book of Predictions*, ed. by David Wallechinsky, *et al.*, Corgi, London, 1982.
Emery, David, ed. *Who's Who in the 1984 Olympics*, Pelham, London, 1984.
Emery, David and Stan Greenberg. *World Sporting Records*, Bodley Head, London, 1986.

Enright, Jim. *Only in Iowa: Where the High School Girl Athlete Is Queen,* Iowa Girls' High School Athletic Union, Des Moines, 1976.

Fletcher, Sheila. *Women First: The Female Tradition in English Physical Education, 1890–1990,* Athlone Press, London, 1984.

Ford, John. *This Sporting Land,* New English Library, London, 1977.

Franks, Violet and Esther Rothblum, eds. *The Stereotyping of Women,* Springer, New York, 1983.

Fraser, Antonia. *The Weaker Vessel: Woman's Lot in Seventeenth-Century England,* Weidenfeld and Nicolson, London, 1984.

Fraser, Dawn. *Gold Medal Girl: The Confessions of an Olympic Champion,* Nicholas Kaye, London, 1965.

Gibson, Althea. 'I Always Wanted to Be Somebody', in *Out of the Bleachers* ed. by Stephanie L. Twin, Feminist Press, Old Westbury, N.Y., 1979.

Giller, Norman. *The Marathon,* Pelham Books, London, 1983.

Glenton, Bill. 'Inside Czechoslovakia', *Tennis,* no. 58, London, June 1986.

Goldberg, B. 'Pediatric Sport Medicine', in *Principles of Sports Medicine,* Williams and Wilkins, Baltimore, 1984.

Golubev, Vladimir. *Soviet Gymnastics Stars,* Progress, Moscow, 1979.

Graydon, Jan. 'But It's More than a Game', *Feminist Review,* vol. 13, Spring 1983.

Green, Tina Sloan *et al.,* eds. *Black Women in Sport,* American Alliance for Health, Physical Education, Recreation and Dance, Reston, Va., 1981.

Greer, Germaine. *The Female Eunuch,* Paladin, London, 1971.

Hare, C. *The Most Illustrious Ladies of the Renaissance,* Harper & Bros, London & New York, 1904.

Hargreaves, Jennifer. 'Women and the Olympic Phenomenon', in Alan Tomlinson and Gary Whannel, eds., *Five Ring Circus,* Pluto, London, 1984.

Harris, Norman *et al.,* eds. *The Sports Health Handbook,* World's Work, Surrey, 1982.

Heaton, Peter. *The Singlehanders,* Michael Joseph, London, 1976

Hemery, David. *Sporting Excellence,* Willow, London, 1986.

Huizinga, J. *Homo Ludens,* Temple Smith, London, 1970.

Jackson, D. W. *et al. International Gymnast,* December 1976.

Johnson, William Oscar and Nancy P. Williamson. 'Whatta-Gal: The Babe Didrikson Story', *A Sports Illustrated Book,* Little, Brown, Boston, 1977.

Kaplan, Jane. *Women and Sports,* Viking, New York, 1979.

Killanin, Lord and John Rodda, eds. *The Olympic Games.* Macdonald & Jane's, London, 1979.

King, Billie Jean with Frank Deford. *The Autobiography,* Granada, London, 1982.

Kochan, A.M. 'Spondylolysis and Spondylolisthesis in Young Athletes', *Coaching Review* 8, November 1985, 64.

Kort, Michele. 'Can Maternity Make You a Better Athlete?', *Women's Sports and Fitness,* Palo Alto, Calif., May 1986.

Kuscik, Nina. 'The History of Women's Participation in the Marathon', Road Runners Club, New York, 1976.

Lefkowitz, Mary R. *Women in Greek Myth,* Duckworth, London, 1986.

Lloyd, Chris and John, with Carol Thatcher. *Lloyd on Lloyd,* Willow, London, 1985.

Loosli, Alvin R. *et al.* 'Nutrition Habits and Knowledge in Competitive Adolescent Female Gymnasts', *The Physician and Sports Medicine,* August 1986.

Lopez, Nancy. *The Education of a Woman Golfer,* Simon and Schuster, New York, 1979.

Macfarlane, Neil. *Sport and Politics,* Willow, London 1986.

Macleod, Iain. 'The Legend that is Koch and Gohr', *Athletics Weekly,* London, 18 October,

Sources and References

1 November and 8 November 1986.

'Maestro: Reminiscences of a Master Sportswoman', BBC Television, 1986. Transmitted 1987.

Mair, Lewine. 'Ladies Tour: A Boom but Not without Problems', *Golf Monthly*, Glasgow, March 1986.

Markel, Robert and Nancy Brooks. *For the Record*, New York, World Almanac, 1985.

Maugham, Ron. 'Men vs. Women', *Running Magazine*, London, January 1987.

Medlycott, James. *100 Years of the Wimbledon Tennis Championships*, Hamlyn, London, 1977.

Midwinter, Eric. *Fair Game*, Allen & Unwin, London, 1986.

Miller Lite Report on American Attitudes Toward Sports. Miller Brewing Co., Milwaukee, WI, 1983.

Navratilova, Martina with George Vecsey. *Being Myself*, Collins, London, 1985.

Oglesby, Carole A., ed. *Women and Sport*, Lea & Febiger, Philadelphia, 1978.

Osborne, Martha Lee, ed. *Woman in Western Thought*, Random House, New York, 1979.

Pannick, David. *Sex Discrimination in Sport*, Equal Opportunities Commission, Manchester, 1983.

Parkhouse, Bonnie L. and Jackie Lapin. *Women Who Win*, Prentice-Hall, Englewood Cliffs, N.J. 1980.

Payne, Howard and Rosemary. *The Science of Track and Field Athletics*, Pelham, London, 1981.

Peters, Mary with Ian Wooldridge. *Mary P.* Arrow, London, 1974.

Pignon, Laurie. 'Kitty Godfree: A Lifetime's Love Affair', *Tennis Great Britain*, Lawn Tennis Association, London, 1986.

Raven, Susan and Alison Weir. *Women in History*, Weidenfeld & Nicolson, London, 1981.

Riggs, Bobby. *Court Hustler*, New American Library, New York, 1974.

Robertson, Max. *Wimbledon: Centre Court of the Game*, BBC, London, 1977.

Robyns, Gwen. *Wimbledon: The Hidden Drama*, David & Charles, Newton Abbot, 1973.

Rosen, Lionel W. *et al.* 'Pathogenic Weight-Control Behaviour in Female Athletes', *The Physician and Sportsmedicine 14*, January 1986.

Russell, Keith. 'Stress or Distress', presented to British Association of National Coaches, 1985.

Sanderson, Tessa. *Tessa: My Life in Athletics*, Willow, London, 1986.

Schickel, Richard. *Common Fame: The Culture of Celebrity*, Pavilion, London, 1985.

Schmolinsky, Gerhardt, ed. *Track and Field*, Sportverlg, 1978.

Seltman, Charles. *Women in Antiquity*, Pan, London, 1956.

Shorter, Edward. *A History of Women's Bodies*, Penguin, London, 1984.

Speroff, L. and Redwine, D.B. 'Exercise and Menstrual Function', *The Physician and Sports Medicine*, no. 8, 1980.

Sport in the GDR: Past and Present, Panorama, DDR, 1984.

Srebnitsky, Alex, APN dispatch to *Soviet Weekly*, 29 September 1986.

Steele, V. A. and White, J. A. 'Injury Amongst Female Gymnasts, 2, *Proceedings of the Society of Sports Sciences*, 1983.

'Injury prediction in Female Gymnasts', *Brit. J. Sports Med.*, 20 March 1986.

'Steroid Abuse', *USA Today*, 6 January 1987.

Straub, William F., ed. *Sport Psychology*, Mouvement Publications, Ithaca, N.Y., 1980.

Suleiman, Susan Rubin, ed. *The Female Body in Western Culture*, Harvard, Cambridge, Mass., 1986.

Swaddling, Judith. *The Ancient Olympic Games*, British Museum, London, 1984.

Tilden, William T. *The Art of Lawn Tennis*, Methuen, London, 1920.

Tinling, Ted. *Sixty Years in Tennis*, Sidgwick & Jackson, London, 1983.

Tomlinson, Alan and Gerry Whannel, *Five Ring Circus*, Pluto, London, 1984.

Turnbull, Alison. 'Does Pregnancy Improve Athletic Performance?', *Running Magazine*, London, October 1986.

╋ Twin, Stephanie L., ed. *Out of the Bleachers: Writings on Women and Sport*, Feminist Press, New York, 1979.

Wade, Virginia with Jean Rafferty. *Ladies of the Court*, Pavilion, London, 1984.

Wakefield, Frances *et al. Track and Field Fundamentals for Girls and Women*, C. V. Mosby, St Louis, 1977.

Watkins, James. 'An Overview of Sports-Related Lower-limb Ephiphyseal Injuries', Scottish School of Physical Education, unpublished, 1986.

╬ Waugh, Auberon. 'Another Voice', *The Spectator*, 12 July 1986.

Weider, Joe, ed. *Bodybuilding and Conditioning for Women*, Contemporary, Chicago, 1983.

Wells, Christine. *Women, Sport, and Performance: A Physiological Perspective*, Human Kinetics, Champaign, Illinois, 1986.

White, Anita White and Celia Brackenridge. 'Who Rules Sport?', paper presented to the *Olympic Scientific Congress*, University of Oregon, 1984.

Willard, Frances. *A Wheel Within a Wheel; How I Learned to Ride a Bicycle*, 1985.

Wooldridge, Ian, ed. *Great Sport Headlines*. Collins, London, 1984.

Zaharias, 'Babe' Didrikson. *Championship Golf*. A. S. Barnes, New York, 1948.

Index

1998